HOMELAND SECURITY LAW: A PRIMER

Since 2001 the U.S. government has been engaged in the delicate balancing act of seeking to protect the country against terrorism, both foreign-connected and wholly domestic, while taking into account a number of constitutional protections that can all too easily be trammelled in the effort to assure domestic security. At the same time the development of these policies has created significant constitutional tension among the three branches of the federal government, especially when the President vigorously asserts claims of sweeping power as commander-in-chief in such a way as to raise warnings about the emergence of an imperial presidency. Simultaneously, the rule of law has been placed under stress as the technological prowess of the government has grown.

This book addresses these topics in an accessible manner, covering the key developments of domestic security law related to terrorism. Tyll van Geel covers the essential elements of homeland security law including: branches of government and institutions involved in counterterrorism law; border control and immigration; surveillance; the searching of computers and cell phones; the prosecution of terrorists for any number of crimes, including cyberterrorism; military detention; the prosecution of unprivileged enemy belligerents in military commissions; and habeas corpus. The book is designed to offer a clear guide to current issues in domestic security in response to terrorism and will be a valuable guide for concerned citizens as well as undergraduate students studying domestic politics or national security.

Tyll van Geel, Northwestern University Pritzker School of Law, J.D.; Earl B. Taylor Emeritus, University of Rochester.

HOMELAND SECURITY LAW

A Primer

Tyll van Geel

Routledge
Taylor & Francis Group
LONDON AND NEW YORK

First published 2019
by Routledge
2 Park Square, Milton Park, Abingdon, Oxon OX14 4RN

and by Routledge
52 Vanderbilt Avenue, New York, NY 10017

Routledge is an imprint of the Taylor & Francis Group, an informa business

British Library Cataloguing-in-Publication Data
A catalogue record for this book is available from the British Library

Library of Congress Cataloging-in-Publication Data
A catalog record for this book has been requested

ISBN: 978-1-138-23804-6 (hbk)
ISBN: 978-1-138-36969-6 (pbk)
ISBN: 978-1-315-29825-2 (ebk)

Typeset in Bembo
by Apex CoVantage, LLC

For Katy, who makes possible a life filled with joy, laughter, and love

CONTENTS

ACKNOWLEDGEMENTS

This volume would not have been possible without the significant work of the commentators, scholars and researchers who have made it their business to stay abreast of this fast-moving body of law on which they report through their online contributions, law review articles, publications for various research centers, and books. The work of many of these scholars can frequently be found at these websites: LawFare, Just Security, Electronic Frontier Foundation, and The Brennan Center for Justice. The reports of the Congressional Research Service are also a very valuable resource. For regular coverage of developments in this area see *The New York Times*, *Washington Post*, *The Guardian*, and *The Intercept*. I also owe thanks to Dean Sudha Setty, Western New England School of Law, for her insights and useful suggestions. This book had its origin in a seminar offered under the auspices of Five College Learning in Retirement, Amherst, MA, an organization that encourages continued reading, learning, and writing.

The writing of this book would not have happened but for the unstinting support, and heroic editorial and copyediting work of Katharine Weinrich van Geel.

ACRONYMS AND ABBREVIATIONS

ACLU	American Civil Liberties Union
ATF	Alcohol, Tobacco, Firearms, and Explosives
ATS	Automated Targeting System
AUMF	Authority to Use Military Force
CBP	Customs and Border Patrol
CFAA	Computer Fraud and Abuse Act
CFR	Code of Federal Regulations
CHS	Confidential human sources
CIA	Central Intelligence Agency
CIPA	Classified Information Procedures Act
CSLI	Cell Site Location Information
CSRT	Combatant Status Review Tribunal
DEA	Drug Enforcement Agency
DHS	Department of Homeland Security
DHS TRIP	DHS Traveler Redress Inquiry Program
DIOG	Domestic Investigations and Operations Guide
DNI	Director of National Intelligence
DOD	Department of Defense
DOJ	Department of Justice
DTA	Detainee Treatment Act
DTO	Designated Terrorist Organization
E.O.	Executive Order
ECPA	Electronic Communications Privacy Act
EFF	Electronic Frontier Foundation
FBI	Federal Bureau of Investigation
FEMA	Federal Emergency Management Agency

FIG	Field Intelligence Groups
FISA	Federal Intelligence Surveillance Act
FISC	Foreign Intelligence Surveillance Court
FISCR	Foreign Intelligence Surveillance Court of Review
FRCP	Federal Rules of Civil Procedure
FTO	Foreign Terrorist Organization
GPS	Global Positioning System
HSC	Homeland Security Council
HSPD	Homeland Security Presidential Directive
HUMINT	Human Intelligence
IC	Intelligence Community
ICE	Immigration and Customs Enforcement
IG	Inspector General (Inspectors General, plural)
IMSI	International Mobile Subscriber Identity-catcher, aka StingRay or Triggerfish
INS	Immigration and Naturalization Service
IRS	Internal Revenue Service
IRTPA	Intelligence Reform and Terrorism Prevention Act
JTTF	Joint Terrorism Task Force
LPR	Lawful Permanent Resident
MAC	Media Access Control address
MCA	Military Commissions Act
MCT	Multiple-Communication Transaction
NCTC	National Counterterrorism Center
NDAA	National Defense Authorization Act
NIT	Network Investigative Technique
NSA	National Security Agency
NSC	National Security Council
NSI	Nationwide SAR Initiative
NSL	National Security Letter
OCL	Office of Legal Counsel
OPR	Office of Professional Responsibility
OSINT	Open Source Intelligence
P/T	Pen Register/Trap and Trace devices
PCLOB	Privacy & Civil Liberties Oversight Board
PFLP	Popular Front for the Liberation of Palestine
PSP	President's Surveillance Program
SAR	Suspicious Activity Reporting
SCA	Stored Communications Act
SLTT	State, Local, Tribal, and Territorial
SRC	Shared Responsibility Committee
SWAT	Special Weapons and Tactics
TECS	Information-Sharing Platform (not an acronym) used by the CBP
TIDE	Terrorist Identities Datamart Environment

TSA	Transportation Security Administration
TSC	Terrorist Screening Center
TSDB	Terrorist Screening Database, aka the Terrorist Watchlist
UDP	Undisclosed Participation
URL	Uniform Resource Locator (aka web address)
USC	United States Code
USG	United States Government

INTRODUCTION

This is a primer on domestic counterterrorism law for informed citizens and students enrolled in a related course. Counterterrorism law deals with foreign-connected jihadist terrorists, domestic jihadist terrorists, and domestic terrorists embracing other extremist ideologies. The book focuses on violent/criminal activity within the U.S. (homeland terrorism) carried out by people or groups of people with a foreign connection, or others with no such connection (domestic terrorists).

Which group poses the greatest danger – foreign-connected jihadist terrorists, domestic jihadist terrorists, or domestic terrorists? In 2015 Assistant Attorney General John P. Carlin said:

> Looking back over the past few years it is quite clear that domestic terrorists and homegrown violent extremists remain a clear and present danger here inside the United States. We recognize that according to at least one study more people died in this country in attacks by domestic extremists than attacks associated with international terrorist groups over the last, say, five to six years.[1]

Between 9/11 and October 2017 right-wing groups killed 68 people and jihadists killed 95 (which includes 49 killed in an Orlando nightclub in 2015).[2]

1 https://www.justice.gov/opa/speech/assistant-attorney-general-john-p-carlin-delivers-remarks-domestic-terrorism-event-co.

2 Daniel L. Byman, *Should we treat domestic terrorists the way we treat ISIS?: What works – and what doesn't* (Foreign Affairs, October 2, 2017), archived at https://www.brookings.edu/articles/should-we-treat-domestic-terrorists-the-way-we-treat-isis-what-works-and-what-doesnt/.

I. Terrorists, unprivileged enemy belligerents, and criminals

"Terrorism" is a term that has been defined in many ways.[3] The Code of Federal Regulations states that terrorism includes "the unlawful use of force and violence against persons or property to intimidate or coerce a government, the civilian population, or any segment thereof, in furtherance of political or social objectives."[4] The federal statutory code has many similar but not identical definitions of terrorism.[5]

Terrorism differs from ordinary criminal activity in that terrorists typically are driven by a cause or ideology, not by self-interested motives such as profit or malice directed toward a specific individual. Malice toward a person may be a hate crime rooted in the victim's race, color, religion, national origin, gender, gender identity, sexual orientation, or disability. Whether a particular hate crime is also a "terrorist" act opens up a complex, gray area.[6]

This book is not just about investigating and prosecuting jihadist terrorists such as the perpetrators of 9/11, who may be U.S. citizens or legal residents, or in the full sense foreign terrorists captured either on a foreign battlefield or in the U.S. This book covers the investigation and prosecution of terrorists motivated by other ideologies as well, such as white supremacists and eco-terrorists. *A note of caution*: a person who in ordinary parlance may be termed a "terrorist" or who fits the definition quoted above may not actually be indicted and prosecuted as a "terrorist," but as a violator of an ordinary criminal law.

A related legal concept used in this book are the terms "unlawful enemy combatant" or "unprivileged enemy belligerent." The "unprivileged enemy belligerent" definition focuses on people who commit hostile acts against the U.S. and do not enjoy or have forfeited the privileges afforded lawful combatants by the law of war (e.g. a uniformed enemy soldier), or forfeited the privileges afforded civilians.[7] Not every unprivileged enemy belligerent is a terrorist and not every terrorist is an unlawful enemy belligerent, but some perpetrators of violence are both. The 9/11 attackers fit both definitions.[8]

The book deals with what some people would call homeland security and others national security. It does not, however, cover what sometimes is included under these headings, like targeting terrorists abroad, the hardening of infrastructures

3 Jerome P. Bjelopera, *Domestic terrorism: An overview*, 3 –7 (Congressional Research Service, August 21, 2017, R44921) (discussing various domestic extremist groups). See, for example, 6 USC §101(18).

4 28 CFR 0.85(l). See, also, 8 USC §1182(a)(3) and 6 USC §101(18).

5 Nicholas J. Perry, *The numerous federal legal definitions of terrorism: The problem of too many grails*, 30 J of Leg 249 (2004).

6 Jerome P. Bjelopera, *Sifting domestic terrorism from hate crime and homegrown violent extremism* (Congressional Research Service Insight, Aug 14, 2017, IN10299); Bjelopera, *Domestic terrorism: An overview*, at 6–7 (cited in note 1).

7 Office of General Counsel, Department of Defense, Law of War Manual, 103–106 (June 2015), archived at https://www.defense.gov/Portals/1/Documents/pubs/Law-of-War-Manual-June-2015.pdf.

8 See description of 9/11 attackers' goals at: https://www.911memorial.org/faq-about-911.

against a terrorist attack, general immigration policy, national security threats of foreign governments, an examination of state and local terrorism efforts, or the mitigation of the consequences of a terrorist attack.

II. Domestic and foreign-connected terrorism

This book's focus is on homeland terrorism, that which occurs primarily within the U.S. "International terrorism" occurs primarily outside the U.S. (50 USC §1801(c) and 18 USC 2331). Terrorism that occurs in the U.S. may be further subdivided and domestic and foreign-connected terrorism can go down different legal tracks. "Foreign-connected" terrorism involves a foreign power or agent of a foreign power.[9] Such an agent is either a "member" of an international terrorist organization or "acts for or on behalf of" a group engaged in international terrorism (50 USC 1801(b)). Note that the phrase "acts for or on behalf of" is somewhat indeterminate.

The distinction between domestic and foreign-connected terrorism is hard to apply when it comes to a lone wolf who acts under the inspiration of a foreign group such as al-Qaeda. Consider the example of Syed Rizwan Farook (citizen) and Tashfeen Malike (legal alien) who killed 14 people in California in December 2015. When a lone wolf is a U.S. person (a citizen or a lawfully admitted alien) the FBI has to determine if the individual really is a lone wolf (in which case FISA would not be available) or is actually an agent of foreign power (in which case FISA would be available since there is a foreign connection; see Chapters 3 and 6). Note when a lone wolf is not a U.S. person, establishing a "foreign connection" is not germane to deciding if FISA is available (50 USC §1801(b)(C)). Also note, Chapter 8 addresses the possibility of a lone wolf being an unprivileged enemy belligerent.

III. Counterterrorism law

A look at the contents pages reveals that counterterrorism law comprises many things. Many themes run through this body of law, including the authority of the President; the relationships of the President, Congress and the judiciary; and significant issues of civil rights and civil liberties. There are, however, two themes that are not given separate or stand-alone treatment in the book, but are nevertheless intertwined with the chapters and deserve to be highlighted next.

IV. The interrelationship between technology and the law

One theme running through the book is the interrelationship between technology and the law. First, changes in technology have created problems for the government. Data that had been stored in the U.S. are now stored outside the U.S., raising

9 50 USC §1801.

the question of the extraterritorial reach of statutes that authorize the government to collect the data. (See Chapter 6.) Another example: because of technological changes, communications that had been collectable without complying with 50 USC §1801 now have to be collected according to §1801 rules, thereby hindering the National Security Agency's ability to conduct surveillance of foreign-based terrorists. (See Chapter 2, and the discussion of §702 in Chapter 3.) Technological limitations of the NSA's surveillance equipment led to a FISA court ruling that part of a surveillance program was unconstitutional. (See discussion of MCTs in Chapter 3.) At the same time, individuals worried about law enforcement have been encrypting the data on their devices, using locked cell phones, the dark web, password protections on devices and prepaid ("burner") cell phones. In an effort to cope with these defenses, legal reforms have been enacted, such as authorizing roving warrants and getting court orders to require companies such as Apple to unlock one of their phones.[10]

Second, law enforcement has increased its technological prowess, raising new legal issues. This aspect of the story pre-dates 9/11, when the FBI placed a microphone on top of a public phone booth to monitor the phone calls of Charles Katz, who was placing illegal bets. The Supreme Court held in *Katz v United States*, 389 US 347 (1967) that monitoring a public phone booth without a warrant violated the Fourth Amendment. Two years later the Supreme Court considered the use of a pen register and trap and trace device in *Smith v Maryland*, 442 US 735 (1979), which could record numbers dialed from a particular phone and concluded that that didn't violate the Fourth Amendment.

Other devices and techniques have raised constitutional issues, e.g. port mirroring to grab copies of network data; keystroke logging; a technology that taps into the Internet's backbone (i.e. coaxial cables and fiber optic cables); powerful search engines that can secretly search massive amounts of electronic data (XKeyscore); metal detectors; GPS tracking devices; cell site simulators (devices that mimic cell phone towers and trick cell phones in the area into transmitting their locations and identifying information to law enforcement); back-scatter x-rays; advanced imaging technology; malware that can penetrate a computer to obtain an anatomized IP address; thermal imaging; Cellebrite, that can grab a cell phone's contents; remote activation of a cell phone or webcam of a computer; forensic software to recover "deleted" files from a computer; and network investigative techniques. Private industry also regularly comes up with new detection devices, such as instruments that can remotely detect if a person is carrying a concealed weapon. In addition to hardware and software, new developments in the mathematics of big data analysis have made the querying and analysis of bulk data more effective.

The capacity of the government to collect, retain, and analyze data has greatly expanded, making possible contact chaining, the creation of social network graphing/

10 Arjun Kharpal, *Apple vs FBI: All you need to know* (CNBC, March 29, 2016), archived at https://www.cnbc.com/2016/03/29/apple-vs-fbi-all-you-need-to-know.html.

diagrams, and community of interest profiles of perhaps every person in the U.S.[11] (See Chapter 3.) New capacities also make possible widespread sharing of information horizontally within the federal government, and vertically between federal, state, and local agencies. (See Chapters 3 and 6.)

V. The rule of law, privacy and liberty under stress

The legal topics taken up in this book raise the question of whether the government's counterterrorism efforts have undermined privacy, have impinged on liberty, and/or have been carried out in conformance with the ideal of the rule of law.

At the heart of the concept of the rule of law is the notion that governmental powers are not exercised through the mere will of individuals; rather, command of the law has primacy, i.e. the U.S. is "a government of laws and not men."

> The most important demand of the Rule of Law is that people in positions of authority should exercise their power within a constraining framework of well-established public norms rather than in an arbitrary, *ad hoc*, or purely discretionary manner on the basis of their own preferences or ideology.[12]

A constraining framework is not created by the person in authority. Additionally, commentators would agree that the hallmarks of the rule of law include:[13] laws are public; legal institutions and procedures should be available to people to uphold their rights against abuses by public and private power; laws are laid down in advance rather than retrospectively; the law is clear (not vague) to enable its comprehension and preclude inconsistent enforcement (i.e. it is possible to foresee how authority will use its power); there is consistency within the body of laws; and there is impartiality in the enforcement of the law. Other requirements of the rule of law are prescribed by the Fifth and Sixth Amendments to the Constitution, e.g., due process of law, and the right to confront and rebut evidence. Article I, Sec 9, cl 3 of the Constitution prohibits ex post facto laws and bills of attainder.

The chapters that follow will show evidence that many of these hallmarks of the rule of law are under stress, if not simply violated.[14] Following 9/11 President Bush launched not just a warrantless mass surveillance program, but also a program that did not entail any prior judicial approval; he claimed his authority to declare individuals "enemy combatants"; established the Guantanamo Bay Detention Camp, and created a trial system of military commissions. In doing this, President Bush

11 James Risen and Laura Poitras, *N.S.A. gathers data on social connections of U.S. citizens* (NYT September 28, 2013), archived at https://www.nytimes.com/2013/09/29/us/nsa-examines-social-networks-of-us-citizens.html.

12 *The rule of law* (Stanford Encyclopedia of Philosophy, Jun 22, 2016), archived at https://plato.stanford.edu/entries/rule-of-law/.

13 See for example, Ronald A. Cass, *The rule of law in America*, 1–22 (Johns Hopkins 2001).

14 See for example, Sudha Setty, *National security secrecy* (Cambridge 2017).

relied on texts that provided little textual guidance regarding his authority (for example, the phrase "commander-in-chief" in Article II of the Constitution and in the authorization to use military force). Bush's claim of authority pursuant to Article II was in large part an effort to avoid having to comply with FISA. (See Chapter 2.) He asserted unconstrained discretion; the only boundaries created were those he invented by and imposed on himself. Legal doctrines were developed in secret by the FISA court and by the Executive, e.g. secret memos authorized torture, secret rules regulated who would be placed on the No Fly list. Crucially, important statutes such as FISA have undefined terms such as the terms "on behalf of," "facilities," "relevant to an ongoing investigation," and "reasonably designed."

Along with the rule of law, privacy and liberty are also under stress. The protections of the Fourth Amendment are lessened in several ways. The collapse of "the wall," discussed in Chapters 3 and 6, allows extensive collaboration and sharing between the NSA and FBI. Courts are relying on vague doctrines, like "totality of the circumstances" when applying the Fourth Amendment. Balancing "tests" hand the courts power not limited by clear rules. The courts have narrowed the situations in which the Fourth Amendment even applies. (Chapter 3, and 6.) Access to the courts to seek redress of claimed violations of rights have been blocked by doctrines such as "standing" and the "state secrets privilege." And a generous interpretation of the doctrine that law enforcement acted in "good faith" opens the door to the use of evidence even if that evidence was collected in violation of the Fourth Amendment.[15]

People are being denied the right to fly based on vague rules and are not provided with an adequate mechanism for redress. Suspicion alone can be the basis for denying someone the liberty to fly and increases the chances of someone being subjected to an FBI "assessment" (Chapter 6). Accountability of both public officials and private companies has been stymied by court rulings and federal legislation, e.g. a law immunizing telecommunications companies from being sued after they used warrantless surveillance. The limitations on who may be detained as an unprivileged enemy belligerent remain unclear (Chapter 8). Procedures used in hearings on petitions for habeas corpus are tilted to favor the government (Chapter 10). Defendants have been denied access to the evidence used against them other than summaries provided by the government (Chapters 7 and 10). And surveillance has been undertaken unevenly when people are targeted based on ethnicity and religion (Chapters 4 and 6). Chapter 1 takes note of various accountability mechanisms and their flaws.

Although living by the rule of law has been under severe stress, the book also illustrates that it has not been abandoned and the law does seek to assure some protections for privacy and liberty. Here are some examples. As is recounted in

15 The following two cases from the 4th and 5th Circuits extend the application of United States v Leon, 468 US 897 (1984) *United States v Kolsuz*, No. 16-4687 *14 (4th Cir 2018); *United States v Molina-Isidoro*, 884 F3d 287 (5th Cir 2018).

Chapter 1, accountability mechanisms are in place. President Bush, under legal pressure from lawyers in the Department of Justice, changed his mass surveillance program (Chapters 2 and 3). Over time increasing efforts have been made to reduce the probability that the communications of unsuspected U.S. persons would be acquired by the mass surveillance programs. Laws are still in place to limit the government sweeping up the mass of data collected by the likes of Google and other participants in corporate surveillance. The Supreme Court has blocked efforts to preclude the availability of the writ of habeas corpus to Guantanamo detainees (Chapter 10) and required changes in the procedures used by military commissions (Chapter 9). Congress has amended surveillance, detainee treatment, and military commission statutes to reign in the discretion of the Executive (Chapters 3, 8, and 9) by laying down new rules to be followed. In the wake of a judicial opinion, redress procedures were improved for those placed on the no fly list (Chapter 5). The usual criminal procedures followed regarding the investigation and prosecution of ordinary crimes are still in force (Chapters 6 and 7). The courts defined somewhat more precisely the definition of an unprivileged enemy belligerent (Chapter 8). Under pressure, President Obama backed away from waterboarding and refined detainment policy (Chapter 8). Finally, mechanisms to assure the transparency of the government continue to be in place and continue to produce public reports on the operations of the government (Chapter 1).

Whether or not these steps have been adequate to protect the hallmarks of the rule of law, privacy, and liberty is not argued in this book. Cited in the footnotes are a number of the many books that address this topic.[16] This book does identify many areas where the law is not firmly settled and could change, in a crisis, especially in the case of foreign-connected terrorism.

16 Id; David Cole and James X. Dempsey, *Terrorism and the Constitution* (New Press 2006); Laura K. Donohue, *The future of foreign intelligence* (Oxford 2016); Jack Goldsmith, *Power and constraint* (W.W. Norton, 2012); Wadie E. Said, *Crimes of terror* (Oxford 2015); Christopher Slobogin, *Privacy at risk* (Chicago 2007).

1
THE COUNTERTERRORISM ENTERPRISE

The United States' governmental apparatus to protect the homeland against foreign-connected and domestic terrorists is huge, involving all three branches of government – executive, legislative and the judicial. According to research by the *Washington Post*, it involves over 1200 governmental agencies and approximately 2000 private companies in 10,000 locations across the United States.[1] The Intelligence Community (IC) expends roughly $71 billion a year, about $18 billion by the military IC and $53 billion by the non-military IC.[2] The effort to combat terrorism is spread across almost every department and agency of the executive branch. This federal effort to make combating terrorism a priority arguably had its start on June 21, 1995, when Presidential Decision Directive No. 39 was issued. It opened with this statement:

> It is the policy of the United States to deter, defeat and respond vigorously to all terrorist attacks on our territory and against our citizens, or facilities, whether they occur domestically, in international waters or airspace or on foreign territory. The United States regards all such terrorism as a potential threat to national security as well as a criminal act and will apply all appropriate means to combat it. In doing so, the U.S. shall pursue vigorously efforts to deter and preempt, apprehend and prosecute, or assist other governments to prosecute, individuals who perpetrate or plan to perpetrate such attacks.[3]

1 Dana Priest and William Arken, *A hidden world growing beyond control* (*Washington Post*, July 19, 2010), archived at http://projects.washingtonpost.com/top-secret-america/articles/a-hidden-world-growing-beyond-control/.

2 Anne Daugherty Miles, *Intelligence community programs, management and enduring issues*, 1 (Congressional Research Service, Nov 8, 2016, R44681).

3 President William Clinton, PPD-No. 39, June 21, 1995, archived at https://fas.org/irp/offdocs/pdd/pdd-39.pdf.

Two agencies focus primarily on foreign-connected terrorism, the Central Intelligence Agency and the National Security Agency. The Federal Bureau of Investigation focuses on both domestic and foreign-connected terrorism. Inevitably, whatever the original primary mission of an agency it may end up dealing with both foreign-connected and domestic terrorism. Given the way budget figures are reported, and the overlapping jurisdiction of the agencies, makes it a Herculean task to determine the absolute dollar figures and percentages of the federal budget allocated to countering foreign-connected terrorism versus domestic terrorism. Chances are, however, that considerably more money is being devoted to the detection, capture and prosecution of foreign-connected terrorists than domestic terrorists. The CIA is focused on foreign terrorists. The NSA's and FBI's total budgets seem to be roughly the same, $10 billion each.[4] Most of the budget of the NSA as well as at least 50% the FBI's budget is devoted to foreign-connected terrorists.[5]

The federal government's homeland security counterterrorism enterprise can be refined by taking note of its three major components: (I) the steering mechanism, (II) the core and, (III) the checking mechanism. The original architects, engineers and builders of the system are Congress, which adopted legislation establishing the system, and the President who also exercised his authority (under Article II and the federal statutes) to create systems and structures.

I. The steering mechanism

The President, the heads of various executive departments such as the Department of Homeland Security and the Department of Justice, and the heads of the divisions under these departments (e.g., the director of Immigration & Customs Enforcement) play a role in formulating counterterrorism policy, setting and allocating the budget, and in steering counterterrorism efforts. Congress too, with its various committees concerned with national security, is a major co-captain of the counterterrorism ship. The judiciary is taken up in Section III below.

The President issues Executive Orders, policy directives, and other memorandums. The most comprehensive policy guidance issued in 1981 was that of President Reagan, E.O. 12333.[6] This order has three parts, one of which addresses the goal of U.S. intelligence efforts and the duties and responsibilities of various agencies and officers, including the intelligence community (IC); a second part lays out principles of intelligence activities; and the third has general provisions and definitions.

4 https://www.statista.com/statistics/283545/budget-of-the-us-national-security-agency/.

5 Devlin Barrett, *FBI investigating 1,000 white supremacist, domestic terrorism cases* (*Washington Post*, September 27, 2017), archived at https://www.washingtonpost.com/world/national-security/fbi-investigating-1000-white-supremacist-domestic-terrorism-cases/2017/09/27/95abff24-a38b-11e7-ade1-76d061d56efa_story.html?utm_term=.64c4a3286938.

6 The order as amended four times is archived at https://fas.org/irp/offdocs/eo/eo-12333-2008.pdf.

Congress passes laws regarding surveillance (e.g., the Wiretap Act[7] and the Foreign Intelligence Surveillance Act), spells out which crimes should be prosecuted as terrorism, specifies the offender and offense jurisdiction of military commissions, specifies the rules of procedures to be used in the military commissions, lays out policies to protect infrastructure, and authorizes and empowers components of the "core." Other laws, such as state wiretapping laws, are the product of state legislatures. Federal courts interpret and apply the Constitution, interpret and apply federal statutes, and also promulgate the Federal Rules of Criminal Procedure and the Federal Rules of Evidence applicable in the federal courts.

Working with the President are several top-level councils – the National Security Council (NSC), and the Homeland Security Council (HSC) whose members are specified by statute.[8] (Also advising the President are two advisors for national and homeland security.) Because these councils are at the apex of the government they include the President and secretaries of relevant executive departments, as well as others appointed by the President. The Director of National Intelligence (DNI) has overall responsibility for intelligence and day-to-day management of the IC; the DNI determines and controls the intelligence budget.[9] Also advising the President and serving at the pleasure of the President are the members of the President's Intelligence Advisory Board who are charged with making recommendations to improve the government's intelligence efforts.

Steering the policies for investigating both domestic and foreign-connected terrorism inside the U.S. are the Department of Justice and the Federal Bureau of Investigation (28 CFR §0.85).

Setting the broad policy directives for the "core" in a nation that embraces adherence to the rule of law necessarily will, and has involved, the advice of legal counsel. Jack Goldsmith claims that over a long period of time a culture has taken hold in the executive branch that he calls a "fiercely legalistic conception of unprecedented wartime constraints on the presidency." He adds that "never in the history of the United States had lawyers had such an extraordinary influence over war policy as they did after 9/11 . . . [because] war itself was encumbered with legal restrictions as never before."[10]

National security legal advice is provided to the President and NSC by, among others:

> [T]he Office of White House Counsel, the Department of Justice (including the Attorney General, Deputy Attorney General, Office of Legal Counsel,

7 18 USC §§2510-2522; 50 USC §§1801-1885c.

8 50 USC §§3021, 3024; 6 USC §§491-496.

9 Miles, *Intelligence community programs, management and enduring issues*, 30 (cited in note 2). The office of the DNI was created in 2004 by the Intelligence Reform and Terrorism Prevention Act, Pub. L. No. 108-458, 118 Stat 3638. See, also, 50 USC §3025.

10 Jack Goldsmith, *The terror presidency*, 91, 129–130 (W.W. Norton 2007).

> and National Security Division), and the Office of the Legal Adviser at the NSC. In addition, national security legal advice is provided directly to individual members of the NSC by department and agency counsel. However, the principal mechanism and source of national security legal advice for the President, NSC . . . is from and through the Office of the Legal Adviser to the National Security Council.[11]

With multiple sources of legal advice, issues arise such as the relationship between the Office of White House Counsel and the Legal Advisor at the NSC, and the relationship between, on the one hand, the attorneys located in the White House, and on the other hand the Attorney General and the Office of Legal Counsel (OCL) in the Department of Justice. At the heart of these relationships lies the question of whether the President should be guided (constrained?) by non-partisan, independent impartial legal advice, or should the President be able to obtain and rely on advice that works backwards from "yes" and then constructs a legal rationale for what the President wants to do.

A word about the OCL.[12] Historically OCL's role has been to provide nonpartisan and independent legal opinions for the President and the executive branch as a whole – even if the President does not like the advice – despite the fact that the OCL operates under the Attorney General who is an appointee and works under the President.[13] The legal opinions from the OCL become binding on the executive branch until countermanded by the President. People acting pursuant to an OLC opinion enjoy civil and criminal immunity. The OCL has followed a number of practices to help assure its autonomy, but arguably its autonomy had been compromised during the Bush administration, when the OCL issued its notorious opinion that waterboarding was neither torture nor a crime, thus authorizing the CIA to move ahead, and eventually leading to the immunity of the CIA personnel who were involved in waterboarding. In 2009 the Office of Professional Responsibility in the Department of Justice concluded that John Yoo, who wrote the "torture memos," had committed "intentional professional misconduct when he violated his duty to exercise independent legal judgment and render thorough, objective and candid legal advice."[14] This finding implied that the OCL had at this historical

11 James E. Baker, *The NSC in transition: Organizing the National Security Council, process and staff in the next administration*, 34 (American Bar Association, Nov 11, 2016), archived at https://www.americanbar.org/content/ dam/aba/images/law_national_security/ABA%20NSC%20Paper%20Final%2011-9-16.pdf.

12 A useful account of the OCL during the Bush administration can be found in, Goldsmith, *The terror presidency* (cited in note 10).

13 The materials that follow draw from: *Developments – Presidential authority*, 125 Harv L Rev 2057 (2012); Goldsmith, *The terror presidency* (cited in note 10).

14 Office of Professional Responsibility, Department of Justice, *Investigation into the Office of Legal Counsel's Memoranda concerning issues relating to the Central Intelligence Agency's use of "enhanced interrogation techniques" on suspected terrorists*, 11 (July 29, 2009), archived at https://www.aclu.org/files/pdfs/natsec/opr20100219/20090729_OPR_ Final_Report_with_20100719_declassifications.pdf.

moment, been politicized. The OCL also issued opinions providing legal justification for the President's Surveillance Program.

Given only the broad-brush guidance of E.O. 12333 and scant statutory authority the Attorney General, FBI, and U.S. Attorneys have self-imposed guidelines for the conduct of investigations and prosecutions. (See Chapters 6 and 7.) These guidelines are a first step toward assuring the FBI and prosecutors operate according to the rule of law, and a balance is struck between, on the one hand, crime prevention and national security, and on the other hand, civil rights and civil liberties.[15]

The Department of Defense also operates under various manuals reflecting its understanding of the law of war and Geneva Conventions.

II. The core

A. *Overview*

The "core" is comprised of all the departments, divisions, agencies, and offices that carry out the counterterrorism program. A wide range of agencies have counterterrorism as part of their mission. Those of central concern in this book, starting at the executive department level, are the Departments of Homeland Security (with multiple components), Defense, State, Treasury, Justice, Energy, and the Office of the Director of National Intelligence. Nested within these departments are the National Intelligence Council, the National Security Agency (NSA), the Federal Bureau of Investigation, Customs and Border Protection, Immigration and Customs Enforcement, the Transportation Security Administration as well as other components that comprise the Intelligence Community (IC), a collaborative arrangement of 16 separate agencies that join together to engage in intelligence activities.[16] The CIA is an independent entity not part of any federal department. [A list of IC intelligence programs and IC leaders can be found in Appendices B and E of the document cited in the accompanying footnote.[17]]

The CIA operating outside the U.S. is "the largest producer of all-source, national security intelligence primarily for the President, Congress, and senior policymakers in the NSC. It manages clandestine HUMINT (human intelligence) collection, covert operations, and OSINT (open source intelligence) across the IC."[18] The collection within the U.S. of foreign intelligence regarding U.S. persons can be carried out by the FBI and NSA with limitations discussed in the book; the CIA may not

15 See, also, Stephen Dycus, Arthur L. Berney, William C. Banks, Peter Raven-Hansen, and Stephen I. Vladeck, *National security law*, 6th ed., 532 (Wolters Kluwer 2016).

16 50 USC §3003(4). See, also, Michael B. Kraft, Edward Marks, *U.S. government counterterrorism: A guide to who does what* (CRC 2012).

17 Miles, *Intelligence community programs, management and enduring issues* (cited in note 2).

18 Id at 9,14.

use surveillance techniques subject to the Fourth Amendment inside the U.S.[19] As for the FBI, it is both an intelligence agency and a law enforcement agency.

With the proliferation of agencies engaged in counterterrorism it should come as no surprise that the legal jurisdiction of these units tends to be joint, overlapping, and blurred, compounded by competition for resources and complex budget arrangements.[20] Accordingly, improving, managing, and coordinating cooperation among this vast intelligence apparatus is a central and continuing focus of the President and the Director of National Intelligence with their oversight responsibility. In this regard, of particular importance for this book is the relationship between the Federal Bureau of Investigation and the National Security Agency taken up in Chapters 5, 6, and 7.

The "core" enterprise has six operational functions: (1) information or intelligence collection; (2) law enforcement and the prosecution of terrorists in civilian courts; (3) protection of infrastructure and responding to and mitigating incidents affecting the infrastructure; (4) border protection and the management of refugees, visas, and removal; (5) the incarceration and prosecution by the military of unprivileged enemy belligerents; and (6) research and development. Each of these functions requires interagency collaboration. There are numerous ways that collaboration could become manifest: collaboration, coordination, merger, integration, networks, and partnerships.[21]

Setting up, managing, and reforming this system has been a work in constant progress over the years. First came the creation of the National Security Council in 1947, the IC in 1981, the Department of Homeland Security in 2002, the Joint Intelligence Community Council in 2004, and the Office of the Director of National Intelligence in 2005 (the authority of which spans across intelligence units located throughout the government).[22] Note that each year the President is required by Congress to submit "a comprehensive report on the national security strategy of the United States" that must include an "evaluation of the balance among the capabilities of all elements of the national power of the United States to support the implementation of the national security strategy."[23]

Within the Executive Department there are seemingly constant changes. For example, in February 2015 President Obama directed the creation of the Cyber Threat Intelligence Integration Center that was to "provide all-source intelligence analysis related to foreign cyber threats and incidents."[24]

19 *Central Intelligence Agency intelligence activities: Procedures approved by the Attorney General pursuant to Executive Order 12333*, January 17, 2017, archived at https://www.cia.gov/about-cia/privacy-and-civil-liberties/CIA-AG-Guidelines-Signed.pdf.

20 Id at 29, 30, 37 Appendices F and G.

21 Frederick M. Kaiser, *Interagency collaborative arrangements and activities: Types, rationales, considerations* (Congressional Research Service, May 31, 2011 R41803).

22 50 USC §3021-3027; 50 USC §3001ff; 6 USC §111.

23 50 USC §3043.

24 https://obamawhitehouse.archives.gov/the-press-office/2015/02/25/fact-sheet-cyber-threat-intelligence-integration-center.

B. Core: information and intelligence collection and related activities

The different governmental entities engaged in the intelligence effort do so for many purposes: to develop the global and domestic strategy to combat and prevent terrorism; to obtain broad long-term data regarding trends – both economic and social – that bear on the forecasting of terrorism activities; to obtain data to aid in more detailed planning and resource allocation to combat terrorism; to obtain information regarding military readiness and capabilities of terrorist organizations; to carry out risk assessments of critical infrastructure; to predict the future of terrorism; to obtain the data necessary to locate, disrupt, and prevent a terrorist plot; to place specific people on watchlists including the No Fly List; to identify specific individuals who should be investigated by the FBI; and to gather the information necessary to bring charges and try specific individuals. Many of these activities will be covered in greater detail in this book.

It is unavoidable that both the kinds of information collected for the above purposes and the methods used to obtain the information are diverse. The categories of information collected include: human intelligence, suspicious activity reports of actual humans, signals or electronic data (especially metadata), content of communications, images of various kinds, financial intelligence, and much more.[25] The NSA constructed a facility to store data at a cost of $1 billion, which has an electrical bill of more than $1 million a month.[26] And this is just the NSA. The Department of the Treasury collects important financial information and banks are required to report on suspicious banking activities (12 CFR §21.11). A list of IC collection disciplines can be found in the report cited in the footnote below.[27]

The intelligence function is executed in a cycle that begins with planning, moves through creating the collection apparatus including hardware, software and personnel, the collection itself, storage, analysis, sharing, and evaluation of the collection function. This intelligence cycle occurs both at the "micro" level within the various departments, divisions, and offices that conduct intelligence work, and at the macro level, meaning the federal government and its state and local partners taken as a whole.[28]

Given the range of data, the information being collected, and the various purposes the intelligence enterprise must serve, it is not surprising that the number of

25 https://nsa.gov1.info/data.

26 Timothy H. Edgar, *Beyond Snowden*, 138 (Brookings Institution Press 2017).

27 Miles, *Intelligence community programs, management and enduring issues*, 48 Appendix A (cited in note 2).

28 See, for example, Mark A. Randol, *The Department of Homeland Security Intelligence enterprise: Operational overview and oversight challenges for Congress* (Congressional Research Service, March 19, 2010, R40602); Mark A. Randol, *Terrorism information sharing and the Nationwide Suspicious Activity Report initiative: Background and issues for Congress* (Congressional Research Service, November 5, 2009, R40901). See, also, Rachel Levinson-Waldman, *What the government does with Americans' data*, 19–22 (Brennan Center For Justice 2013); Michael Price, *National security and local police* (Brennan Center 2013), archived at https://www.brennancenter.org/sites/default/files/ publications/NationalSecurity_LocalPolice_web.pdf.

governmental and private entities involved is significant. A study by the *Washington Post* noted above concluded that there were 17 government organizations engaged in human intelligence; 26 engaged in collecting what the study called technical intelligence; 36 engaged in counterintelligence; 25 involved in addressing terrorist financing; and 39 agencies engaged in analysis. Further, some 1000 private companies were under contract to provide assistance, half of which worked with the National Security Agency.

For there to be an effective counterterrorism effort, these separate buckets of information needed to be analyzed, disseminated, and shared as promoted by statutes adopted after 9/11, 6 USC §§481–485, and §§101-125. Since 9/11 Congress and the President together have been beating the drum of data sharing among the agencies.[29] Effective sharing is not easy, requiring both bureaucratic changes and technological changes to assure compatibility among machines, software, and databases. The explosion of data places increased demands on the analytical capabilities of the government.

For the purposes of this book, the four agencies of greatest significance regarding intelligence are the NSA, the National Counterterrorism Center (NCTC), the FBI, the Terrorist Screening Center (TSC), and agencies associated with these central four agencies. (The Department of Homeland Security also owns and operates the TECS (not an acronym), an information sharing platform of particular use in the screening of travelers by the Customs and Border Patrol.)

The NSA, the largest agency in the IC, has its own databases compiled through its own surveillance activities (Chapters 2 and 3). As noted above, the NSA maintains a 1 million square feet data center.[30] It does not act on these data by seizing or detaining suspects, but passes the data on to the President, the National Security Council, the military services, the Department of Homeland Security, the members of the Intelligence Community, foreign partners, and the FBI.[31]

Turning to the National Counterterrorism Center:

> The Director of the National Counterterrorism Center shall establish and maintain within the National Counterterrorism Center a Directorate of Intelligence which shall have primary responsibility within the United States Government for analysis of terrorism and terrorist organizations (except for purely domestic terrorism and domestic terrorist organizations) from all sources of intelligence, whether collected inside or outside the United States.[32]

The NCTC has access to and is provided information from multiple databases in the hands of the FBI, CBP, NSA, CIA, and also receives from other federal agencies

29 6 USC §485; 50 USC §3381; 6 USC §121; 6 USC §124a; 6 USC 124c.

30 https://nsa.gov1.info/utah-data-center.

31 https://www.nsa.gov/what-we-do/customers-and-partners/. See, also, Dycus, Berney, Banks, Raven-Hansen, and Vladeck, *National security law*, 6th ed., at 508 (cited in note 14).

32 50 USC §3056(i).

nominations of people to be included on the, Terrorist Identities Datamart Environment (TIDE).[33]

> [TIDE] is the USG's central repository of information on international persons and groups with known or suspected links to terrorist activities. TIDE incorporates information derived from credible intelligence developed by USG [United States Government] agencies to support terrorist screening systems across the USG.[34]

What behavior leads a person to be nominated for TIDE?

Types of conduct that warrant inclusion in TIDE include persons who:

- Commit international terrorist activity.
- Prepare or plan international terrorist activity.
- Gather information on potential targets for international terrorist activity.
- Solicit funds or valuables for international terrorist activity or a terrorist organization.
- Solicit membership in an international terrorist organization.
- Provide material support (e.g., safe house, transportation, or training) to a known or suspected terrorist or foreign terrorist organization.
- Are members of or represent a foreign terrorist organization.[35]

After reviewing and enhancing the TIDE data, the NCTC exports terrorist identifiers to the Terrorist Screening Center and multiple agencies are able to request information from the NCTC.

Before discussing the Terrorist Screening Center, a few words need to be said about the FBI. The FBI investigates domestic and foreign-connected terrorism and collects its own data, but in addition, works with other agencies, and those agencies may supply the FBI with further data. The FBI and the NSA are discussed in Chapters 6 and 7.

There are 104 FBI-sponsored JTTFs, which have been described as follows:

> JTTFs are locally based, multi-agency teams of investigators, analysts, linguists, SWAT experts, and other specialists who investigate terrorism and

33 NCTC, *Overview of NCTC's data access as authorized by the 2012 Attorney General guidelines* (no date), archived at https://www.dni.gov/index.php/nctc-newsroom/nctc-transparency/item/1723-overview-of-nctc-s-data-access-as-authorized-by-the-2012-attorney-general-guidelines; Jerome P. Bjelopera, Bart Elias, Alison Siskin, *The Terrorist Screening Database and preventing terrorist travel* (Congressional Research Service, November 7, 2016, R44678). See, also, Levinson-Waldman, *What the government does with Americans' data*, 19–22 (cited in note 29).

34 In Focus, *National Counterterrorism Center (NCTC)* (Congressional Research Service, August 18, 2017, IF10709).

35 NCTC, *Terrorist Identities Datamart Environment (TIDE)*, June 30, 2016.

> terrorism-related crimes. Seventy-one of the more than 100 JTTFs operated by DOJ and the FBI were created since 9/11. Over 4,400 federal, state, and local law enforcement officers and agents—more than four times the pre-9/11 total—work in them. These officers and agents come from more than 600 state and local agencies and 50 federal agencies.[36]

The Bureau of Alcohol, Tobacco, Firearms and Explosives (ATF) and the Internal Revenue Service participate in the JTTFs.

> The FBI considers JTTFs "the nation's front line on terrorism." They "investigate acts of terrorism that affect the U.S., its interests, property and citizens, including those employed by the U.S. and military personnel overseas." As this suggests, their operations are highly tactical and can involve developing human sources (informants) as well as gathering intelligence to thwart terrorist plots. JTTFs also offer an important conduit for the sharing of intelligence developed from FBI-led counterterrorism investigations with outside agencies and state and local law enforcement.[37]

The fusion centers (perhaps 77 of them[38]) are run by state and local authorities and focus on the collection and "fusing" of terrorism-related information from many sources, including federal databases.[39] The Department of Homeland Security says the fusion centers "operate as state and major urban area focal points for the receipt, analysis, gathering, and sharing of threat-related information between federal, state, local, tribal, territorial (SLTT), and private sector partners."[40] The National Strategy for Information Sharing states that fusion centers "will serve as the primary focal points within the state and local environment for the receipt and sharing of terrorism-related information."[41] Fusion centers have a broader purpose than terrorism, namely, to address "all crimes" and consolidate information on "all hazards" such as tornadoes. Yet the centers are linked to the federal Information Sharing Environment, an important computer-based system for sharing information. There are issues regarding the quality of information fusion centers obtain locally and share with the federal government.[42]

36 Jerome B. Bjelopera, *The Federal Bureau of Investigation and terrorism investigations*, 13 (Congressional Research Service, April 24, 2013, R41780).

37 Jerome B. Bjelopera, *Domestic terrorism: An overview*, 4 (Congressional Research Service, August 21, 2017, R44921).

38 https://www.aclu.org/other/more-about-fusion-centers.

39 *Fusion center guidelines: Developing and sharing information and intelligence in a new era*, August 2006, archived at http://it.ojp.gov/documents/fusion_center_guidelines_law_enforcement.pdf.

40 https://www.dhs.gov/state-and-major-urban-area-fusion-centers.

41 General Accounting Office, *Information sharing*, April 2013, GAO-13-471, at 16, archived at https://www.gao.gov/products/GAO-13-471.

42 Price, *National security and local police*, 1, 20–21, 23 (cited in note 29).

The JTTFs and fusion centers work with each other and are "often located in the same building." JTTFs conduct investigations while fusion centers do not. But they have some overlapping responsibilities that can create competition for information, promote confusion about the rules, and thereby lead to the proliferation of bad data without adequate oversight.[43]

Field Intelligence Groups (FIGs) perform a function that overlaps with that of the fusion centers but has a focus that moves beyond the region, state and locality to the national and international stage; it combines the expertise of special agents, language analysts, and surveillance specialists. "FIGs are teams of FBI intelligence analysts, special agents, language analysts, and financial analysts, among others, working in each of the 56 FBI field offices to analyze information from cases in their field offices and share intelligence locally and nationally."[44]

Piled on top of the fusion centers and JTTFs is the Nationwide Suspicious Activity Reporting Initiative (SAR), a federal effort to create a system for consolidating into a shared space suspicious activity reports from around the nation submitted by local law enforcement agencies. This system is legally rooted in the 2004 Intelligence Reform and Terrorism Prevention Act (IRTPA)[45] and President Bush's National Strategy for Information Sharing. A suspicious activity is "observed behavior reasonably indicative of pre-operational planning related to terrorism or other criminal activity."[46] Thus if one of the approximately 750,000 sworn police officers in the U.S. observes someone taking photos of the superstructure of a bridge, this may be reported as a suspicious activity, especially if the person moves off when approached.[47] These reports are then vetted by a fusion center or JTTF and then, if the information meets the SAR criteria (as established by the Director of National Intelligence), it ends up in a "shared space" which is available to law enforcement officials at all levels of government through various sharing systems such as the FBI's Guardian system.

The FBI's "Shared Responsibility Committees" (SRCs), a recent development, have been described as locally based arrangements whereby social service workers, teachers, mental health professionals, religious figures, and others "interdict" young

43 Id at 17.

44 Id at 54.

45 6 USC §485; Jerome P. Bjelopera, *Terrorism information sharing and the Nationwide Suspicious Activity Reporting initiative: Background and issues for Congress*, 1 (Congressional Research Service, December 28, 2011, R40901).

46 https://www.hsdl.org/?abstract&did=9093; See, also, Fact sheet: Update to suspicious activity reporting functional standard provides greater privacy and civil liberties protections, May 21, 2009, archived at https://www.dni.gov/files/ISE/documents/DocumentLibrary/SAR/ISE-SAR_Functional_Standard_V1_5_Fact_Sheet.pdf.

47 Information Sharing Environment (ISE) Functional Standards (FS) Suspicious Activity Reporting (SAR) Version 1.5.5, ISE-FS-200, Issued by the Office of the Director of National Intelligence Program Manager, Information Sharing Environment, at 48, archived at https://www.dni.gov/files/ISE/documents/DocumentLibrary/SAR/ SAR_FS_1.5.5_IssuedFeb2015.pdf; Duren Banks, et. al., *National sources of law enforcement employment data*, 2 table 1 (U.S. Department of Justice, Bureau of Justice Statistics, April 26, 2016, revised October 4, 2016), NCJ 249681, archived at https://www.bjs.gov/index.cfm?ty=pbdetail&iid=5600.

people they believe are on a radicalization path. Those identified would in turn be discussed by community leaders and FBI representatives. Critics say the program is simply another FBI informants program.[48]

Turning back now to the Terrorist Screening Center (TSC), which is a multi-agency organization administered by the FBI and created by President Bush in 2003 after 9/11.[49] The TSC compiles and maintains the Terrorist Screening Database (TSDB) also known as the terrorist watchlist, and:

> [I]ncludes biographic identifiers for those known either to have or be suspected of having ties to terrorism. In some instances it also includes biometric information on such people. It stores hundreds of thousands of unique identities. Portions of the TSDB are exported to data systems in federal agencies that perform screening activities such as background checks, reviewing the records of passport and visa applicants, and official encounters with travelers at U.S. border crossings.[50]

It is from the TSDB that the No Fly and Selectee lists and other lists are developed (see Chapter 5) to ultimately be used by screeners issuing visas, and the Transportation Security Administration (TSA) whose employees screen people prior to being allowed to board an airplane.

An important purpose behind collecting all this information is to engage in data mining. Federal law specifically authorizes the Department of Homeland Security to engage in data mining, 6 USC §121(d)(13). Contact-chaining applied to meta-data (e.g., telephone numbers) is a standard technique to uncover sleeper cells, conspirators. A related law is the Privacy Act of 1974 that regulates disclosure of data, and access to it, 5 USC §552a. The law also requires agencies to list the permissible "routine" uses of the data, which must be compatible with the purposes for which the data were originally collected.

C. *Core: law enforcement and the prosecution of terrorists*

Law enforcement responsibilities are found in many federal agencies (as well as in state and local law agencies). This book focuses on four law enforcement agencies, the FBI, Customs and Border Patrol (CBP), U.S. Immigration and Customs Enforcement (ICE), and Transportation Security Administration (TSA). The Attorney General of the U.S. has the "primary investigative authority for all Federal

48 Murtaza Hussain and Jenna McLaughlin, *FBI's "Shared responsibility committees" to identify "radicalized" Muslims raise alarms* (Intercept, April, April 9, 2016), archived at https://theintercept.com/2016/04/09/fbis-shared-responsibility-committees-to-identify-radicalized-muslims-raises-alarms/.

49 Jerome P. Bjelopera, Bart Elias, and Alison Siskin, *The Terrorist Screening Database and preventing terrorist travel*, 1 (Congressional Research Service November 7, 2016, R44678).

50 Id at Summary.

crimes of terrorism."[51] The FBI has "lead agency responsibility" in investigating all crimes that involve terrorist activities or preparation for those activities, and reports on same to the Attorney General, 28 CFR §§0.85(l), 0.85a. A bill (S. 2148) has been proposed that would create offices within the Department of Justice and within the FBI especially dedicated to investigating and prosecuting domestic terrorism.

Other agencies may from time to time deal with terrorist-related activity, for example the Drug Enforcement Agency and the ATF. The fusion centers noted above are vehicles for sharing information, while the JTTFs led by the FBI coordinate federal counterterrorism investigations throughout the U.S., involving federal, state, and local agencies. The JTTFs are comprised of over 500 state and local agencies and 55 federal agencies (the Department of Homeland Security, the U.S. military, Immigration and Customs Enforcement, and the Transportation Security Administration, to name a few). The 104 JTTFs as described by the FBI "do it all: chase down leads, gather evidence, make arrests, provide security for special events, conduct training, collect and share intelligence, and respond to threats and incidents at a moment's notice."[52] Another joint enforcement effort is the National Cyber Investigative Joint Task Force with 20 partnering agencies to go after terrorists and criminals mounting cyber threats.[53] The number of federal employees with arrest and firearm authority in 2008 was approximately 120,000, with by far and away the largest numbers employed by the CBP (36,863); Bureau of Prisons (16,835); the FBI (12,760); and ICE (12,446).[54]

D. Core: the other operational functions

There are a number of other operational functions of the federal enterprise: (a) border protection and the management of refugees and immigrants; (b) airline security; (c) the protection of infrastructure, responding to and mitigating terrorist incidents by both civilian and military authorities;[55] and (d) the detainment, interrogation and prosecution of unprivileged enemy belligerents. Later chapters of this book will take up border protection (Chapter 4), airline security (Chapter 5), infrastructure with the focus on cybersecurity (Chapter 7) and unprivileged enemy belligerents (Chapters 8 through 10).

Finally, the government needs to engage in research and development in order to keep up with the moving target that is terrorism; this gets the government into the funding many projects, both "soft" and "hard" science projects. To name a few, here's a partial list of research endeavors: data mining and machine learning; the psychology of radicalization; biometrics; all aspects of information technology; spying apparatus to be used for the Internet or even at the street level; sensor technology; forecasting;

51 18 USC §2332b(f).

52 https://www.fbi.gov/investigate/terrorism/joint-terrorism-task-forces.

53 https://www.fbi.gov/investigate/cyber/national-cyber-investigative-joint-task-force.

54 Brian A. Reaves, *Federal law enforcement officers, 2008* (U.S. Department of Justice, Bureau of Justice Statistics, July 2012, NCJ 238250), archived at https://www.bjs.gov/index.cfm?ty=pbdetail&iid=4372.

55 See William C. Banks and Stephen Dycus, *Soldiers on the home front* (Harvard 2016).

language; speech recognition, and face and object recognition.[56] Research is a component of many of the players in the government's counterterrorism enterprise – the Office of the Director of National Intelligence, the National Security Agency, and the FBI. For example, the FBI houses a Counterterrorism and Forensic Science Research Unit whose research areas include DNA, chemical analysis, microbial forensics, and more.[57] The Intelligence Advanced Research Project Activity in the Office of the Director of National Intelligence works on forecasting, machine learning, superconducting, computing technologies, and "innovative approaches to gain access to denied environments," and much more.[58]

III. Overseeing and constraining the counterterrorism enterprise

The federal counterterrorism enterprise is subject to internal and external legal and non-legal constraints. What these constraints are is the focus of this section. The effect of these constraints in protecting, on the one hand, the rule of law, and civil rights and liberties, or, on the other hand, in frustrating the effort to protect national security, is a separate empirical and normative question briefly addressed at the end of this section.[59]

The Brennan Center has concluded that many state and local intelligence programs lack adequate oversight. "While federal agencies operate under the watch of independent inspectors general, there is often no equivalent for state and local information sharing ventures. Very few local governments have built the kind of oversight structures that should accompany such a significant expansion of police functions."[60]

A. The mechanisms

In recent years a most visible check on the system has been the free press and non-governmental organizations such as the American Civil Liberties Union, Electronic Frontier Foundation, Lawfare, Just Security, the Center for Constitutional Rights, the Brennan Center for Justice, Georgetown's Center on National Security and Law, the Brookings Institute, and others. These organizations, armed with the Freedom of Information Act[61] and assisted by whistleblowers, launch important legal challenges and play a big role in reporting on and exposing the operations of the system.

Oversight and checking was potentially enhanced by a provision of the FISA Amendments Reauthorization Act of 2017 that extends protection against retaliation to employees of contractors with the IC, including the FBI, who "lawfully disclose"

56 See The research project of the Intelligence Advanced Research Projects Activity (IARPA), archived at https://www.iarpa.gov/. See, also, James Bamford, *The shadow factory*, 320, 325, 327, 334 (Doubleday 2008).
57 Kraft Marks, *U.S. government counterterrorism: A guide to who does what*, 253 (cited in note 15).
58 https://www.iarpa.gov/.
59 See, for example, Jack Goldsmith, *Power and constraint* (W.W. Norton 2012); Sudha Setty, *National security secrecy* (Cambridge 2017).
60 Price, *National security and local police*, 20–21 (cited in note 29).
61 5 USC §552.

information they "reasonably believe" evidences violation of any federal law or an abuse of authority.[62] Under the law the whistleblower is protected when making a report to one of several specific officials, e.g., the DNI, an inspector general, the head of the contracting agency, a congressional intelligence committee, the FBI Office of Professional Responsibility, or the Office of Special Counsel. The new law also increased the penalty for unauthorized removal and retention of classified documents from one to five years;[63] Snowden's revelations would not have been protected.

Congress has played an important role in overseeing and checking the executive branch of the government. A history of surveillance in the United States would not be complete without telling the story of how various congressional investigations of the intelligence system have impacted the system.[64] Today there is a permanent select committee in the House and Senate to conduct oversight of U.S. intelligence activities. Congress has, to an extent, sought to assure its oversight responsibility by incorporating into statutes a requirement that periodic reports be made to it. During the course of the President's (Mass) Surveillance Program (Chapter 2) between October 2001 and January 2007, the NSA conducted 49 briefings for members of Congress and staff. Interestingly, it appears no Congress person suggested that the NSA should stop the program.[65]

Agencies are obligated to make regular reports to Congress. For example, under the Federal Data Mining Reporting Act of 2007 agencies are required to report their data mining activities to Congress, 42 USC §2000ee. The Government Accountability Office audits and evaluates programs for Congress, 31 USC §701 et seq.

After Edward Snowden's revelations in 2013 regarding the then secret surveillance activities of the NSA, Congress in 2015 passed the USA Freedom Act, which imposed a new set of reporting and disclosure requirements on the Director of National Intelligence, the Attorney General, and the Director of the Administrative Office of United States Courts. The law required that steps be taken to undertake declassification reviews of FISA court orders and opinions; reports had to be issued to Congress regarding applications and certifications submitted to FISA courts; and all related data had to be posted on the Internet, including data regarding national security letters.[66] Additionally, people subject to FISA orders or National Security Letters now could publish aggregate data about the orders or NSLs (50 USC §1874). Article III courts were required to report annually on the number of wiretaps authorized under Title III of the Omnibus Crime Control and Safe Streets Act of 1968.[67]

62 50 USC §3234 (amended by Pub L 115-118, January 19, 2018).

63 18 USC §1924(a) (amended by Pub L 115-118, January 19, 2018).

64 Richard A. Best Jr., *Proposal for intelligence reorganization 1949–2004* (Congressional Research Service, September 24, 2004, RL32500); Loch K. Johnson, *A season of inquiry revisited: The Church Committee confronts America's spy agencies* (University of Kansas Press 2015).

65 Offices of the Inspector General, Department of Defense, Department of Justice, Central Intelligence Agency, National Security Agency, Office of the Director of National Intelligence, *Report on the President's Surveillance Program*, Volume I 26–27 (July 10, 2009).

66 USA Freedom Act, PL 114-23 (2015).

67 18 USC §2519(3).

The Department of Justice was required to report on: the number of requested orders for the use of pen register/trap and trace devices (a method of electronic surveillance discussed in Chapter 3); the status of U.S. persons or residents detained on suspicion of terrorism; the number of applications made for electronic surveillance for foreign intelligence purposes; and the number of applications for the production of business records for foreign intelligence and international investigations.[68]

The USA Freedom Act gives Congress the option on an ad hoc basis of requesting specific reports and holding hearings on specific troubling issues for purely investigative purposes, with a view to writing legislation. The Senate Intelligence Committee conducted a five-year inquiry into the CIA's harsh detention and interrogation practices that used, among other things, waterboarding, a technique widely labeled as torture. (See Chapter 8.) It was then that Congress adopted the Detainee Treatment Act, which sought to limit the use of torture, albeit not by the CIA. Another example: Congress, in the face of severe concerns regarding the surveillance activities of an administration, passed legislation to check and control those abuses. The original FISA was a product of this history. Since FISA's enactment in 1978, Congress has amended FISA several times both to legalize aspects of the President's Surveillance Program, but also more recently, to reign in the efforts of the administration to obtain in bulk "tangible things" (telephony metadata) of innumerable innocent Americans. (See Chapter 3.) In 2018 Congress again substantively amended FISA and imposed additional reporting requirements regarding the substantive reforms, and also required the Attorney General to report annually on the number of applications and number of subjects targeted under FISA.[69]

What about the third branch of the government, the judiciary? The judiciary plays an oversight role when suits are filed by individuals claiming, for example, that their Fourth Amendment rights have been violated, or when the government is required by federal statute to come to the judiciary for authorization, such as to obtain a search warrant under the Fourth Amendment, or to obtain authorization to engage in electronic surveillance under FISA or the Wiretap Act. In the context of a criminal trial the judiciary blocks the use of illegally obtained evidence and testimony.

The judiciary, however, has not always made itself available to those seeking to block the government's surveillance activity. Article III of the Constitution limits the jurisdiction of the federal courts to "cases" or "controversies." This has traditionally been interpreted to mean, among other things, that only people who have actually been injured by the government, a doctrine called "standing," may bring suit. The Supreme Court has adopted a narrow view of who meets the standing requirement.[70] For example, to have standing to challenge a surveillance program the plaintiff must have information about the NSA's targeting practices and be able to establish that they have been targeted or that targeting of them is certainly impending, an obviously high hurdle given the secrecy surrounding the NSA's

68 18 USC §3126; 28 USC §509; 50 USC §§1807 and 1862(c).

69 50 USC 1807, 50 USC 1846, 50 USC 1881a (as amended by Pub L 115-118, January 29, 2018).

70 *Clapper v Amnesty Int'l US*, 133 S Ct 1138, 1147, 1148 (2013).

targeting practices. Courts have upheld governmental claims of secrecy in blocking suits by those subject to extraordinary rendition.[71]

The Supreme Court did block the effort of the Bush administration to deny access to the writ of habeas corpus to the Guantanamo detainees (Chapter 10), and proceedings in the lower federal courts have served to help air out and reveal how the surveillance programs in fact operate (Chapter 3).

The FISA court operates under a number of constraints noted by Professor Setty:[72] the judges have had to rely entirely on the facts and presentations made by the government since the court has no investigative capacity of its own and proceedings before the court are not adversarial. A partial reform correcting these procedural limitations was instituted when Congress required the presiding FISA court judges to designate at least five people to serve as amici curiae in the proceedings before the court.[73] The amici curiae are there to provide the court with legal arguments that advance the protection of individual privacy and liberties, among other topics. The amicus curiae who has a security clearance "may have access" to classified information.

Checking mechanisms also exist within the executive branch itself. As a result of the Inspector General Act there are offices of inspectors general located in the Department of Justice, National Security Agency, Central Intelligence Agency, and the Department of Homeland Security.[74] Inspectors General (IGs) "head permanent, nonpartisan, and independent offices that conduct audits, investigations, and other evaluations of federal department and agency programs and operations."[75] Pursuant to the law an IG has considerable authority to carry out "audits and investigations" leading to recommendations designed to promote economy, efficiency, effectiveness, and to prevent fraud and abuse.[76] (The law specifically directed the inspector general of the Department of Justice to report on the FBI's querying procedures of data collected pursuant to §702 (See Chapter 3).[77]) Armed with that authority the IG in the Department of Justice executed a series of investigations regarding a variety of surveillance and information gathering activities of the FBI under the Foreign Intelligence Surveillance Act.[78] A working draft dated March 29, 2009 of a report by the

71 *Mohamed v Jeppesen Dataplan*, 614 F3d 1070 (9th Cir 2010); *El-Masri v United States*, 479 F3d 296 (4th Cir 2007).

72 Sudha Setty, *Surveillance, secrecy, and the search for meaningful accountability*, Stan J Intl L 69, 84 (2015).

73 50 USC §1803(i). The FISA Amendments Reauthorization Act of 2017 authorizes their compensation. Pub L. 115-118, §106.

74 5 USC App. 3.

75 Wendy Ginsberg and Michael Greene, *Federal inspectors general: History, characteristics, and recent Congressional actions*, 1 (Congressional Research Service June 2, 2016, R43814).

76 5 USC Title 5, Appendix, Inspector General Act of 1978, archived at https://www.gpo.gov/fdsys/pkg/USCODE-2011-title5/html/USCODE-2011-title5-app-inspector.htm.

77 50 USC §1881a(m)(2).

78 See, for example, Office of the Inspector General, U.S. Department of Justice, *A review of the Federal Bureau of Investigation's activities under Section 702 of the Foreign Intelligence Surveillance Act Amendments of 2008* (September, 2012), archived at https://oig.justice.gov/reports/2015/o1501.pdf; Office of the Inspector General, U.S. Department of Justice, *A review of the FBI's use of pen register and trap and trace devices under the Foreign Intelligence Surveillance Act in 2007 through 2009*, Executive Summary (June 2015), archived at https://oig.justice.gov/reports/2015/o1506.pdf.

NSA's IG regarding President Bush's President's Surveillance Program (PSP) – the initial controversial mass suspicionless program of the NSA (addressed in Chapters 2 and 3) – was made available online by the American Civil Liberties Union.[79] And the IG of the CIA issued a critical report on CIA interrogation and detention practices.[80]

Presidential Policy Directive 28 requires a member of the IC to facilitate oversight over the implementation of safeguards protecting personal information; when a significant compliance issue occurs involving personal information of any person, regardless of nationality, the issue has to be reported to the Director of National Intelligence, who is to determine what, if any, corrective actions are necessary.

There are two mechanisms in the Department of Justice. Of particular importance is the Office of Legal Counsel (OCL) discussed above. The Department of Justice's Office of Professional Responsibility (OPR) has jurisdiction to investigate misconduct of department attorneys regarding the exercise of their authority to investigate, litigate, or provide legal advice.[81] 28 CFR §0.39(a)(1). OPR investigated the department attorneys who wrote the "torture" memo authorizing waterboarding (Chapter 8).[82] The report concluded that the authors of the memo had committed professional misconduct. However, the Associate Deputy Attorney General, David Margolis, on January 5, 2010 rejected that conclusion, thus closing the investigation of Yoo and Bybee.[83]

Central Intelligence Agency employees have an obligation to inform the CIA's general counsel about violations of law and agency rules, and heads of departments or agencies must report to the Attorney General information and allegations regarding violations of federal criminal laws by officers and employees of the government.[84]

The Privacy and Civil Liberties Oversight Board (PCLOB) was established by E.O. 13353 on August 27, 2004, following the recommendation of the National Commission on Terrorist Attacks Upon the United States (9/11 Commission) that "there should be a board within the executive branch to oversee adherence to the guidelines we recommend and the commitment the government makes to defend our civil liberties."[85] Today the PCLOB is authorized by a federal statute that establishes the PCLOB as a five-member bipartisan board with six-year terms appointed by the President with the advice and consent of the Senate.[86] A central purpose of the PCLOB is to "ensure that liberty concerns are appropriately considered in the development and implementation of laws, regulations, and policies related to efforts

79 https://www.aclu.org/files/natsec/nsa/20130816/NSA%20IG%20Report.pdf.

80 Goldsmith, *Power and constraint* at 103 (cited in note 59).

81 28 CFR §0.39; 28 CFR §0.39a(a)(1).

82 Department of Justice, Office of Professional Responsibility, *Investigation into the office of legal counsel's memoranda concerning issues relating to the Central Intelligence Agency's use of "enhanced interrogation techniques" on suspected terrorists* (July 29, 2009), archived at https://www.hsdl.org/?abstract&did=28555.

83 Eric Lichtblau and Scott Shane, *Report faults 2 authors of Bush terror memos* (*New York Times*, February 19, 2010), archived at http://www.nytimes.com/2010/02/20/us/politics/20justice.html.

84 28 USC §535(b); A. John Rasdan, *Quis custodiet ipsos custodes: The CIA's office of general counsel?* 2 J Natl Sec L & Pol 201, 210 (2008).

85 U.S. National Commission on terrorist attacks upon the United States, *The 9/11 Commission report*, 395 (GPO 2004), archived at https://www.9-11commission.gov/report/911Report.pdf.

86 42 USC §2000ee.

to protect the Nation against terrorism."[87] To achieve that purpose the PCLOB is required to review proposed legislation, review the implementation of new and existing legislation, continually review regulations and policies, and determine if the information sharing practices of the executive branch "appropriately protect privacy and civil liberties" and adhere to officially promulgated information sharing guidelines issued under 6 USC §485, which, in turn, must ensure the protection of privacy and civil liberties. The PCLOB has authority to achieve its mission by means of issuing subpoenas approved by the Attorney General and is required to issue reports to Congress and the President not less frequently than semi-annually. Among the reports the PCLOB has issued are reports on surveillance programs operated pursuant to Sections 215 702 of the Foreign Intelligence Surveillance Act. These reports can be found using the search feature on the PCLOB webpage.[88] While the PCLOB cannot itself command reform, it can provide publicity and attention to the issues it addresses, thus possibly triggering pressure on the President and Congress. PCLOB reports have also found their way into judicial proceedings, thus informing the judiciary about its deliberations. As of this writing the PCLOB is in danger of collapsing, with only one current member out of five seats.

By federal law, 42 USC 2000ee-1, various agencies including the NSA and FBI must designate a senior officer to assist the agency regarding privacy and civil liberties concerns when developing or implementing policies related to terrorism.[89] They are also periodically to investigate and review the agency to assure the agency is adequately considering privacy and civil liberties, and to assure the agency has adequate procedures to respond to complaints regarding privacy and civil liberties. The law prohibits reprisals for making a complaint or disclosing information to the officers. The privacy and civil liberties officers are to make periodic reports that are made available to the public.[90]

The Intelligence Community has its own Office of Civil Liberties, Privacy and Transparency headed by the Civil Liberties Protection Officer who reports to the Director of National Intelligence. And the Intelligence Community has sought to be more transparent with its webpage entitled *IC on the Record*, through which it declassifies documents.

The Joint Intelligence Community Council in the Office of the Director of National Intelligence is responsible for, among other things, evaluating the performance of the Intelligence Community.[91]

In 2013 the Director of National Intelligence was directed by President Obama to form an ad hoc review group – the President's Review Group on Intelligence and Communications Technologies – in the wake of the Snowden revelations. In December 2013, the Review Group issued its report entitled "Liberty and Security in a Changing World," which recommended, among other things, amendments to

87 42 USC §2000ee(c)(2).

88 https://www.pclob.gov/.

89 42 USC §2000ee-1(a) (as amended by Pub L 115-118, the FISA Amendments and Reauthorization Act of 2017).

90 The reports of the Office of Privacy and Civil Liberties of the Department of Justice are archived at https://www.justice.gov/opcl/reports.

91 50 USC §3022.

the Foreign Intelligence Surveillance Act and the use of National Security Letters in order to enhance privacy protection, especially of United States persons.

B. Effectiveness

Many of these mechanisms work only after-the-fact. The President acts first, as President Bush did in establishing the President's Surveillance Program (Chapter 2), and then congressional, judicial, and executive branch mechanisms (such as the IGs), kick in. It is beyond the scope of this book to get into a cost-effectiveness assessment of the law in this area, but here are some questions that might be addressed: (a) What effect did these mechanisms have on Presidents Bush, Obama, and Trump? For example, can the modifications by Bush of his initial counterterrorism efforts be attributed to these mechanisms? Professor Jack Goldsmith answers "yes."[92] (b) Are some of these mechanisms more potent than others in affecting policy changes? The answer in this case is certainly "yes." Take several examples. Few would doubt the importance of the whistleblowing of Edward Snowden and related reportage in the free press. While the ordinary federal courts have served, to an extent, to limit the counterterrorism program (as discussed in subsequent chapters), there are concerns with how the secret Foreign Intelligence Surveillance Court has carried out its supervisory role when reviewing requests from the President to engage in surveillance regulated by FISA. The court charged with ruling on the legality of the administration's surveillance requests over the years has basically acquiesced to those requests. Professor Setty reports that between 1979 and 2012, the FISA court received over 30,000 surveillance applications from the government and rejected fewer than 0.1% of them. And in 2012 the FISA court authorized all 1788 requests to conduct electronic surveillance.[93]

Yet Timothy H. Edgar says that the data reported above give a misleading impression.[94] He says surveillance applications before they are formally filed are shared with the court in a process that often results in a change in the application in order to meet the court's objections. If the objections cannot be met the application is withdrawn. And he says even Snowden's disclosures "revealed no intentional targeting of American journalists, political figures, or activists."[95] Yet he does recommend improvements, such as providing the FISA court with skilled technologists, and reforms to prevent a right-leaning Chief Justice with the authority to appoint FISA court judges from packing the court with right-leaning judges.[96]

Congress has repeatedly amended applicable laws and imposed on the executive branch a number of reporting requirements, yet even Jack Goldsmith has said members of Congress have not carried out the oversight function well.[97]

92 Goldsmith, *Power and constraint* (cited in note 59).

93 Id at 75 and 83.

94 Edgar, *Beyond Snowden*, at 129 (cited in note 26).

95 Id at 130; 50 USC §1803(a) (authority of the Chief Justice to appoint sitting federal judges as members of the FISA court).

96 Id at 125, 130.

97 Goldsmith, *Power and constraint*, at 91 (cited in note 59).

2

PRESIDENT BUSH AND MASS SURVEILLANCE

Mass surveillance without a judicially-authorized Fourth Amendment warrant or any other approval of a court started with President Bush's authorization of October 4, 2001. This chapter covers the initial three years of the President's Surveillance Program (PSP) from October of 2001 to March of 2004. During this period, the administration claimed authority for the program based on the President's authority under Article II of the Constitution, creating separation of powers tensions. The program was exclusively focused on foreign-connected terrorism as defined in the introduction, not domestic, a fact that is important regarding its compliance with the Fourth Amendment. (See Section V.) Starting in March 2004 the administration transitioned to reliance on Foreign Intelligence Surveillance Act (FISA) authority; Chapter 3 will pick up the story at that point.

Section I discusses the concept of mass surveillance. Section II outlines the information collected by the PSP, which for a time was known by NSA's code name Stellar Wind.[1] Section III addresses the President's Article II authority, Section IV takes up the Authorization to Use Military Force, Section V briefly addresses the PSP and the Fourth Amendment, and Section VI the PSP as it relates to FISA.

I. Mass surveillance

Mass surveillance involves acquiring hundreds of millions of communications yearly, year after year, regardless of whether the sender or receiver is specifically suspected of anything. While actual mass surveillance programs have tended to focus on

1 Office of the Inspector General, National Security Agency Central Security Service, Working Draft *ST-09-0002*, 10, n.3 (March 24, 2009) (hereinafter Working draft), archived at https://www.aclu.org/files/natsec/nsa/20130816/ NSA%20IG%20Report.pdf.

foreign-connected terrorists, the single most important statute involved, FISA, is written in such a way that it could be used to obtain communications of domestic terrorists and criminals motivated by any number of ideologies. (See Chapter 3 and 6.)

Mass surveillance yields a "bulk collection" of data, which has been defined as a collection of data, a significant portion of which pertains to identifiers (telephone numbers, mobile phone subscribers, IP addresses, email addresses) that were not targets at the time of acquisition.[2] In contrast, "targeted" collection tries to avoid collecting the communications of parties without criminal or national security value. David S. Kris uses the concept of a "relevance-ratio," namely, the ratio of terrorist-related communications to the total number of communications. A bulk collection's relevance-ratio is much lower than that of a targeted collection.[3]

Mass surveillance may be carried out without the use of discriminants (specific identifiers, selection terms), or by means of a very general discriminant ("anyone with an email address served by aol.com," or a key word such as al-Qaeda, or a person reasonably believed to be outside the U.S.). Additionally, for technological or operational reasons, data of a person not targeted may be acquired.[4] Mass surveillance is typically carried out without complying with the procedural protections of the Fourth Amendment required in ordinary criminal law enforcement efforts, albeit the surveillance may still be legally permissible under the Fourth Amendment and FISA.

Why mass surveillance? Presidential Policy Directive 28 on January 17, 2014 said that intelligence in bulk was to be used for the purposes of detecting and countering espionage, various threats to the United States, cybersecurity, and transnational criminal threats. [The data could not be used for the purpose of suppressing dissent, discriminating against individuals, or affording competitive advantage to U.S. companies.] The directive notes that: "Locating new or emerging threats and other vital national security information is difficult, as such information is often hidden within the large and complex system of modern global communications. The United States believes it must consequently collect signals intelligence in bulk." Stated more colloquially, the U.S. needs the haystack in order to acquire the needle that is somewhere in that haystack. That needle may be a terrorist, a terrorist sleeper cell, or even an ordinary criminal. The data collected end up in the hands of the FBI and federal prosecutors for law enforcement purposes, and in the National Counterterrorism

2 National Research Council, *Bulk Collection of Signals Intelligence: Technical Options*, S-1, 2-9 (National Academy Press 2015), archived at https://www.nap.edu/catalog/19414/bulk-collection-of-signals-intelligence-technical-options.

3 Cited in Stephen Dycus, Arthur L. Berney, William C. Banks, Peter Raven-Hansen, and Stephen I. Vladeck, *National Security Law*, 6th ed., 760 (Wolters Kluwer 2016).

4 Executive Office of the President, Presidential Policy Directive-28 states that: "References to signals intelligence collected in 'bulk' mean the authorized collection of large quantities of signals intelligence data which, due to technical or operational considerations, is acquired without the use of discriminants (e.g., specific identifiers, selection terms, etc.)." Executive Office of the President, Presidential Policy Directive/PPD-28 (2014), at note 5 §2.

Center and the Terrorist Screening Center for the purpose of constructing the No Fly and Selectee Lists. (See Chapter 5.) Arguably, we have become a "national surveillance state" that "features the collection, collation, and analysis of information about populations both in the United States and around the world."[5]

To help understand how mass surveillance works, contrast it with the requirements for obtaining a court order to engage in ordinary wiretapping under the Wiretap Act.[6] An application for a wiretap order must be directed toward finding evidence regarding one of a specific number of listed criminal offenses; must include descriptions of the facilities to be targeted, the identity of a person, if known, whose communications are to be intercepted, proof of probable cause that the communications to be collected concern the listed offense(s), and a description of the type of communication to be intercepted. Furthermore, these interceptions are limited in time – no longer than 30 days.[7] (There are provisions of FISA that are specifically used for targeted surveillance.[8] But even NSA's targeted programs may collect massive amounts of data.[9])

Mass surveillance departs from the focused nature of wiretapping under the Wiretap Act in a number of ways. Mass surveillance focuses on gathering foreign intelligence, a very broad concept, thus it is not limited to obtaining evidence regarding specific crimes, as is required by the Wiretap Act.[10] Mass surveillance is not premised on prior suspicion of specific criminal wrongdoing by an identified individual or group. (It can result and, indeed, has resulted in the collection of communications of people who pose no security risk and communications unrelated to foreign intelligence. See discussion of §215 and §702 in Chapter 3.) Mass surveillance is less strictly time limited than surveillance under the Wiretap Act. One type of mass surveillance, upstream mass surveillance – especially when conducted outside the U.S. and discussed more fully later – is, in effect, like opening a fire hydrant and grabbing all the water flowing out and storing it in large tanks to be searched through at a later date. (A FISA court has said that upstream Internet collection constitutes only 9% of the NSA's collection, with the rest obtained perhaps under PRISM and other programs.[11])

II. The President's Surveillance Program (PSP)

The President's Surveillance Program was initiated after 9/11 because the administration concluded existing surveillance efforts were not collecting information thought to be essential to discovering al-Qaeda sleeper cells within the U.S. Missing

5 Jack M. Balkin, *The Constitution in the National Surveillance State*, 93 Minn L Rev, 1, 3 (2008).

6 18 USC §§2510-2522.

7 18 USC §2518.

8 50 USC §1804.

9 Amos Toh, Faiza Patel, and Elizabeth Goitein, *Overseas Surveillance in an Interconnected World*, 18 (Brennan Center for Justice at NYU School of Law 2016), archived at https://www.brennancenter.org/sites/default/files/publications/Overseas_ Surveillance_in_an_Interconnected_World.pdf.

10 18 USC §2516.

11 Memorandum Opinion and Order 15 (FISC April 26, 2017), archived at https://www.dni.gov/files/documents/icotr/51117/ 2016_Cert_FISC_Memo_Opin_Order_Apr_2017.pdf.

information consisted of communications between terrorists outside the U.S. and their communicants inside the U.S. The methods needed to obtain this information ran up against FISA, because FISA made it illegal without a court order to collect *from wires* (a crucially important method of transmitting communications) *inside the U.S.*[12] Furthermore, preparing the papers for a FISA court order and getting the order took a long time; the time between preparing the papers for the court and the time the data were in hand was four to six weeks. Targets could change their telephone numbers and email addresses before the FISA gave approval to the NSA to target them. Thus it was decided to not strictly adhere to FISA. To accomplish this, Bush cited his Article II authority under the Constitution and authorized the NSA to move forward with an expanded collection program that allowed the NSA to collect communications from wires in the U.S., even those communications with one communicant in the U.S.[13] The general counsel of the NSA and John Yoo, Deputy Assistant Attorney General in the Office of Legal Counsel, concluded that the PSP was legal.[14]

Detailed information regarding the PSP is not yet available, but it appears President Bush expanded the authority of the NSA to acquire four kinds of intelligence information. Two kinds included the contents of (i) telephone communications and (ii) Internet communications, both of which had to be "based on the factual and practical considerations of everyday life [that] there are reasonable grounds to believe [redaction] that such communication originated or terminated outside the United States and a party to such communication is a group engaged in international terrorism, or activities in preparation therefore, or *any* agent of such a group, or . . ."[15]

A description of this collection effort was included in a filing of a suit against the NSA. This litigation, *Jewel v NSA,* is still ongoing and is addressed in Chapter 3.

> The plaintiffs in that case provided the court the following description of how one aspect of PSP worked. The collection, a collaboration between AT&T and the NSA, was executed in a special room of AT&T in which there was access to fiber optic cables and switches that allowed access to AT&T's Internet traffic. And the program involved intercepting and copying all communications passing through something called the WorldNet Internet Room in an AT&T facility in the U.S. (What was collected included the content of

12 Id at 5.

13 Id at 3-8. See James Bamford, *The Shadow Factory*, 115 (Doubleday 2008); Charlie Savage, *Power Wars*, 180, 182–184 (Little, Brown & Company 2015).

14 Id at 184; Working draft, at 9 (cited in note 1).

15 Offices of the Inspector General, Department of Defense, Department of Justice, Central Intelligence Agency, National Security Agency, Office of the Director of National Intelligence, *Report on the President's Surveillance Program*, Volume I, 7–8, 11–12 (July 10, 2009) (quoting the President's Authorization of November 2, 2001) (hereinafter Volume 1), archived at https://oig.justice.gov/reports/2015/PSP-09-18-15-full.pdf.

telephone calls, emails, instant messages, and Web communications as well as metadata.[16])

The cables in the WorldNet Internet Room were connected to a "splitter cabinet." The "splitter cabinet" split the light signals from the WorldNet Internet service in two, making two identical copies of the data carried on the light signal. The splitter cabinet directed one copy of the light signal through fiber optic cables into a secret room built on AT&T premises, but controlled by the NSA, while allowing the other copy to travel its normal course to its intended destination. The split cables carried both domestic and international communications of AT&T customers, as well as communications from users of other non-AT&T networks that passed through the Folsom Street Facility. The use of the splitter cabinet to create an identical copy resulted in the wholesale acquisition by the government of AT&T customers' Internet communications.[17]

The plaintiffs also stated that there was evidence of similar installations in at least five other cities in the U.S. Once acquired the communications including those to, from and/or between Americans; even those without foreign intelligence value were stored in a government database.

This collection effort was in a sense "targeted" since the NSA was collecting communications of people outside the U.S. already suspected of links to terrorism.[18] The President had authorized the NSA to obtain all communications with one end in Afghanistan or communications where one communicant was engaged in or preparing for acts of international terrorism.[19] (Content collection involving the targeting of non-U.S. persons outside the U.S., even when one end was in the U.S., ultimately was authorized by §702, discussed in Chapter 3.)

PSP also involved the collection of two categories of metadata: telephony metadata such as the telephone number from which a call was made and that to which the call was made; and email metadata (header/router/addresses).[20] The following analogy is often used to explain the difference between content and metadata: consider an ordinary letter and its envelope. The message written on the paper inside the envelope is "content," whereas the information that appears on the envelope is the metadata, e.g., a mailing address, a return address. It is often noted, however, that this analogy is at best a loose one when it comes to explaining the difference

16 Complaint for Plaintiffs, *Jewel v National Security Agency* Docket No C 08 4373 (D NCal filed September 18, 2008), archived at https://www.eff.org/files/filenode/jewel/jewel.complaint.pdf.

17 Plaintiff's Federal Rule of Evidence Section 1006 Summary of Voluminous Evidence Filed in Support of Their Motion for Partial Summary Judgment and Opposition to the Governments' Cross-Motion Case No. 08-CV-4373-JSW *6-8(DC NCal filed December 9, 2012), archived at https://www.eff.org/files/filenode/jewel_conformed_summary_of_evidence.pdf.

18 Savage, *Power Wars*, at 186 (cited in note 13).

19 Working draft, at 1, 7, 16–17 (cited in note 1).

20 Id at 12. See, also, Volume I, at 7–8 (cited in note 15).

between content and metadata when one considers technology such as the telephone, email, and Web search histories.

The President authorized the collection of metadata (i) when one communicant was outside the U.S.; (ii) for which no communicant was known to be a U.S. citizen; or (iii) there were articulable facts giving reason to believe the communication related to international terrorism, or activities in preparation therefore.[21] NSA's authority to collect metadata was thus extremely broad. Under (i) all communications with a communicant outside the U.S. could be collected. Under (iii) any communication that may "relate" to international terrorism could be acquired.[22] In this way the amount of data available for contact chaining analysis used to find sleeper cells (say, at the request of the FBI) was enormously increased.[23]

Metadata were collected through the voluntary cooperation of private companies.[24] Interestingly the legality of part of this program was subsequently questioned by Jack Goldsmith, head of the Department of Justice's Office of Legal Counsel. He concluded that existing law permitted the collection of telephony metadata, but that the connection of Internet metadata was a violation of FISA.[25] This controversy ultimately led to a change in how telephony and Internet metadata were collected, and it changed the legal basis for the collection of the two kinds of metadata. (See Chapter 3 for discussions of 50 USC §1842 and Internet metadata, and §215 and telephony metadata.)

A fifth category of information, foreign-to-foreign communications, was acquired directly off of cables often located in the United States. This method of collection rested on what was dubbed "transit authority," in that these wholly foreign communications were not subject to FISA or the Fourth Amendment, and were only transiting the U.S.[26] The collection of this information did not require special authorization by Bush.

Finally, under the PSP for one month (October to November 2001) the NSA was also authorized by the President to acquire the content of wholly domestic communications.[27]

Note: The PSP was not the only collection activity of the NSA. The NSA operating under E.O. 12333 was also in the business of collecting communications wholly outside the U.S. that could sweep up, say, all the telephone conversations of a particular country. (See Chapter 3.)

Each of the five PSP intelligence activities not only involved its own method(s) of information acquisition but also raised distinct legal issues. Starting in March 2004

21 Id at 1, 8. See, also, Volume I, at 7–8 (cited in note 15).
22 Volume I, at 8, 12 (cited in note 15); Working draft, at 13 (cited in note 1).
23 Working draft, at 13 (cited in note 1).
24 Id at 29–30, 33–34.
25 Savage, *Power Wars*, at 164, 192–194 (cited in note 13).
26 Id at 173, 186; Working draft, at 4, 15 (cited in note 1).
27 Id at 184.

the Bush administration shifted its claim of legal authorization from Article II/AUMF (the Authorization to Use Military Force) to FISA and the AUMF. The shift was aided, importantly but not exclusively, by amendments to FISA. The shifting of various programs to reliance on FISA is touched on in Chapter 3 and has been described in various books.[28]

III. The President's Article II authority

Before turning to FISA, President Bush relied on a claim of Article II authority for the PSP. Did President Bush have the authority pursuant to Article II of the Constitution to do what he did, given the absence of Congressional authorization? A memorandum from the Congressional Research Service broached this topic this way:

> Foreign intelligence collection is not among Congress's powers enumerated in Article I of the Constitution, nor is it expressly mentioned in Article II as a responsibility of the President. Yet it is difficult to imagine that the Framers intended to reserve foreign intelligence collection to the states or to deny the authority to the federal government altogether. It is more likely that the power to collect intelligence resides somewhere within the domain of foreign affairs and war powers, both of which areas are inhabited to some degree by the President together with the Congress.[29]

This quote assumes that the President does have Article II authority regarding foreign intelligence collection, but is that authority in the "vesting" clause, or in the commander-in-chief clause?[30] In other words, is the authority to collect foreign intelligence an aspect of the "executive" power vested in the President, or is it part of the President's authority as commander–in-chief? Or perhaps neither, but rather arises from the "structure" of the Constitution, or perhaps the President enjoys what some call "inherent" authority as head of state.

John Yoo, who served in the Department of Justice at the time of the initiation of the PSP, was an advocate of broad presidential authority. He argued that because the President bears the constitutional duty to ensure the security of the United States, he has the power.[31] Jack Goldsmith rephrased the argument of the administration

28 See, for example, Timothy H. Edgar, *Beyond Snowden*, 38–45 (Brookings Institution Press 2017).

29 Elizabeth B. Bazan and Jennifer K. Elsea, *Presidential authority to conduct warrantless electronic surveillance to gather foreign intelligence*, 3–4 (Congressional Research Office, January 5, 2006).

30 Const, Art II, §1, cl.1; Const, Art II, §2, cl.1.

31 John C. Yoo, Deputy Assistant Attorney General, U.S. Department of Justice to Judge Colleen Kollar-Kotelly, U.S. District Court 20 (May 17, 2002), archived at https://www.justice.gov/olc/page/file/936196/download. See, also, Letter from William E. Moschella, Assistant Attorney General to the Honorable Pat Roberts, Chairman Senate Select Committee on Intelligence, December 22, 2005, archived at https://www.justice.gov/sites/default/files/ag/legacy/2007/01/11/surveillance6.pdf.

this way: Given that the President swears to preserve, protect, and defend the Constitution, built into the Constitution is a presidential emergency power to do just that, a power that Congress may not limit during war time.[32] In 2014 Yoo explicitly argued that the U.S. was at war with al-Qaeda and the President's commander-in-chief authority encompassed Bush's warrantless mass surveillance program.[33]

Then there is this "structural" argument from the Bush administration: because of the structural advances of the Executive Branch, the President as commander-in-chief has a grant of war power that includes "the authority to use secretive means to collect intelligence for the conduct of foreign affairs and military campaigns."[34]

Justice Department lawyers also invoked claims of "inherent constitutional authority to order warrantless foreign intelligence surveillance." The founders, so went the claim, "intended the President to be clothed with all authority necessary to carry out the responsibilities assigned to him as commander-in-chief and Chief Executive."[35] Central to that authority, arguably, would be intercepting communications of the enemy, enemies who very well may reside in the United States, as did the 9/11 attackers. (Whether or not Congress may regulate the exercise of this authority is addressed in Section VI.f.)

These and other similar formulations of the argument for Presidential authority to engage in foreign intelligence surveillance within the United States were buttressed with historical references to the surveillance activities of earlier Presidents such as Franklin Roosevelt during World War II – surveillance that, incidentally, was targeted and did not involve the kind of mass surveillance involved in the PSP.[36] Furthermore, support was claimed based on lower court precedent.[37]

While no one seems to have argued that the President is wholly without authority under Article II to authorize the collection of foreign intelligence, Louis Fisher, a noted writer on Presidential authority, has been particularly alarmed by two of the lines of argument in support of the President's authority. First, Fisher has raised the alarm regarding the claim of Presidential "inherent powers." He begins his analysis with the premise that: "The purpose of a Constitution is to specify and confine governmental power to protect individual rights and liberties. That objective is undermined by claims of open-ended authorities that are not easily defined or circumscribed. The assertion of 'inherent' powers ushers in a range of vague and

32 Jack Goldsmith, *The terror presidency*, 79, 82–83, 85 (W.W. Norton 2007).

33 John C. Yoo, *The legality of the National Security Agency's bulk data surveillance programs*, 10 ISJLP 301, 319–324 (2014).

34 U.S. Department of Justice, *Legal authorities supporting the activities of the National Security Agency described by the president*, 7 (January 19, 2006) (hereinafter Legal authorities), archived at https://www.justice.gov/archive/opa/docs/ whitepaperonnsalegalauthorities.pdf.

35 Office of Legal Counsel, U.S. Department of Justice, *Memorandum for the attorney general re: review of the legality of the Stellar Wind program*, 37 (May 6, 2004) (hereinafter Goldsmith memorandum), archived at https://www.hsdl.org/?abstract&did=757725.

36 Legal authorities, 7 (cited in note 33).

37 Id at 8.

abstruse sources. What 'inheres' in the president?"[38] "Inherent" can introduce other properties, including attributes that suggest being superior, exclusive, and enduring."

> The claim and exercise of inherent powers move a nation from one of limited powers to boundless and ill-defined authority. The assertion of inherent power in the president threatens the doctrine of separated powers and the system of checks and balances. Sovereignty moves from the constitutional principles of self-government, popular control, and republican government to the White House.[39]

Thus whether, and if so, to what extent the President enjoys "inherent emergency powers" are questions not finally settled by Supreme Court precedent. In perhaps the most famous case on the topic, a majority of the Court rejected President Truman's claim of emergency power to seize steel mills to assure the continued production of steel needed for the Korean War. The decision came against a backdrop of multiple statutes in which Congress spelled out what could be done should steel production cease because of a work stoppage.[40] Three justices said the President could not act in this emergency absent specific authorization from Congress, which did not exist in this case. Four other justices, while denying Truman authority in this case, did not delimit the authority of the President to act in future emergencies even in the absence of a statute authorizing the emergency action.[41] In any event, even if the President were to have inherent emergency powers, the definition of the term "emergency" remains unsettled, as does the scope of the emergency authority.[42]

Fisher expressed similar concerns regarding the administration's "sole organ" argument. Fisher's central point was that:

> The "sole organ" doctrine seems to support a plenary, exclusive, and inherent authority of the president in foreign relations and national security, an authority that overrides conflicting statutes and treaties. The theory appears to carry special weight because its author is John Marshall, a member of the House in 1800 and later chief justice of the Supreme Court. The theory is developed in an important foreign affairs case, United States v. Curtiss-Wright. However, when Marshall's speech is read in context, he did not advocate an independent, inherent presidential power over external affairs.[43]

38 Louis Fisher, *Invoking inherent powers: A primer*, 37 Presidential Stud Q 1, 2 (March 2007).

39 Id.

40 *Youngstown Co v Sawyer*, 343 US 579 (1952).

41 Louis Fisher, *Presidential war power*, 3 ed. revised, 115 (University Press of Kansas 2013).

42 See Stephen Dycus, Arthur L. Berney, William C. Banks, Peter Raven-Hansen, and Stephen I. Vladeck, *National security law*, 6th ed., 123–126 (Wolters Kluwer 2016) (reviewing statutory emergency powers).

43 Louis Fisher, *The law: Presidential inherent power: The "sole organ" doctrine*, 37 Presidential Stud Q 1, 140 (March 2007).

Fisher's concerns point to an important point regarding the arguments made in support of the President's authority to collect foreign intelligence. These arguments, of course, seek not only to support the claim that the President has Article II authority, but also to carry the message that Congress is precluded from encroaching on this power, and to read the Fourth Amendment so as to not lay too heavy a hand on the President.

IV. The authorization to use military force (AUMF)

After 9/11 President Bush sought sweeping authority from Congress:

> That the President is authorized to use all necessary and appropriate force against those nations, organizations or persons he determines planned, authorized, harbored, committed, or aided in the planning or commission of the attacks against the United States that occurred on September 11, 2001, and *to deter and pre-empt any future acts of terrorism or aggression against the United States.* [italics added][44]

With this language, Bush asked for authority to act not only against the 9/11 perpetrators but also against any future acts of terrorism by anyone or any nation.

Congress adopted a narrower authorization P.L.107-40, 115 Stat. 224 (2001) that the Bush administration cited, along with Article II, as authority for the PSP.

> That the President is authorized to use all necessary and appropriate force against those nations, organizations, or persons he determines planned, authorized, committed, or aided the terrorist attacks that occurred on September 11, 2001, or harbored such organizations or persons, in order to prevent any future acts of international terrorism against the United States by such nations, organizations or persons.[45]

The problem for the President was that the AUMF neither expressly amended FISA nor expressly granted the President authority to carry out domestically the collection of foreign intelligence. To deal with this problem the Department of Justice asserted that: "In the field of foreign affairs, and particularly that of war powers and national security, congressional enactments are to be broadly construed where they indicate support for authority long asserted and exercised by the Executive Branch."[46] The authorization "to use all necessary and appropriate force" should thus be read to include all the incidents of conducting war and that of course historically has included surveillance of the enemy, a critical and traditional tool for

44 https://www.everycrsreport.com/reports/RS22357.html.

45 Reported as a note to 50 USC §1541.

46 Legal authorities, at 11 (cited in note 33).

finding the enemy. Further, the AUMF presupposes that the President will "determine" who planned, authorized or committed the attacks on 9/11, hence again surveillance power is being granted. "Given that the agents who carried out the initial attacks resided in the United States and had successfully blended into American society and disguised their identities and intentions until they were ready to strike, the necessity of using the most effective intelligence gathering tools against such an enemy, including electronic surveillance, was patent."[47]

V. The PSP and the Fourth Amendment: a brief note

The effort to avoid any meaningful constraints by the Fourth Amendment on the President has taken two forms: (a) the Fourth Amendment simply does not apply; and (b) even if it does, it does not preclude the PSP. Before examining these points, a few words about the Fourth Amendment.

The Fourth Amendment to the Constitution protects privacy by prohibiting unreasonable searches and seizures by the Government.

> The right of the people to be secure in their persons, houses, papers, and effects, against unreasonable searches and seizures, shall not be violated, and no Warrants shall issue, but upon probable cause, supported by Oath or affirmation, and particularly describing the place to be searched, and the persons or things to be seized.

The Fourth Amendment has been interpreted many ways over the years, but bottom line there is no question that it applies to electronic eavesdropping and surveillance.[48] Given this, it seems strange to ask whether the Fourth Amendment has any bearing on the permissibility of the PSP. But John Yoo and Robert J. Delahunty believe it does not. An internal Department of Justice memorandum they wrote asserted that "we think that the better view is that the Fourth Amendment does *not* apply to domestic military operations designed to deter and prevent terrorist attacks."[49] They argue that "the original understanding of the Fourth Amendment was aimed primarily at curbing law enforcement abuses."[50] "In the circumstances created by the September 11 attacks, the Constitution provides the government with expanded powers to prosecute the war effort," declaring that activities such as 9/11 "can readily be described as 'war.'"[51] "[W]ar has exigencies that cannot

47 Id at 12.

48 *Katz v United States*, 389 US 347 (1967).

49 Memorandum for Alberto Gonzales, Counsel to the President and William J. Haynes, General Counsel, Department of Defense from John C. Yoo, Deputy Assistant Attorney General and Robert J. Delahunty, Special Counsel, Re: Authority for Use of Military Force to Combat Terrorist Activities Within the United States, 25 (October 23, 2001), archived at https://www.justice.gov/sites/default/files/olc/legacy/2009/08/24/memomilitaryforcecombatus10232001.pdf.

50 Id at 23.

51 Id at 3.

readily be enumerated or described which may render it necessary for a commanding officer to subject loyal citizens, or persons who though believed to be disloyal have not acted overtly against the government, to deprivations that would under ordinary circumstances be illegal."[52] To further buttress this line of thought, the memorandum offers the hypothetical example of a report that terrorists had concealed a massive bomb in an apartment building. To prevent a disaster the commander should be able immediately to seize the building and detain, search, and interrogate everyone found inside, which, the memo claims, if done for ordinary law enforcement purposes, would most likely be held to be a Fourth Amendment violation. [In that same memo, Yoo and Delahunty argued that Article II authorized the use of the military domestically against terrorists, and that the Authorization to Use Military Force, quoted above, also provided authority to deploy troops domestically in response to 9/11. In October of 2008 another Office of Legal Counsel memo refuted in substantial part the Yoo/Delahunty memo.[53]]

The Yoo/Delahunty argument, of course, has enormous potential to wholly block the protections of the Fourth Amendment whenever the President declares a war against, say, drugs, or right-wing hate organizations. Perhaps for this reason this line of argument has not been embraced by the courts, at least to date. Assuming the Fourth Amendment remains applicable to a program such as the PSP even in the face of significant domestic and international terrorist operations, might it still in fact bar or constrain the PSP? Chapter 3 takes a close look at Fourth Amendment doctrine, where it is examined in light of mass surveillance pursuant to FISA. Suffice it to say here that the Fourth Amendment doctrine does not require the President to obtain a warrant prior to conducting a search for foreign intelligence, and the basic requirement that warrantless searches be "reasonable" is sufficiently flexible that much of what a President may want to do may very well survive scrutiny in the courts. This was the position of Assistant Attorney General William E. Moschella who stated that: "Intercepting communications into and out of the United States of persons linked to al Qaeda [*sic*] in order to detect and prevent a catastrophic attack is clearly *reasonable*."[54]

As noted above, the domestic "upstream" surveillance aspect of the PSP has been challenged in court in *Jewel v NSA* on Fourth and First Amendment grounds; in addition, several federal statutes may have been violated. As of this writing a federal court has ordered the government to provide all relevant evidence needed to prove or disprove that the plaintiffs were subject to NSA surveillance by tapping into the Internet backbone (cables).[55]

52 Id at 30 quoting from *Commonwealth ex. rel. Wadsworth v Shortall*, 55 A 952, 955 (Pa 1903).

53 Id at 4, 20. William C. Banks and Stephen Dycus, *Soldiers on the home front*, 222–223 (Harvard 2016).

54 Letter from William E. Moschella, Assistant Attorney General to the Honorable Pat Roberts 4 (cited in note 31). See, also, Yoo, *The legality of the National Security Agency's bulk data surveillance programs*, at 318 (cited in note 32).

55 Cindy Cohn, *Judge orders government to provide evidence about internet surveillance* (Electronic Frontier Foundation, May 23, 2017), archived at https://www.eff.org/deeplinks/2017/05/judge-orders-government-provide-evidence-about-Internet-backbone-upstream.

VI. The PSP and the Foreign Intelligence Surveillance Act (FISA)

The PSP was launched against the background of a complex surveillance regulatory scheme known as the Foreign Intelligence Surveillance Act (FISA).[56] (Chapter 3 addresses the relationship between FISA and E.O. 12333 on which the PSP relied.)

> FISA provides a statutory framework regulating when government agencies may gather foreign intelligence through electronic surveillance or physical searches, capture the numbers dialed on a telephone line (pen registers) and identify the originating number of a call on a particular phone line (with trap and trace devices), or access specified business records and other tangible things. Authorization for such activities is typically obtained via a court order from the Foreign Intelligence Surveillance Court (FISC), a specialized court created to act as a neutral judicial decisionmaker in the context of FISA.[57]

FISA was adopted in 1978 in the aftermath of "revelations of illegal spying and other activities by U.S. intelligence agencies, including the FBI and CIA, and by the IRS and the military. These agencies sought to target and disrupt politically active domestic groups (principally civil rights and anti-war organizations), and they engaged in widespread warrantless surveillance."[58]

FISA's existence forces the consideration of a number of questions pertaining to the PSP: (a) Were there aspects of the PSP that were simply outside the reach of FISA's requirements? (b) FISA authorizes surveillance without a court order in an emergency – why did Bush not use this authority? (c) To the extent that aspects of PSP fell within the scope of FISA, did they comply with FISA? (d) Did Congress intend for FISA to be the exclusive means by which those surveillance efforts were to be carried out? (e) If so, how did the Bush administration seek to avoid having to comply with FISA as originally written? One argument was that the Authorization to Use Military Force (AUMF) amended FISA, thus giving the President the authority he needed. (f) But if the AUMF argument is not availing, would enforcement of FISA to constrain the President be an unconstitutional violation of the separation of powers, an unconstitutional infringement on the President's Article II authority?[59] [Note – there is another important law regulating electronic surveillance and eavesdropping by private individuals and law enforcement that has stricter controls than FISA and is not directed to the collection of foreign intelligence.[60] This law's central role is the investigation of ordinary crimes.]

(a) The full story behind the PSP has not yet been made public, thus it is hard to determine how far beyond the scope of FISA the PSP was. Be that as it may, FISA does

56 50 USC Chapter 36.

57 William L. Painter, *Selected issues in homeland security policy for the 114th Congress*, 8 (Congressional Research Office, May 19, 2015, R44041).

58 Dycus, Berney, Banks, and Vladeck, *National security law*, 6th ed., at 634 (cited in note 42).

59 Id at 89–95.

60 18 USC §§2510 to 2522 known as Title III of the Omnibus Crime Control and Safe Streets Act of 1968.

not apply when all parties to a wire or radio communication are outside the United States, neither did it apply, at the time of the PSP, to the targeted surveillance of someone located abroad even if the person were a U.S. citizen. [Revisions to FISA since the PSA, however, have added provisions regarding the surveillance of U.S. persons outside the United States.[61]] When a sender and recipient were both outside the U.S. but communicated using wires located in the U.S., those communications collected under the PSP were not subject to FISA.[62] (This involves the so-called transit authority.) International communications of a United States person are covered by FISA 50 USC §1801(f)(1), but only if the interception entailed an intentional targeting of that person. Thus, when the PSP targeted non-U.S. persons reasonably believed to be outside the U.S. and when that surveillance effort incidentally collected the communications of U.S. persons, FISA did not regulate that incidental collection. In short, these aspects of the PSP were beyond the scope of FISA, and therefore could not violate it. Hence legal challenges to these pieces of the PSP would have to be based on, say, the Fourth Amendment, or a claim could be made that the PSP was beyond the Article II authority of the President.

(b) Assuming aspects of the PSP did fall within the scope of FISA, the President might have made use of his emergency authorization to engage in surveillance without first obtaining a court order before acting.[63] To use this authority the Attorney General needed reasonably to determine that there was an emergency and that there was a factual basis for the issuance of a court order prior to seeking the court order. (Within seven days of the start of the surveillance a court order must be sought.) The administration seems to have concluded that these requirements did not allow the administration to act immediately, and without delay.[64] And perhaps the administration also feared that it would ultimately not obtain court approval.

(c) Assuming a surveillance activity did fall within the scope of FISA, was that activity in compliance with FISA? In his letter to the FISA judge, John Yoo made this cautious and hedged admission: "We do not believe an electronic surveillance program, undertaken in response to the September 11, 2001 attacks, could fully satisfy FISA standards."[65] There was severe conflict within the Bush administration with members of the Department of Justice who insisted that the bulk collection of Internet metadata was a violation of FISA and that the FISA requirements be adhered to. Members of the President's White House staff insisted on going forward under the President's Article II authority and ignored FISA. This conflict led to the now well documented hospital room crisis of March 10, 2004, in which White House Counsel Alberto Gonzales and Chief of Staff Andrew Card confronted James Comey, Jack Goldsmith, and Patrick Philbin from the Department of Justice

61 50 USC §1881b; 50 USC §1881c.

62 Savage, *Power wars*, at 173 (cited in note 13). So-called "transit authority" is a legally complex topic taken up later in the book.

63 50 USC §1805(e). See, also, 50 USC §1805(f).

64 Dycus, Berney, Banks, and Vladeck, *National security law*, 6th ed., at 674 (cited in note 42) (quoting remarks of Attorney General Alberto R. Gonzales).

65 Yoo, Deputy Assistant Attorney General, U.S. Department of Justice to Judge Colleen Kollar-Kotelly, at 6 (cited in note 31).

over an effort to get the bedridden and seriously ill Attorney General John Ashcroft to sign off on another Presidential authorization of the PSP. Ashcroft refused, saying he did not agree that the PSP was legal, and deferred to Comey who was at that point the acting Attorney General. Ultimately President Bush signed the authorization without Ashcroft's signature, but shortly afterwards made important changes in the program in an attempt to bring it in line with FISA.[66] The precise legal problems with the PSP are interesting and important but will not be examined here in order to continue the main line of the narrative of this portion of the chapter.[67]

Regarding collecting content, FISA 50 USC §1801 applied to the collection inside the U.S. of wire communications. The PSP program involved the collection of telephone communications between the U.S. and Afghanistan, thus triggered the application of 50 USC §1801 when collection occurred in the U.S; accessing – in the U.S. – Internet communications of foreign targets involved FISA. But national security required getting hold of what foreign targets were saying to their U.S-based correspondents quickly. Complying with §1801 required considerable paperwork and an exacting judicial process, hence complying with §1801 was deemed to be too costly. To get around the FISA problem the President authorized collection under his Article II authority.[68] (Ultimately the issue was addressed by the adoption of FISA Amendments Act and §702, discussed in Chapter 3.)

(d) The PSP's violation of FISA might not have been a legal problem if Congress had not intended FISA to be the *exclusive* means for collecting foreign intelligence domestically. 18 USC §2511(2)(f) says: "The Foreign Intelligence Surveillance Act of 1978 shall be the *exclusive means* [italics added] by which electronic surveillance, as defined in section 101 of such Act, and the interception of domestic wire, oral, and electronic communications may be conducted." Scholars have wrestled with the meaning of the italicized phrase; a standard treatise on FISA concludes that FISA was designed "to curb the practice by which the Executive Branch may conduct warrantless electronic surveillance on its own unilateral determination that national security justifies it." The authors note that as far as the President's constitutional power is concerned, there is no avoiding the preclusive intent of the exclusivity provision.[69] The authors also note that a white paper of the Department of Justice reached the same conclusion when it stated: "Congress therefore enacted a regime intended to supplant the President's reliance on his own constitutional authority."[70]

(e) FISA was thus, on its face, a law with which the administration needed to be in compliance. But the administration came up with a workaround argument that began

66 Volume I, at 44 (cited in note 15), Charlie Savage, *Power wars*, at 190 (cited in note 13).

67 For a discussion of the legal issue surrounding the collecting of email metadata, see Julian Sanchez, *What the Ashcroft "hospital showdown" on NSA spying was all about* (Ars Technica, July 29, 2013), archived at http://arstechnica.com/tech-policy/2013/07/what-the-ashcroft-hospital-showdown-on-nsa-spying-was-all-about.

68 Working draft, at 3–7 (cited in note 1).

69 David S. Kris and J. Douglas Wilson, *National security investigations & prosecutions*, 15-8 (Thomson-West 2007).

70 Legal authorities, at 20 (cited in note 33).

with reliance on 50 USC §1809(a)(1), which prohibits any person from intentionally "engag[ing] . . . in electronic surveillance under color of law *except as authorized by statute* [italics added]." "Because FISA's prohibitory provision broadly exempts surveillance 'authorized by statute,' the provision demonstrates that Congress did not attempt to regulate through FISA electronic surveillance authorized by Congress through a subsequent enactment."[71] The administration interpreted the term "statute" to include subsequent statutes even if that subsequent statute did not expressly and specifically say it was amending FISA. The administration then went on to claim that the AUMF qualified as such a statute and should be interpreted as authorizing the PSP and in effect amending FISA.[72] (See the discussion of the AUMF above.)

Arguments from scholars and one dissenting judge have been mounted against this reading of the AUMF. It made little sense that Congress, without explicitly saying so, amended FISA with a statute that did not say it was an amendment of FISA. Louis Fisher noted that: "Amendments to statutory law must be explicit and evident, with clear understanding by all lawmakers as to what is at stake. Amendments are not made by implication, with Members unaware of what they are voting on."[73]

Furthermore, Congress had no need to amend FISA since FISA already included a provision for dealing with surveillance during war time, 50 USC §1811. And when the AUMF was adopted, almost simultaneously Congress was amending FISA by means of the Patriot Act in 2001,[74] a law that did not grant the President the authority claimed to have been granted by the AUMF. As two scholars of electronic surveillance put it: "It is hard to read the AMUF as authorizing electronic surveillance in light of the nearly simultaneous enactment of the Patriot Act."[75]

(f) If the AUMF does not serve to assure the compliance of the PSP with FISA, a fundamental constitutional issue arises that cannot be ducked. May Congress impose FISA, thereby constraining and regulating the President's exercise of his Article II authority?

Congress's authority here *might* be unquestioned if FISA merely enacted precisely the minimum (not more) requirements of the Fourth Amendment (and First Amendment).[76] Of course, if the President had Article II authority to ignore the Fourth Amendment (as discussed above), then even imposing only Fourth Amendment requirements on the President would, arguably, be unconstitutional.[77] Additionally, FISA's requirements might, arguably, exceed the requirements of the Fourth Amendment; if this is the case, then the President would be compelled by FISA to

71 Id.

72 Pub L No 107-40, §2(a), 115 Stat 224, 224 (September 18, 2001) (reported as a note to 50 USC §1541).

73 Statement by Louis Fisher, *Constitutional limitations on domestic surveillance*, appearing before the House Committee on the Judiciary, 5 (Law Library of Congress June 7, 2007), archived at https://fas.org/irp/congress/2007_hr/060707fisher.pdf.

74 The Patriot Act, P.L. 107-56, 115 Stat 272.

75 Kris and Wilson, *National security investigations & prosecutions*, 15-25, 15-26 (cited in note 69).

76 Yoo, *The legality of the National Security Agency's bulk data surveillance programs*, at 319 (cited in note 32) (arguing that FISA offered the President a deal – comply with FISA and courts will agree the search was reasonable under the Fourth Amendment, i.e., FISA offers the President a safe harbor).

77 Id at 319-324 (arguing that FISA cannot limit the President to protect national security through surveillance).

do more than the Fourth Amendment requires. Consequently, the serious question raised at the outset of this subsection arises also in this situation: Is FISA an unconstitutional infringement of the President's Article II authority?

Justice Jackson answered a parallel question in his famous concurring opinion from *Youngstown Sheet & Tube Co. v Sawyer* (the Steel Seizure Case) when he warned that:

> Courts can sustain exclusive presidential control in such a case only by disabling the Congress from acting upon the subject. Presidential claim to a power at once so conclusive and preclusive must be scrutinized with caution, for what is at stake is the equilibrium established by our constitutional system.[78]

Justice Jackson's warning grew out of the constitutional structure that gives both the President and Congress a role in national defense. The President is commander-in-chief, but Congress declares war, raises and pays for the military, makes rules for the government and regulation of the military, organizes the military, provides for governing the military, and, in connection with these powers, makes all laws that shall be necessary and proper for carrying into execution these powers.[79] The conjoint authority of President and Congress is further underscored by Article II Section 2 which empowers the President to make treaties, but only with the advice and consent of two-thirds of the Senate. Given this constitutional structure, paraphrasing Justice Jackson, courts can sustain exclusive presidential control of surveillance only by disabling Congress from acting on the subject.

A May 6, 2004 memorandum by Jack Goldsmith of the Office of Legal Counsel in the Department of Justice took the position that the President's "core exercise of commander in chief" authority regarding surveillance during an armed conflict could not be interfered with by Congress and, in any event, Congress lacked authority under Article I to regulate in this area. These two points aside, when it came to the President's actual management of a military campaign Congress had no authority to interfere.[80]

In two significant articles, David J. Barron and Martin S. Lederman tackled this difficult topic by framing the question this way and arrived at a different conclusion: "[W]hether, as a matter of original constitutional understanding and longstanding constitutional practice, operational or tactical matters are in fact within the exclusive, and preclusive, province of the commander in chief."[81] They quickly add that this question is distinct from the question of whether the President has constitutional authority to defy a statute if he concludes that it is unconstitutional, or whether he is obliged to obey it unless and until a court declares it unconstitutional.

Their question plunges the two authors into a close examination of the original understanding of the Constitution and of the constitutional text itself. They conclude that the effort to premise executive defiance of the legislature on original understanding

78 *Youngstown Sheet & Tube Co v Sawyer*, 343 US 579, 637-638 (1952) (Jackson, J. concurring.).

79 US Const Art I, §8.

80 Goldsmith memorandum, at 37–49, 51–53 (cited in note 34).

81 David J. Barron and Martin S. Lederman, *The commander in chief at the lowest ebb – Framing the problem, doctrine, and original understanding*, 121 Harv L. Rev 689, 695 (2008). See, also, by the same authors, *The commander in chief at the lowest ebb – A constitutional history*, 121 Harv L Rev 941 (2008).

has little "Founding-era evidence supporting the notion that the conduct of military campaigns is beyond legislative control and a fair amount of evidence that affirmatively undermines it."[82] They examine historical practice in the second of the two articles where they "explain that no post-Founding historical consensus has ever developed among the political branches in favor of the President's preclusive power over the conduct of campaigns."[83] After exhaustive examination of the evidence regarding original intent and historical consensus, Barron and Lederman reach this conclusion:

> In other words, the argument for a substantive preclusive power must proceed, if at all, by defending a reversal of our constitutional tradition in more frankly normative and functional terms – as to which, we believe, traditional concerns about unchecked executive power provide forceful rejoinders. Thus stripped of its assumed roots in a supposedly longstanding tradition, and considered in light of the long pattern of executive acceptance of constraining statutes, the Administration's recent assertion of – and action in reliance upon – a claim of preclusive war powers is revealed as an even more radical attempt to remake the constitutional law of war powers than is often recognized.[84]

Conclusion

Given the ambiguity of Article II, the uncertainties surrounding the applicability of the Fourth Amendment, and the ambiguity of the Fourth Amendment, the door seems open to a President instituting a vast domestic surveillance program. The other branches of government – Congress and the judiciary – have a choice at this point. They may work with and enable the President in mounting this program, or serve to constrain and limit the President. FISA represents an effort on the part of Congress to impose some constraints on the President, but Congress has also, arguably, served as a Presidential enabler when, for example, it adopted the AUMF. The judiciary has also played the roles of handmaiden and watchdog. Members of President Bush's own administration have also played this dual role with John Yoo writing memos justifying the PSP, and other members such as Attorney General Ashcroft and James Comey putting up resistance to a specific aspect of the PSP.

This chapter has focused on the President and surveillance, i.e., the PSP. Of course, surveillance is only one aspect of the President's efforts to deal with terrorism. Domestic counterterrorism efforts of the government have included many more components that also entail important constitutional issues and raise issues regarding the authority of the President. To mention only one example: President Bush's program made possible designating U.S. citizens as unprivileged (unlawful) enemy belligerents, making their detainment by the military possible and making their prosecution by the military in military commissions possible. The difficult constitutional issues this caused was inherited by Presidents Obama and Trump; they are addressed in Chapters 8, 9, and 10.

82 Id at 696.
83 Id at 697.
84 Id at 697–698

3

MASS SURVEILLANCE TODAY

Mass surveillance that began with the President's Surveillance Program (PSP) – see Chapter 2 – has evolved over the years. This evolution entailed both a change in the legal authorities used to support the program, and a reduction of the scope of materials collected. This latter change reflects a rebalancing of the interests in domestic security and privacy. The chapter focuses on the most recent iteration of "mass surveillance," a term that is defined in Chapter 2.

Section I describes the technology behind carrying out seven mass surveillance programs. Section II outlines the debate regarding mass surveillance. Section III starts a discussion of the law of mass surveillance by addressing the links between FISA, E.O. 12333, and the Electronic Communications Privacy Act. (Take note that mass surveillance based on FISA initially focuses on foreign-connected terrorists, including unprivileged enemy belligerents (Chapter 8), not domestic terrorists. But as discussed, FISA may also end up being used to investigate domestic terrorism.) Sections IV through VI look at FISA and the bulk collection of metadata and the content of communications. The concluding section VII looks at the Fourth Amendment and the collection of metadata and content under FISA.

I. How bulk databases were/are made

What follows is a rough outline of how bulk data sets were and are generated.[1] (What follows does not apply to all data gathering programs of the NSA.) These descriptions focus on the technology of collection, not on legal authorization.

1 See, also, https://www.dailydot.com/layer8/nsa-spy-prgrams-prism-fairview-blarney/#blarney; https://nsa.gov1.info/surveillance/.

One important source of data for the NSA is provided by international partners such as Great Britain. Also, by means of technology not revealed, the NSA intercepts every cell phone call made "to, from, and within the Bahamas, Mexico, Kenya, the Philippines, and Afghanistan."[2] These external collections may of course gather up phone calls of U.S. citizens located in the target countries. Next:

> The NSA obtains a wide range of information transmitted, stored, and accessed on the Internet. Under a program codenamed MUSCULAR, the NSA works with the United Kingdom's intelligence agency, General Communication Headquarters (GCHQ), to tap into the cables connecting internal Yahoo and Google networks to gather information – including email address books and contact lists – from hundreds of millions of customers.[3]

Satellite collection grabs up international phone calls and emails between the U.S. and Afghanistan.[4]

Upstream content collection involves tapping into the backbone of the Internet, namely, coaxial and fiber optic cables.[5] Oakstar and its component programs obtain data from *foreign access points* such as undersea coaxial cables,[6] occasionally requiring the use of submarines.[7] Since this collecting occurs outside the U.S., U.S. persons whose communications are collected would be protected by the Fourth Amendment, not by FISA.

Another upstream program involves telecommunications firms tapping into network switches *located on U.S. soil*, to acquire content and metadata of foreign-to-foreign communications flowing past for the NSA (this is termed transit authority). The Bush administration said FISA did not apply to transit messages, only E.O. 12333 did.[8] [One-third of all communications entering and leaving the country are such transit messages. A large share of intra-African communications pass through U.S. switches, as well as nearly all Latin American communications.[9]]

2 Amos Toh, Faiza Patel, and Elizabeth Goitein, *Overseas surveillance in an interconnected world*, 5 (Brennan Center for Justice at NYU School of Law 2016), archived at https://www.brennancenter.org/sites/default/files/publications/Overseas_ Surveillance_in_an_Interconnected_World.pdf.

3 Id at 5–6.

4 Charles Savage, *Power wars*, 180 (Little, Brown & Company 2015).

5 Ashley Gorski and Patrick C. Toomey, *Unprecedented and unlawful: The NSA's "upstream surveillance"* (Just Security, September 19, 2016), archived at https://www.justsecurity.org/33044/unprecedented-unlawful-nsas-upstream-surveillance/.

6 https://nsa.gov1.info/surveillance/. See, also, *NSA's global interception network* (Electrospaces.net, December 3, 2013), archived at https://electrospaces.blogspot.com/2013/12/nsas-global-interception-network.html; https://www.dailydot.com/layer8/nsa-spy-prgrams-prism-fairview-blarney/#so; Jeff Larson, Julia Angwin, Henrik Moltke and Laura Poitras, *A trail of evidence leading to AT&T's partnership with the NSA* (ProPublica, August 15, 2015), archived at https://www.propublica.org/article/a-trail-of-evidence-leading-to-atts-partnership-with-the-nsa.

7 https://nsa.gov1.info/surveillance/.

8 See Savage, *Power wars*, at 173 (cited in note 4).

9 James Bamford, *The shadow factory*, 207, 209 (Doubleday 2008).

A different domestic *upstream* program (Internet content and metadata) began with the President's Surveillance Program and became the subject of an ongoing suit (*Jewel v NSA*) discussed below. How that collection process worked previous to the adoption of FISA §702 is described in Chapter 2. Following the decision of the Bush administration to rely for legal authority on FISA and after the adoption of §702, domestic upstream collection proceeds as follows: According to the Privacy and Civil Liberties Oversight Board (PCLOB) the NSA first identifies selectors that are sent to a United States electronic communication service provider to acquire communications that are transiting through circuits that are used to facilitate Internet communications, what is referred to as the "Internet backbone." After these data are collected, Internet transactions are "first filtered to eliminate potential domestic transactions, and then are screened to capture only transactions containing a tasked selector. Unless transactions pass both these screens, they are not ingested into government databases filtered by the NSA."[10]

An especially important program (not an upstream program) is called PRISM, which operates by the government asking companies to turn over targeted communications.[11] (Discussed below.) As of mid-2011 91% of the Internet communications the NSA acquired in a given year were obtained through PRISM. More NSA reports were based on PRISM than on any other collection program.[12] FISA §702 is the applicable law.

For a time, pen register and trap and trace devices were used. Historically, a pen register was a device used to mechanically record the numbers dialed on a telephone, whereas a trap and trace device could collect phone numbers that had called a specific telephone number. The modern P/T does the same thing now with software applied to Internet communications. The P/T does not collect the content of a communication.

The last database collection method to be described is an important one, FISA §215. It involves the government going to communication providers and directly obtaining, based on a FISA court order, massive amounts of customers' telephony metadata the companies have stored.[13] Under the court order the companies "must provide the NSA with all call detail records generated by those companies." This is equivalent to metadata regarding communications over the Internet. "The NSA

10 Privacy and Civil Liberties Oversight Board, *Report on the surveillance program operated pursuant to Section 702 of the Foreign Intelligence Surveillance Act*, 36–37 (July 2, 2014), (herein after PCLOB 702), archived at https://www.pclob.gov/library/702-Report.pdf. See, also, Frances J. Fleisch, National Security Agency, *Jewel v Nat'l Sec. Agency*, No. 08-cv-4373-JSW (N.D. Cal. Dec. 20, 2013), archived at https://www.dni.gov/files/documents/1220/NSA%20Fleisch%202013%20Jewel%20 Shubert% 20Declaration%20Unclassified.pdf.

11 Id at 33. Glenn Greenwald, *No place to hide*, 110 (Metropolitan Books 2014).

12 Id at 111.

13 Privacy and Civil Liberties Oversight Board, *Report on the telephone records program conducted under Section 215 of the USA Patriot Act and on the Operations of the Foreign Intelligence Surveillance Court*, 21–24 (January 23, 2014), archived at https://fas.org/irp/offdocs/pclob-215.pdf. See *American Civil Liberties Union v Clapper*, 785 F3d 787 (2d Cir 2015).

uses the calling records it obtains under Section 215 to attempt to identify communications among known and unknown terrorism suspects, particularly those located inside the United States."[14]

II. The debate: mass surveillance in the balance

How persuasive is this argument? Mass surveillance serves our national security and does no harm to people who have nothing to hide; it is like a long-term care health insurance policy with a (modest?) premium.

Here are three reasons why mass surveillance might be undertaken: A bulk database of communications metadata is useful for contact chaining, the tracking of networks of contacts among targets, and finding sleeper cells. A bulk collection helps track targets who often change phones or email accounts. Bulk collections allow analysts to assemble a picture of a previously unknown group following a terrorist attack.[15] The data may also be useful to track down after-the-fact perpetrators of terrorism.

Has mass surveillance actually worked in generating leads leading to the prevention of terrorism? It turns out that obtaining evidence to support the value of mass surveillance is difficult because so much of the program is classified.[16] To the extent that there have been publicly available evaluations, the reports of success are modest. Charlie Savage, based on information obtained under the Freedom of Information Act, found that the FBI concluded that 1.2% of the leads have proved useful. The NSA has claimed that it had successfully thwarted more than 50 attacks, but ProPublica could not find evidence to support this claim.[17] In any event, it is possible that mass surveillance has prevented a few terrorist attacks, the potential size and magnitude of which is not publicly known.

The law permits NSA-acquired data to be shared with other agencies in the government, notably the National Counterterrorism Center, the Terrorist Screening Center, Customs and Border Protection, the Transportation Security Agency, and the FBI. Some of these agencies, e.g. the FBI, have direct access to the NSA's raw (unminimized) data.[18] Thus NSA data help protect air safety through the creation of the No Fly List, and has been used in the criminal prosecution of individuals identified as terrorists.

On the other side of the scale, is there a price to be paid for mass surveillance? Arguably "yes." It may weaken the protections of the Fourth Amendment afforded

14 Id at 25.

15 Timothy H. Edgar, *Beyond Snowden*, 139–141 (Brookings Institution Press 2017).

16 Lauren Kirchner, *What's the evidence that mass surveillance works? Not much* (ProPublica, November 18, 2015), archived at https://www.propublica.org/article/whats-the-evidence-mass-surveillance-works-not-much.

17 Id.

18 Raw Sigint Availability Procedures, January 2017, archived at https://fas.org/sgp/othergov/intel/sigint-raw.pdf; https://nsa.gov1.info/partners/index.html. See, also, 6 USC §485.

defendants in ordinary criminal prosecutions. Fourth Amendment rules regarding mass surveillance are a marked departure from the rules in civilian criminal law. To the extent that mass surveillance yields evidence used in a criminal prosecution, it may serve as a way around the usual Fourth Amendment protections afforded a defendant.

Professor Neil M. Richards argues that mass surveillance has other deep-cutting negative consequences.[19] To the extent that it discourages freedom of speech (another empirical question), it blunts the benefits of free speech: the marketplace of ideas, the ferreting out of truth through dialogue, self-actualization and personal growth, and making democracy possible. Mass surveillance hands private information to public officials, which then can be used to blackmail people (this was the FBI's plan when it undertook surveillance of Martin Luther King). A mass of collected data may be analyzed using "big data" techniques, and then can be used to classify people for favorable or unfavorable treatment. (Recall that the No Fly and Selectee Lists are discussed in Chapter 5.) Mass surveillance can foster conformity; here Professor Reid takes note of the philosopher Jeremy Bentham's idea of Panopticon:

> [A] prison designed around a central surveillance tower from which a warden could see into all of the cells. In the Panopticon, prisoners had to conform their activities to those desired by the prison staff because they had no idea when they were being watched.[20]

Bentham's Panopticon is more than the depiction of a fictional negative utopia. The U.S. itself started down this road in the previous century when both the FBI and the CIA undertook domestic surveillance programs to keep tabs on the activities of the New Left and the anti-Vietnam war movement.[21] As for the future of mass surveillance, one need only look at developments in the Republic of China where a massive data-based system is in the process of being implemented that will result in each citizen being afforded a "social credit" score that will indicate how trustworthy they are. An untrustworthy person will not be allowed to rent a car, borrow money, will experience lower Internet speeds, have restricted access to restaurants, and be barred from certain jobs.[22] The social credit score will be combined with a massive visual surveillance system that employs facial recognition software that will enable the government to visually track specific individuals; surveillance data of an individual's behavior will be combined with the social

19 Neil M. Richards, *The dangers of surveillance*, 126 Harv L Rev 1934 (2013).

20 Id at 1948.

21 Laura K. Donohue, *The future of foreign intelligence*, 5 (Oxford 2016).

22 Rachel Botsman, *Big data meets big brother as China moves to rate its citizens* (Wired, October 21, 2017), archived at http://www.wired.co.uk/article/chinese-government-social-credit-score-privacy-invasion.

credit data to develop an assessment of them and then to look at their connections with other people.[23]

As noted below, the NSA is now engaged in social network graphing and creating community of interest profiles.

III. The law: FISA, E.O.12333, and the Electronic Communications Privacy Act (ECPA)

Three sets of law are relevant to bulk collection: E.O. 12333, FISA, and the Electronic Communications Privacy Act (ECPA), creating potential conflicts among the three. The first of these conflicts is avoided by the provision in E.O. 12333 that says surveillance must comply with FISA or ECPA when those laws apply to the surveillance. That is, when FISA and ECPA overlap with E.O. 12333, those laws are controlling; surveillance under E.O. 12333 may not violate those statutes.[24] In other words, E.O 12333 controls only surveillance activities not covered by FISA or ECPA.[25] As for FISA and ECPA, if the collection satisfies FISA's definition of electronic surveillance, or alternatively involves the acquisition of foreign intelligence from international or foreign communications, then the ECPA does not prohibit the collection and conflict is avoided.[26]

IV. FISA overview

Here is a quick overview of the FISA itself (which has been amended many times over the years). FISA provisions are directed to what the FBI would call "foreign (connected) terrorism." (See Introduction.) FISA establishes a set of procedures for surveillance aimed at gathering "foreign intelligence." Foreign-connected intelligence is information regarding foreign powers or agents of foreign powers (50 USC §1801(e)). FISA's targets are defined by their status as a foreign power or as an agent of a foreign power, not by whether the target has committed a crime, unlike ordinary criminal wiretap law. [An agent of a foreign power can be a U.S. person (50 USC 1801(b)(2).] Section 1861 also can be used to obtain foreign-connected

23 Simon Denyer, *Beijing bets on facial recognition in a big drive for total surveillance* (Washington Post, January 7, 2018), archived at https://www.washingtonpost.com/news/world/wp/2018/01/07/feature/in-china-facial-recognition-is-sharp-end-of-a-drive-for-total-surveillance/?utm_term=.e5058e543157.

24 E.O. 12333, as amended, §2.5, §2.8, archived at https://fas.org/irp/offdocs/eo/eo-12333-2008.pdf.

25 The precise relationship of FISA and E.O. 12333 is a complex topic. See Toh, Patel, and Goitein, *Overseas surveillance in an interconnected world*, 39 (cited in note 2); Savage, *Power wars*, at 174–177 (cited in note 4); https://www.lawfareblog.com/understanding-deeper-history-fisa-and-702-charlie-savages-power-wars-fiber-optic-cables-and-transit; https://nsa.gov1.info/surveillance/. Toh, Patel, and Goitein, *Overseas surveillance in an interconnected world*, 5–7 (cited in note 2).

26 18 USC §2511(2)(f).

intelligence not involving a U.S. person and foreign intelligence to protect against "international terrorism" that might involve a U.S. person.

What started out as a foreign-connected intelligence investigation may also bring to the surface evidence of an ordinary crime entailing domestic terrorism. (See discussion of "the wall" in Section VII.A.2.)

Except for emergencies, authorization to conduct the surveillance must first be obtained from the secret Foreign Intelligence Surveillance Court (FISC) established by FISA. Provisions of importance for mass surveillance are highlighted in bold:

50 USC §§1801-1809 – Electronic surveillance for foreign intelligence **§1805**.
50 USC §§1822-1826 – Physical searches for foreign intelligence.
50 USC §§1841-1846 – Pen registers and trap and trace devices (aka P/T) **§1842**.
50 USC §§1861-1862 – Business records and other tangible things for foreign intelligence (aka **§215**).
50 USC §§1881a – Targeting non-U.S. persons outside the U.S. (aka **§702**).
50 USC §§1881b-1881c – Targeting U.S. persons outside the U.S.

V. FISA and the collection of metadata

The mass collection of metadata between 2001 and 2004 was addressed in Chapter 2. Two statutes are directed specifically at the collection of metadata, FISA §1842 and what is called §215.

A. Telephony and Internet metadata: FISA §1842 – pen register/trap and trace (P/T)

In 2001, working with private sector partners after authorization from the President, the NSA began to collect Internet metadata. *Email* metadata included information about the session (network address, time, duration) and message data information (to, from, time, length). *Browsing* metadata would include personal IP, and the IP matched with past pages visited. Conflict erupted within the Bush administration regarding the legality of this collection effort, ultimately leading the administration to try using 50 USC §1842 to achieve the same thing.[27] Section 1842 is limited to obtaining foreign intelligence not concerning a U.S. person, and to protect against "international terrorism" as defined in 50 USC §1801(c).

Thus the administration sought authorization from a FISA court.[28] The application for authority for the NSA to collect with P/T was filed on behalf of the NSA by the Attorney General. Because of the Supreme Court's decision in *Smith v Maryland*, 442 US 735 (1979), the information collected by the historic devices

27 Savage, *Power wars*, 193 (cited in note 4). See, also, 50 USC §1801(f).

28 Office of the Inspector General, National Security Agency Central Security Service, Working Draft ST-09-0002 at 38 (March 24, 2009), (hereinafter Working draft), archived at https://www.aclu.org/files/natsec/nsa/20130816/NSA%20IG% 20Report.pdf.

(telephones) did not enjoy Fourth Amendment protection; the Court concluded in *Smith* that callers did not have a reasonable expectation of privacy in the metadata their calls generated. That is to say, since the caller had "voluntarily conveyed numerical information to the telephone company and 'exposed' that information to its equipment in the ordinary course of business," telephone users did not have reasonable expectations of privacy in their telephony metadata. (This is the so-called "third party doctrine." As discussed in Chapter 6, Section V, the Supreme Court importantly reinterpreted the doctrine in 2018 regarding the collection of cell site location information. The implications of that interpretation for the collection of browsing metadata are not clear. It is possible the decision may lead to requiring a warrant in order to obtain cell site location data.) Accordingly, use of the P/T was not a search, and was not subject to the Fourth Amendment.

The use of P/T for bulk collection started in July 2004 after FISA court approval. One feature of the story is the willingness of the FISA court to extend coverage of P/T from telephone to email metadata.[29] The court also made bulk collection possible by agreeing with the Bush administration that the statutory requirement that P/T surveillance be "relevant to an ongoing investigation to protect against international terrorism" could be interpreted so broadly that everybody's data were relevant. In effect, the court said that the NSA and the FBI needed a huge body of data if the agencies were to carry out the analytical task of "contact chaining," designed to find the needle in the haystack – the terrorist hiding in the general population. The large batch of data was "relevant" to these fishing expeditions – "relevant" because it might encompass information that reasonably might lead to the discovery of directly relevant information.[30] The court went on say the bulk collection did not violate the Fourth Amendment because the government's need was compelling and immediate.[31]

The government ended P/T bulk collection in 2011 and turned to other methods for collecting the same data.[32] Today it accesses Internet metadata via its foreign collection of metadata and through PRISM and, presumably, upstream programs discussed below.[33]

In 2015 with the adoption of the USA Freedom Act, the FISA P/T law was amended to preclude bulk collection of either telephony or Internet metadata. Under the revised law the application had to include a "specific selection term" to be used as the basis for the use of the pen register or trap and trace device.

29 Opinion and Order, No. PR/TT [redacted] (FISC [date redacted]), archived at https://www.dni.gov/files/documents/1118/ CLEANEDPRTT%202.pdf.

30 Id at 39, 49–50. The data could be used for contact chaining. National Security Agency, *Pen register/trap and trace FISA NSA Review*, 10 (January 2010), archived at https://epic.org/foia/doj/pen-reg-trap-trace/EPIC-FISA-PEN-REGISTER-FOIA-RELEASE-08082014-33.pdf.

31 Id at 54.

32 https://icontherecord.tumblr.com/post/70683717031/dni-announces-the-declassification-of-the.

33 Timothy Edgar, *Bulk NSA internet program shows the complete incoherence of surveillance law* (Lawfare, November 20, 2015), archived at https://www.lawfareblog.com/bulk-nsa-Internet-program-shows-complete-incoherence-surveillance-law.

B. Telephony metadata: §215

The NSA made a significant effort to acquire bulk telephony metadata.[34] Telephony metadata includes the length of the call, the phone number from which the call was made, the identity of the communications device, the number called, a phone's calling-card numbers, trunk identifier, but not the voice(s) of the communicant(s) or the content of what was said. By all accounts telephony metadata is an especially valuable kind of data for understanding the behavior of potential terrorists, their habits in daily life, and their network of supporters and conspirators. With the use of analytical tools the NSA can carry out contact chaining, and thus develop the network of contacts linked to a targeted number as well as identify additional numbers. "When the NSA identifies communications that may be associated with terrorism, it issues intelligence reports to other federal agencies such as the FBI, that work to prevent terrorist attacks."[35] That is, the FBI would be "tipped." Dissemination of these data is subject to the rules of a presidential directive, namely the United States Signals Intelligence Directive SP0018, which prescribes rules for the dissemination of information about U.S. persons to assure compliance with the Fourth Amendment.

The story of the collection of telephony metadata has several acts to it. Act One – a bulk collection program occurs through voluntary collaboration between the government and telecommunications companies. This was part of the President's Surveillance Program enacted by Bush claiming Article II authority. (See Chapter 2.) Act Two – in 2006 the Bush administration sought and obtained approval to continue under the auspices of FISA §215.[36] (This was accomplished by the Attorney General requesting a court order that required companies to deliver bulk metadata to the NSA.[37]) Section 215 (50 USC §1861(b)(2)(A)) at the time allowed the collection of "tangible things" (i.e., a broad range of records) based on "reasonable grounds" if the records were "*relevant*" to "*an authorized investigation*" to obtain "foreign intelligence information" not concerning a U.S. person or to "protect against international terrorism." Despite the italicized statutory language, the government's applications did not link the applications to a single investigation. Since the program operated and was approved by a FISA court, it involved the collection

34 Under 50 USC §1861, the FBI obtained, on behalf of the NSA, a FISA court order that required telephony metadata be delivered to the NSA. Privacy and Civil Liberties Oversight Board, *Report on the telephone records program conducted under Section 215 of the USA Patriot Act and on the Operations of the Foreign Intelligence Surveillance Court*, at 21–22, 42, 45 (cited in note 13).

35 Id at 8.

36 Letter from Ronald Weich to the Hon Diane Feinstein and the Hon Saxby Chambliss (February 2, 2011), archived at https://www.dni.gov/files/documents/2011_CoverLetters_Report_Collection.pdf.

37 Department of Justice, Office of the Inspector General, *A review of the FBI's use of Section 215 Orders: Assessment of progress in implementing recommendations and examination of use in 2007 through 2009*, 46ff (May, 2015), archived at https://www.oversight.gov/sites/default/files/oig-reports/o1505.pdf.

of ALL metadata from various companies on an ongoing indefinite basis basically on the grounds that all these records were relevant to counterterrorism in general, i.e., there is only one enormous investigation to which the data are relevant. (See *ACLU v Clapper* mentioned below.)

Act Three – the program came under legal attack in the courts. Act Four – FISA §215 was amended in 2015 by the USA Freedom Act in response to the concerns regarding the program. Act Five is now being written.

Acts One and Two are historically interesting, but for our purposes we jump to Act Three. Over the years the FISA court has renewed §215 authorizations 41 times. In January 2014 the Privacy and Civil Liberties Oversight Board issued a report on §215 expressing doubts about the efficacy of the program in stopping terrorism, concluding that the program had serious implications for both privacy and civil liberties, that it was in deep tension with the statutory language, and recommending an end to the §215 bulk collection program.[38] In May 2015 the Second Circuit Court of Appeals held that the program violated §215.[39] Again the statutory requirement that the collection be relevant to an authorized investigation became important; here the court noted there was no specific investigation identified by the government. The court therefore concluded that there was no evidence in the text of the law or elsewhere that Congress intended for the statutes to authorize "the bulk collection of every American's toll-billing or educational records and to aggregate them into a database."[40] On June 2, 2015, one month after the May decision, Congress passed the USA Freedom Act, which amended §215.

The USA Freedom Act required that an application for data had to include "a specific selection term," which was to be the basis for what tangible things were collected.[41] The statute defines "specific selection term" to mean "a term that specifically identifies a person, account, address, or personal device, or any other specific identifiers; and is used to limit, to the greatest extent reasonably practicable, the scope of tangible things sought consistent with the purpose for seeking the tangible things." To further limit any effort at bulk collection the statute precludes the use of the following as selection terms – an electronic communication service provider per se, a broad geographic region, city, county, state, zip code, or area code "when not used as part of a specific identifier."[42]

The revised statute contains terms and language that may leave the door open to at least some form of mass collection. The term "relevant to an authorized investigation"

38 Privacy and Civil Liberties Oversight Board, *Report on the telephone records program conducted under Section 215 of the USA Patriot Act and on the Operations of the Foreign Intelligence Surveillance Court*, at 12,16 (cited in note 13).

39 *American Civil Liberties Union v Clapper*, 785 F3d 787 (2d Cir 2015). But see *In Re Application of the Federal Bureau of Investigation Misc. 15-01*, 2015 WL 5637562 (FISC June 29, 2015).

40 Quotations from Id at 812, 814, 816, and 818.

41 50 USC §1861(b)(2)(A).

42 50 USC §1861(k)(4).

remains in the statute. Many terms or identifiers may be used. And collection can move beyond the specific selection term originally used in the application.

> Whereas a standard order under Section 215 would produce only those records that are responsive to an approved [specific selection term], an order seeking telephone records for an international terrorism investigation can also be used to produce a second set of telephone records that are not themselves responsive to an approved [specific selection term], but that are connected to one of the records that was directly produced by an [specific selection term]. For example, if Alice called Bob, and Bob also called Charles, then a single Section 215 order that used Alice's phone number as [a specific selection term] could obtain records of the call to Bob as well as records of the call from Bob to Charles.[43]

To make use of this "hop," the government would provide facts "showing" there was a "reasonable articulable suspicion" the specific selection term was associated with, say, an agent of a foreign power who was engaged in international terrorism.[44]

USA Freedom Act amendments of §215 has reduced the collection of records. In 2014, the year prior to the Act, the NSA collected billions of records per day; in 2016, by targeting 42 suspects, the NSA collected 151 million call records. The 150 million records were collected as follows: the NSA is informed by one company that target number #123 phoned 300 numbers; another company says target #123 phoned 200 numbers, and so on. Each of those 500 numbers phoned other numbers. In this cascading way, total call records reached 150 million.[45]

VI. FISA and collecting the content of communications

Mass content collection began with the PSP and the targeting of communications that originated or terminated outside the U.S. in cases where there was a reason to believe a party to the communication was engaged in terrorism. Originally the collection was based on the President's Article II authority, but in 2006 this part of the PSP was brought under FISA authority.[46]

A. FISA §1805

Starting late in 2006 the Bush administration turned to an expansive interpretation of the term "facility" as used in 50 USC §1804 and §1805 as a way to continue

43 (Name redacted), *Amendments to the Foreign Intelligence Surveillance Act (FISA) expiring on December 15, 2019*, 4 (Congressional Research Service, April 11, 2016, R40138).

44 50 USC §1861(b)(2)(C)(ii).

45 Director of National Intelligence, *Statistical transparency report*, 19–20 (April 2017), archived at https://www.dni.gov/files/icotr/ic_transparecy_report_cy2016_5_2_17.pdf.

46 Offices of the Inspector General, Department of Defense, Department of Justice, Central Intelligence Agency, National Security Agency, Office of the Director of National Intelligence, *Report on the President" Surveillance Program*, Volume I, 57 (July 10, 2009), (hereinafter Volume I), archived at https://oig.justice.gov/reports/2015/PSP-09-18-15-full.pdf.

content collection. These provisions were part of the original FISA that authorized and regulated what can best be described as a traditional wiretap. The law authorized electronic surveillance to collect foreign intelligence from targets who were either agents of foreign powers or foreign powers themselves.

Under the law the government had to include in its application facts to justify the belief that "each of the *facilities* or places at which the electronic surveillance is directed is being used, or is about to be used, by a foreign power or an agent of a foreign power."[47] The administration's gambit was to argue that the term "facility" should not be read just in the traditional sense, meaning a specific telephone number or email address, but would also include a "general gateway" or "cable head."[48]

On January 10, 2007 the administration got what it sought regarding the interpretation of the term "facility" when the FISA court signed two separate orders regarding foreign and domestic content collection.[49] The court did impose a restriction that the administration found hard to live with, and thus it abandoned this bulk collection program,[50] and instead pursued amending FISA again to allow collecting communications of foreign targets when one communicant was in the U.S.[51] First came the Protect American Act[52] and then the FISA Amendments Act of 2008, which in effect codified the earlier statute and enacted §702 (50 USC §1881a).

B. §702 and mass content collection

Section 702 is the statutory authority that permitted collecting the content of communications of a massive number of U.S. persons. As discussed in Chapter 2, §702 had its origin in President Bush's effort to avoid complying with 50 USC §1801 when acquiring inside-the-U.S. communications of foreign targets in touch with U.S. correspondents. First Bush relied for this authority on Article II, but ultimately relied on §702 after passage of the FISA Amendments Act of 2008 and Section §702.[53] Section 702 was recently extended to December 31, 2023.[54]

47 50 USC §1804(a)(3)(B).

48 Laura K. Donohue, *Section 702 and the collection of international telephone and internet content*, 38 Harv J of L & Pub Pol 117, 132 (2015); Working draft, at 40–42 (cited in note 28).

49 Id at 117, 133.

50 Working draft, at 42 (cited in note 28); https://www.efForg/nsa-spying/timeline.

51 50 USC §1881a (referred to herein as §702 as the provision was numbered in Public Law 110-261 entitled the Foreign Intelligence Surveillance Act of 1978 Amendments Act of 2008). See, also, 50 USC §188b and §188c regarding the targeting of U.S. persons outside the United States.

52 FISA Amendments Reauthorization Act of 2017, Pub L No 110-55, 121 Stat. 552, codified at 50 USC §§1805a and 1805b.

53 Donohue, *Section 702 and the collection of international telephone and internet content* (cited in note 48) (with a history of §702).

54 Id at §201.

1. *About §702*

Section 702 focuses on collecting *foreign intelligence* from targets who are *non-U.S. persons reasonably believed to be outside the U.S.* The targeting of these non-U.S. persons may only occur if the government has reason to believe those people possess, are expected to receive, or are likely to communicate, foreign intelligence.[55] The surveillance power of §702 is underscored by these points: (a) there is no requirement that the target be a foreign power or the agent of a foreign power, or has committed a crime; (b) the government need not identify the facilities or places where the collection will occur; (c) the communications of people who are in touch with the targets will be "incidentally" collected; (d) any type of communication (radio, wire, Internet) may be monitored; and (e) the FISA court only reviews the targeting procedures, not the selection of individual targets, to assure the procedures comply with FISA and the Fourth Amendment.

> The required process for the surveillance of non-U.S. persons outside the U.S. is comprised of four steps: (1) guideline adoption and procedure determinations; (2) the filing of a joint certification with the FISA court by the Attorney General and the Director of National Intelligence; (3) judicial review of the certification and the proposed targeting and minimization procedures, and then possibly the order from the court; and, finally (4) orders or directives to an electronic communication service to provide information and/or assistance.[56] This process gets repeated at short intervals, especially step (3) when the FISA court re-examines the new application to see that it complies with the statute and the Fourth Amendment, and also addresses possible non-compliance issues regarding previous orders.[57]

Regarding step (3), the FISA court approves "procedures" and never specifically approves the individuals who are targeted, or the facilities (email address or telephone number) "tasked," i.e., used. The role of the FISA court is only to assure that these procedures are reasonably designed so that when properly executed by the NSA the FISA legal requirements are complied with – namely, that only non-U.S. persons outside the U.S. are targeted and the information collected is foreign intelligence. As part of step (4) NSA analysts use the approved procedures to identify email address(es) and telephone numbers to be used and to determine whether they are used by non-U.S. persons outside the U.S. After this the collection is carried out.[58]

The analysts work under NSA guidelines to assure compliance with the statute – no intentional targeting of any person known to be in the U.S., no targeting of a U.S.

55 Privacy and Civil Liberties Oversight Board, *Report on the surveillance program operated pursuant to Section 702 of the Foreign Intelligence Surveillance Act*, at 22 (cited in note 10).

56 50 USC §1881a(h); *United States v Duggan* 743 F2d 59 (2d Cir 1984).

57 See, for example, Memorandum and Order (FISC November 6, 2015), archived at https://icontherecord.tumblr.com/post/ 143070924983/release-of-three-opinions-issued-by-the-foreign.

58 Privacy and Civil Liberties Oversight Board, *Report on the surveillance program operated pursuant to Section 702 of the Foreign Intelligence Surveillance Act*, at 24–33 (cited in note 10).

person reasonably believed to be outside the U.S., no intentional acquiring of wholly domestic communications, and prohibiting what is called "reverse targeting":

> [The NSA] may not intentionally target a person reasonably believed to be located outside the United States if the purpose of such acquisition is to target a particular, known person reasonably believed to be in the United States.[59]

In 2016 alone 106,469 people were §702 targets.[60]

As discussed below, millions of domestic communications and communications of U.S. persons do end up being acquired, an advantage from a government interested in finding sleeper cells, criminals and domestic terrorists. However it also means communications of innocent people are swept up; consequently, the provision has been controversial but was nevertheless renewed until December 31, 2023. What is called "incidental collection" is virtually built into §702 in that when the NSA grabs the communication of a non-U.S. person outside the country it is very possible the other communicant is a U.S. person in the U.S., "incidentally" collected.

Under the policies of both the Obama and Trump administrations, the NSA may retain, not destroy, and disseminate §702-acquired information even pertaining to U.S. persons and domestic communications if: the communication is reasonably believed to contain significant intelligence information or reasonably believed to contain evidence of a crime that has been, is being, or is about to be committed.[61] Similarly if the communication indicates that the United States person may be an agent of a foreign power, may be engaged in international terrorist activities, may be believed to contain evidence that a crime has been, is being, or is about to be committed, must be given to the Attorney General pursuant to E.O. 12333. The NSA is also authorized to provide the FBI raw (unminimized) communications acquired pursuant to §702 based on targets identified by the FBI. And what appears to be a significant modification by the Obama administration, a January 2017 order regarding access to raw NSA data, even raw §702 data, may be requested by the FBI from the NSA.[62] In turn the FBI's own minimization procedures authorize it to disclose to federal prosecutors FISA-acquired information, including raw FISA-acquired information, as well as information derived therefrom.

The NSA is also authorized to distribute raw information acquired under §702 to the National Counter Terrorism Center (NCTC), which is a central depository of terrorism-related data and is a source for the data that feed into the No Fly and

59 50 USC §1881a(f), and §1881a(b). See. Glenn Greenwald, *FISA Court oversight: A look inside a secret and empty process*, The Guardian, U.S. Edition (June 18, 2013), archived at https://www.theguardian.com/commentisfree/2013/jun/19/ fisa-court-oversight-process-secrecy.

60 *Statistical transparency report*, at 7 (cited in note 45).

61 Jeff Sessions, Attorney General of the United States, *Minimization procedures used by the National Security Agency in connection with acquisitions of foreign intelligence information pursuant to Section 702 of the Foreign Intelligence Surveillance Act of 1978, as Amended* (March 29, 2017), archived at https://www.dni.gov/files/documents/icotr/51117/2016-NSA-702-Minimization-Procedures_Mar_30_17.pdf.

62 Raw Sigint Availability Procedures (cited in note 18).

Selectee Lists. The NCTC obtains this information by requesting the NSA to send raw information that use individual §702 selectors. Thus, the NCTC has access to the bulk data collected under the huge PRISM program.[63] The NSA is, however, not authorized to share raw information obtained by NSA's *upstream* Internet collection (described below) with the NCTC.

As a result of the FISA court ruling discussed in Section VII.C., NSA may now query its own §702 data using identifiers of known U.S. persons. In that section, Fourth Amendment issues related to the query and dissemination of §702 are also addressed.

2. PRISM

Under PRISM, the government acquires communications by going to Microsoft, Yahoo, Google, Facebook, Paltalk, AOL, Skype, YouTube, and Apple asking for/demanding targeted emails, chats (video and voice), photos, VoIP communications, file transfers, video conferencing, log-ins, online social networking details, and more that is stored in their facilities. A version of PRISM had its origin prior to the passage of §702 as part of Stellar Wind.[64] Today PRISM arises under §702 with the NSA targeting non-U.S. persons believed to be outside the U.S., but since it is collecting "to and from communications" of these targets, it is possible that one of the communicants is located in the U.S. (incidental collection), and that communicant might be a U.S. person. That person may be an innocent, but perhaps an ordinary criminal, or a domestic or foreign terrorist.

PRISM is an enormously important mass surveillance.[65] As suggested above, the NSA may share raw data from PRISM with the FBI, the CIA, and the National Counterterrorism Center.[66] The constitutionality of PRISM, discussed below, under both the Fourth Amendment (privacy) and First Amendment (freedom of association) has been raised in a court challenge.[67]

3. Upstream – U.S. and upstream-external collection

The NSA's upstream acquisition efforts go by various names – Oakstar, Stormbrew, Blarney, and Fairview.[68] These programs vary somewhat, but the focus here first is on collecting Internet data from cables in the U.S. (upstream-U.S., e.g., Blarney),

63 Memorandum opinion and order 36-40 (FISC April 26, 2017), archived at https://www.dni.gov/files/documents/icotr/ 51117/2016_Cert_FISC_Memo_Opin_Order_Apr_2017.pdf.

64 Greenwald, *No place to hide*, at 110 (cited in note 11). Edgar, *Beyond Snowden*, at 39–40, 115–119 (cited in noted 15) (discussing Stellar Wind and §702).

65 Id at 111; PCLOB 702, at 32–33 (cited in note 10).

66 Sessions, Attorney General of the United States, *Minimization procedures used by the National Security Agency in connection with acquisitions of foreign intelligence information pursuant to Section 702 of the Foreign Intelligence Surveillance Act of 1978, as Amended*, §6(c) (cited in note 61).

67 *In re Directives*, 551 F3d 1004 (DC Cir 2008); *Schuchardt v President of the United States*, 839 F3d 336 (3d Cir 2016).

68 https://nsa.gov1.info/surveillance/.

and, second, on collecting Internet data from key points outside the U.S (upstream-external, e.g., Oakstar).

The upstream method for collecting communications has evolved over the years in a way that has reduced the likelihood that the communications of U.S. persons would be acquired. How that happened follows.

Inadvertent collection – the NSA assumes that if a person is not known to be a U.S. person, the individual is a non-U.S. person. This assumption of course can lead to what is termed an "inadvertent" collection.[69] Additionally and significantly, communications of U.S. persons were collected in several ways under the upstream programs.

1. A U.S. person communicates by telephone or Internet with a foreigner located abroad *who has been targeted.* The government refers to this as "**incidental**" collection [to and from targeting].
2. A U.S. person sends or receives an Internet communication routed internationally that includes a reference to a selector such as an email address used by a foreigner who has been targeted. The government refers to this as "**about**" collection.
3. A U.S. person sends or receives an Internet communication that is embedded within the same "transaction" as a different communication that meets the requirements for acquisition (because it is to or from a targeted foreigner or includes a reference to the communications identifier of a targeted foreigner). The government refers to these transactions containing more than one separate communication as "multiple-communication transactions" or "**MCTs**."[70]

Acquisition under PRISM does not involve "about" collections, or MCTs, even though PRISM is based on §702.

Incidental collection continues today. Section 702 expressly authorizes the NSA to collect the communications of non-U.S. persons reasonably believed to be outside the U.S., and in doing so the person in communication with the legal target may be a U.S. person, and hence that person's communication is acquired. The fact that the U.S. person is in touch with the target is likely to be of great interest to the NSA and to the FBI. From a counterterrorism perspective these incidental collections are clearly important as they may lead to, for example, the discovery of sleeper cells within the United States, ordinary criminals, and domestic terrorists. Thus, as far as FISA is concerned, incidental collection is a lawful acquisition. But then two legal questions arise: What are the implications of FISA's minimization rules for the handling of these incidental collections? And what does the Fourth Amendment have to say about both the constitutionality of the acquisition and minimization?

69 Donohue, *Section 702 and the collection of international telephone and internet content*, at 158 (cited in note 42).

70 Privacy and Civil Liberties Oversight Board, *Report on the surveillance program operated pursuant to Section 702 of the Foreign Intelligence Surveillance Act*, 86–87 (cited in note 10).

The Privacy and Civil Liberties Oversight Board (PCLOB) noted that incidental collections were accomplished in the absence of the protections that accompany traditional FISA (50 USC §1805) or criminal electronic surveillance (18 USC §2518), namely, the approval of a judge:

> [W]ho independently assesses the legitimacy of the targeting and must be persuaded that the government's beliefs about the person and/or communications facility being targeted are supported by probable cause. By providing a neutral check on the government's authority to conduct electronic surveillance, these protections help assure innocent U.S. persons that their conversations will not be incidentally acquired in the course of improper surveillance directed at another person.[71]

The PCLOB goes on to note that NSA collection policy combined with technological prowess results in hundreds of millions of Internet communications being acquired, and even if U.S. person communications are a small percentage of the total, the absolute number of U.S. communications acquired "could be considerable." Minimization requirements intended to minimize acquisition of information regarding nonconsenting U.S. persons (50 USC §1801 (h)) to some degree compensate for the possibility of broad incidental collection. While the existence of minimization rules may temper the privacy impact of incidental collection, the scope of that collection may also bear on whether the minimization rules are adequate. The present lack of knowledge about the range of incidental collection under Section 702 therefore hampers attempts to gauge whether the program appropriately balances national security interests with the privacy of U.S. persons.[72]

The NSA has announced that it will no longer engage in "about" collection, but it could renew the effort under newly enacted procedures. Since "about" collection could be resurrected, a few words about its previous use are in order. Professor Donohue has noted that FISA is silent regarding whether only information held by the target may be obtained, or whether communications in which the target is referred to, may be obtained.[73] This is a loophole in the law, which the NSA has exploited, saying that it means it may seek to acquire communications "about the target" even if the communication is not to or from the target. Thus the NSA will collect not just email to or from the target's email account (e.g., badguy@ISP.com), but in addition, any other communication that happens to mention badguy@ISP.com. In other words, wholly domestic communications – communications between U.S. communicants – might also be acquired.[74]

"About" collection was very controversial. It was more likely than other collections to acquire wholly domestic communications and the communications of

71 Id at 115–116.

72 Id at 116.

73 Donohue, *Section 702 and the collection of international telephone and internet content*, 159 (cited in note 48).

74 Id at 161–164.

people about whom the government had no prior suspicion.[75] In April 2017 the NSA announced it would discontinue "about" collections.[76] Nevertheless Congress, anticipating that "about" collections might be renewed, specified in the FISA Amendments Reauthorization Act of 2017 several steps that needed to be taken in addition to obtaining a FISA court order. Prior to reenacting the about collection, the DNI and Attorney General had to notify Congress prior to restarting the program and hold off implementing it for 30 days, giving Congress time to review the program. The statute did not give Congress the authority to block renewed "about" collection.[77]

The likelihood of acquiring domestic communications when "about" collection was ongoing was increased because of multi-communication transactions (MCTs). To paraphrase the *New York Times*, MCTs are bundles of discrete messages that are packaged and travel as a bundle through the Internet.[78] One of those messages might contain a reference to the selector, e.g., badguy@ISP.com. When the NSA acquires the message "about" the badguy@ISP.com selector, it ends up acquiring the whole bundle of messages. In 2011 a FISA court required the NSA to do a better job of minimizing after-the-fact acquisition of MCTs, and the NSA complied.[79] After the NSA stopped collecting "about" communications, the risk of collecting MCTs was further reduced, and today the NSA says it will destroy an entire MCT if even a single discrete communication within the MCT is from a domestic sender to a solely domestic recipient.[80]

VII. Mass surveillance and the Fourth Amendment[81]

Bulk collection of telephony and Internet metadata and the contents of Internet communications has raised serious concerns regarding the invasion of privacy protected by the Fourth Amendment:

> The right of the people to be secure in their persons, houses, papers, and effects, against unreasonable searches and seizures, shall not be violated, and no warrants shall issue, but upon probable cause, supported by oath or affirmation, and particularly describing the place to be searched, and the persons or things to be seized.[82]

75 Id at 119–122.

76 https://www.nsa.gov/news-features/press-room/press releases/2017/nsa-stops-certain-702-activites.shtml.

77 FISA Amendments Reauthorizataion Act of 2017, Pub L 115-118 amending 50 USC §1881(b).

78 Charlie Savage and Scott Shane, *Secret court rebuked N.S.A. on surveillance* (New York Times, August 21, 2013), archived at http://www.nytimes.com/2013/08/22/us/2011-ruling-found-an-nsa-program-unconstitutional.html.

79 [Case title redacted] 2011 WL 10945618 (FISC Oct 3, 2011).

80 Memorandum opinion and order ,15, 23–27 (cited in note 63).

81 See. USSID SP0018, January 25, 2011, archived at https://www.dni.gov/files/documents/1118/CLEANEDFinal% 20USSID%20SP0018.pdf (signals intelligence policies and procedures to assure compliance with the Fourth Amendment).

82 US Const Amend I V.

To date somewhat less attention has been paid to the implications of bulk collection on freedom of speech and freedom of association. Nevertheless, surveillance of communications can also impair the exercise of these rights as people fear to speak out and form associations that the government is tracking.

Note: Massive bulk collection efforts outside the U.S. of the communications of non-U.S. persons not communicating with someone in the U.S. are authorized by E.O. 12333, and are not protected by the Fourth Amendment.

Do the collection (A), retention (B), querying (C), and analysis (D) of communications of non-suspects located in the U.S. violate the Fourth Amendment? The following discussion takes up these topics, but does not address two serious obstacles facing any plaintiff seeking to challenge a mass surveillance program in a court, obstacles that may preclude ever getting a hearing on the challenge.[83] These two doctrines – "standing" and the "state secrets privilege" – are serious impediments to holding the government accountable before the judiciary; they are briefly discussed in the Introduction.

A. Collection

1. Is collection a search/seizure?

The Fourth Amendment would have no bearing on the constitutionality of bulk collection programs if they did not constitute a "search" or "seizure." This is both a complicated question and not settled in the law.[84] Perhaps any data or communication sent to and through a communications system owned by a third party loses its Fourth Amendment protection. (See discussion in Chapter 6, Section V.) But even if the sender continues to have a reasonable expectation of privacy, it may not constitute a "search or seizure" if the data are merely duplicated, duplication does not interfere individual's possession of his or her data, and it is not examined by a human. Robert Litt, while conceding mass collection of Internet content is technically a search, makes this argument: if the government collects the content of communications, scans it for content it is lawfully entitled to collect, and no one (no

83 STANDING: *American Civil Liberties Union v Clapper* (cited in note 13) (standing recognized); *Klayman v Obama*, 957 F Supp.2d 1 (D DC 2013), vacated and remanded, 800 F3d 559 (DC Cir 2015) (standing recognized); *Schuchardt v President of the United States*, 839 F3d 336 (3d Cir 2016) (standing recognized); *In re Directives* (cited in note 67) (the standing of Yahoo recognized to mount a challenge based on the Fourth Amendment on behalf of customers); *Wikimedia Foundation v NSA*, 857 F3d 193 (4th Cir 2017) (standing recognized). Cases in which standing was not recognized: *Clapper v Amnesty Int'l US*, 133 SCt 1138 (2013); *ACLU v Nat'l Sec Agency*, 493 F3d 644 (6th Cir 2007).

STATE SECRETS DOCTRINE: *ACLU v Nat'l Sec Agency*, 493 F3d 644 (6th Cir 2007); *Jewel v NSA*, 2015 US Dist LEXIS 16200 (DNDCal Feb 10, 2015). See, also, *Klayman v Obama*, 957 F Supp 2d 1 (2013), vacated and remanded, 800 F3d 559 (DC Cir 2015). Suda Setty, *National security secrecy: Comparative effects on democracy and the rule of law* (Cambridge 2017).

84 *Digital duplications and the Fourth Amendment*, 129 Harv L Rev 1046, 1048 (2016).

human) sees the other content, or even knows it exists, where is the actual privacy harm?[85] Professor Donohue has a different view:

> [T]he collection of information *is* a search. Consistent with [the] reasonable expectation of privacy test, it is access to the information that violates the private sphere. If the government were to mount a camera in your bedroom and to record everything that you do there – *promising* not to look at it unless it had a *really good reason* to do so – it would still be an invasion of your privacy. . . . [I]ndividuals change their behavior when what they do and say is monitored by the government. One is inherently *not* free when what one does, who one loves, with whom one shares one's passions, and what those passions are, are recorded by government.[86]

When it comes to the collection of content (PRISM, upstream), collection clearly seems to be a search. Whether it nevertheless is permissible is another issue explored below.

The Donohue argument faces an important obstacle when applied to the collection of metadata (§215) as discussed in Chapter 2 using the mailing address on the envelope analogy. The claim that looking at and collecting metadata (the address) is not a "search" is: (a) For there to be a search the plaintiff must have a reasonable expectation of privacy regarding the information being collected. (b) When a person voluntarily discloses information to a third party such as the postal service, a telephone company, or an ISP, they cannot claim a reasonable expectation of privacy of that data. (c) It thus follows that the government collecting the telephone numbers one calls and gets calls from, the email addresses one sends email to and gets mail from, subscriber information records, credit card charges, and IP addresses one uses or connects with, is not a search. In each case, using the technology involves the "voluntary" disclosure of the metadata to a third party.[87] This non-search argument was made by John Yoo in his letter to Judge Kollar-Kotelly in defense of the PSP insofar as it collected metadata.[88] Note also that a significant number of courts have rejected the claims of criminal defendants challenging the use of pen registers and the collection of their metadata stored in the computers of telecommunication companies on Fourth Amendment grounds.[89]

85 Robert S. Litt, *The Fourth Amendment in the information age*, Yale L J Forum 15 (April 27, 2016), archived at https://www.yalelawjournal.org/forum/fourth-amendment-information-age. See, also, Orin S. Kerr, *Fourth Amendment seizures of computer data*, 119 Yale L J 700 (2010) (noting the ambiguity of the case law and offering a doctrinal solution).

86 Laura K. Donohue, *The future of foreign intelligence, privacy and surveillance in a digital age*, 131 (Oxford 2016).

87 The starting point for this line of argument is *Smith v Maryland*, 442 US 735 (1979).

88 John C. Yoo, Deputy Assistant Attorney General, U.S. Department of Justice to Judge Colleen Kollar-Kotelly, U.S. District Court, 13 (May 17, 2002), archived at https://www.justice.gov/olc/page/file/936196/download.

89 *United States v Moalin*, Crim. No. 10-4246, 2013 WL 6079518 *5-8 (SD Cal. November 18, 2013) (holding that bulk telephony metadata collection does not violate Fourth Amendment); *United States v Forrester*, 512 F3d 500, 510 (9th Cir 2008) (no Fourth Amendment rights in IP addresses); *United States v Fregoso*, 60 F3d 1314, 1321 (8th Cir 1995) (stored telephone records and subscriber information not protected).

In 2018, however, the Supreme Court broadened the concept of a search. The Court ruled obtaining at least seven days or more of a person's historical cell site location information was a search since obtaining this batch of data violated the person's legitimate expectation of privacy in the record of their physical movements.[90] In so ruling, the Court placed an effective limit on third party doctrine of *Smith v Maryland*. The implications of this decision for the collection of other types of data is an important question to be settled in future years. (For more on this case see, Chapter 6, Section V.)

One Federal District Court in *Klayman v Obama* developed work around the *Smith v Maryland* decision that, after the 2018 Supreme Court opinion, might find favor in the Supreme Court. In *Klayman*, the court ruled that the mass collection of metadata under 50 USC §1861 (Section 215 of the Patriot Act) was a search.[91] Judge Leon formulated the issue that he had to grapple with as follows: "The threshold issue that I must address, then, is whether plaintiffs have a reasonable expectation of privacy that is violated when the Government indiscriminately collects their telephony metadata along with the metadata of hundreds of millions of other citizens without any particularized suspicion of wrongdoing, retains all of that metadata for five years, and then queries, analyzes, and investigates that data without prior judicial approval of the investigative targets."[92] In answering with an emphatic "yes," Judge Leon made the following findings. The program here was, in effect, a joint intelligence operation between the government and private companies that had been in effect for five years and was likely to continue indefinitely into the future. Advanced technology gave the government the capacity for long-term storage of the data collected along with the possibility of continued mining of the data. Available for mining was a huge quantity of information about each individual that could yield a wealth of information about family, political, professional religious and sexual associations. [That the program is a search does not by itself mean it violates the Fourth Amendment; that issue will be discussed below.]

Judge Leon's conclusion that the mass collection of metadata is a search is supported by scholars who argue that the analogy between the old-fashioned telephone and the modern electronic world and massive NSA collection is not comfortable.[93] However, Robert S. Litt, General Counsel in the Office of the Director of National Intelligence, disagrees with Judge Leon. He argues that *Smith v Maryland* is still controlling, and "I find it hard to understand the alchemy by which information that you choose to disclose to a third party develops an expectation of privacy because you have chosen to disclose a lot of that information."[94]

The Ninth Circuit Court of Appeals followed Litt's reasoning in allowing the government to say the Fourth Amendment was not triggered by the collection of

90 *Carpenter v United States*, No. 16-402 (U.S. June 22, 2018) (slip opinion).

91 *Klayman v Obama* (cited in note 83).

92 Id at 30.

93 Laura K. Donohue, *The future of foreign intelligence, privacy and surveillance in a digital age*, Chapter 2 (cited in note 86) See, also, Privacy and Civil Liberties Oversight Board, *Report on the telephone records program conducted under Section 215 of the USA Patriot Act and on the Operations of the Foreign Intelligence Surveillance Court*, at 116–128 (cited in note 13).

94 Litt, *The Fourth Amendment in the information age*, at 11 (cited in note 85).

a target's IP address, to/from addresses of emails, and the volume of messages sent from the target's account.[95] Transactional data [billing records, customer Internet use, banking transactions, credit card records] – often collected using national security letters (NSLs; see Chapter 6) – also do not enjoy Fourth Amendment protection. More controversial is the collection of URLs, as this data reveals websites viewed by a person and even specific pages of an online publication, e.g., how to print a 3D plastic weapon, or the speech of a white supremacist.

2. *Should a warrant have been obtained prior to collecting?*

This discussion assumes that the government has engaged in a search. FISA does not require a warrant based on probable cause, and the Fourth Amendment by its own terms does not require a warrant before a search may be executed. The Fourth Amendment only lays down the grounds for issuing a warrant – probable cause *if* a warrant is to be issued. One has to turn to case law (precedent) to determine when a warrant is required prior to searching, and when it is not required, one must turn to precedent to determine if FISA violates warrant-requirement rules.

The Supreme Court has left open the question of whether there is a "foreign intelligence exception" to the warrant requirement that allows the President/government to engage in warrantless surveillance "with respect to the activities of foreign powers, within or without this country."[96] Several lower courts, however, have recognized such an exception "when the object of the search or the surveillance is a foreign power, its agent, or a collaborator."[97]

In 2002 the Foreign Intelligence Surveillance Court of Review upheld as reasonable under the Fourth Amendment FISA's procedures (18 USC §1805) even though a warrant was not required, and even when seeking foreign intelligence was merely "a purpose" and not "the" primary purpose.[98] Prior to this ruling a policy – dubbed "the wall" – required that NSA surveillance have the collecting of foreign intelligence as its "primary purpose."[99] Now the warrantless procedures of FISA could

95 *United States v Forrester*, 512 F3d 500 (9th Cir 2008). The Second, Third, and Eighth Circuits have also held that the Fourth Amendment does not protect the IP address: https://www.insideprivacy.com/united-states/litigation/second-circuit-in-silk-road-appeal-no-fourth-amendment-protection-in-ip-addresses-under-the-third-party-doctrine/.

96 *United States v U.S. Dist. Court for E Dist of Mich*, S Di v, 407 US 297, 308 (1972) (*Keith*).

97 *United States v Truong Dinh Hung*, 629 F2d 908, 915 (4th Cir 1980); *United States v Butenko*, 494 F2d 593 (3rd Cir 1974); *United States v Brown*, 484 F2d 418 (5th Cir 1973), cert. denied, 415 US 960 (1974); *United States v Butenko*, 494 F2d 593 (3d Cir 1974) (en banc), cert. denied sub nom. *Ivanov v United States*, 419 U.S. 881 (1974). But see *Zweibon v Mitchell*, 516 F2d 594 (DC Cir 1975), cert denied, 425 US 944 (1976). Of particular significance here is the recognition of special needs beyond the normal need for criminal law enforcement. In these situations, the warrant and probable-cause requirement are said to be impractical. See *Griffin v Wisconsin*, 483 US 868, 872 (1987). The FISA review court relied on this doctrine. *In re Directives* at 1010 (cited in note 67).

98 *In Re Sealed Case*, 310 F.3d 717, 725–727, 734 (DC Cir 2002).

99 A useful history of "the wall" and its collapse can be found in: Scott J. Glick, *FISA's significant purpose requirement and the government's ability to protect national security*, 1 Harv Nat Sec J 87 (2010).

be used to obtain evidence of an ordinary crime (including domestic terrorism) as long as it also had obtaining foreign intelligence as "a purpose." In fact, the primary purpose of using FISA could be for ordinary crime enforcement; the data collected could be used in a criminal prosecution; and the FBI and the NSA could coordinate its collection.[100] (See 50 USC §1806(k), specifically authorizing coordination.)

Instead of a warrant, the original FISA (18 USC §1805) only requires a finding of probable cause that the target is a foreign power or an agent of a foreign power, and a probable cause finding regarding the facility; it does not require a probable cause finding that a crime has been committed. A long line of courts has held these findings are sufficient to satisfy the Fourth Amendment.[101]

Furthermore, §702 has no requirement that "the government demonstrate probable cause to believe that a Section 702 is a foreign power or agent of a foreign power as is required under traditional FISA. Rather the categories of information being sought must meet the definition of foreign intelligence."[102]

In a ruling regarding the constitutionality of the warrantless §702 PRISM program, the Foreign Intelligence Surveillance Court of Review (FISCR) concluded that the program fell within the special needs/foreign intelligence exception to the warrant requirement.[103] The FISCR upheld the exception to the warrant because PRISM had as "a purpose" collecting foreign intelligence, even if it also had an ancillary criminal law purpose. Recall the sweep of materials under PRISM that included the incidental collection of communications of U.S. persons. Whether PRISM meets the reasonableness test of the Fourth Amendment is addressed below in Section 3.

The "a purpose" requirement[104]

Obtaining evidence of an ordinary crime or domestic terrorism normally requires a warrant, and in fact may be the primary purpose of a search, as noted above.[105] This means that if foreign intelligence is discovered, what started out as an ordinary law enforcement investigation could be covered by FISA and thus avoid the need for a warrant. (A FISA court order would have to be obtained.) And what started out as a foreign intelligence investigation (foreign terrorism) could be continued under the FISA even after its primary purpose became a criminal investigation (domestic terrorism).[106] Either way, a FISA search may end up dealing with domestic terrorism, not exclusively

100 *United States v Wen*, 477 F3d 896 (7th Cir 2006).

101 Id; *United States v Pelton*, 835 F2d 1067 (4th Cir 1987); *United States v Cavanagh,* 807 F2d 787 (9th Cir. 1987); *United States v Duggan*, 743 F2d 59 (2d Cir 1984); *United States v Elshinaway*, ELH-16-0009 (D. Md. March 20, 2017).

102 PCLOB 702, at 25 (cited in note 10).

103 *In Re Directives* at 1010–1012, 1015 (cited in note 67).

104 *In Re Sealed Case* (cited in note 98).

105 Id at 734; James G. Carr and Patricia L. Bellia, *The law of electronic surveillance*, 2015 ed., §9.31, at 488 (Thomson Reuters 2015).

106 Stephen Dycus, Arthur L. Berney, William C. Banks, Peter Raven-Hansen, and Stephen I. Vladeck, *National security law*, 6th ed., 612 (Wolters Kluwer 2016).

foreign-connected terrorism. Given the possibility of the NSA sharing data with the FBI, this represents yet another part of the story of how the Fourth Amendment might be circumvented. [This important point will be taken up again in Chapter 7.]

As noted, the decision of the FISCR regarding PRISM refused to require a warrant. The plaintiffs in attacking an upstream program in *Jewel v NSA* also attempted to have the court require a warrant, arguing that the special needs/foreign intelligence exception to the warrant should not apply to mass surveillance. The plaintiff's Fourth Amendment claim was dismissed for lack of standing because they could not establish that *their* communications had actually been collected.[107]

3. *Is bulk collection "reasonable"?*

Now we get to the heart of the matter: are the government's bulk collection programs – PRISM, upstream collections, §215 – consistent with the Fourth Amendment? The Amendment provides that even if a warrant is not required, "searches" must not be unreasonable.

The ultimate measure of the constitutional permissibility of a search is reasonableness, and the reasonableness of a search "is determined by assessing, on the one hand, the degree to which it intrudes upon an individual's privacy and, on the other hand, the degree to which it is needed for the promotion of legitimate governmental interests."[108] A three-pronged formulation of the test lists these factors to be considered: (1) "the nature of the privacy interest allegedly compromised" by the search," (2) "the character of the intrusion imposed" by the government, and (3) "the nature and immediacy of the government's concerns and the efficacy of the [search] in meeting them."[109] This is not an easy framework within which to work, and it seems to be a framework that decidedly favors the government when it comes to national security. As one commentator phrased it: "The greater the government interest that is involved, the greater the intrusion that may be permitted, as long as the privacy protections are sufficient in light of the stated governmental interest."[110] Nevertheless, one needs to ask whether the particular program is effective, and perhaps also whether it goes further than necessary in serving the government's interest.

Metadata bulk collection – §215

Robert Litt argued for the reasonableness of bulk collection of metadata by claiming there was no actual harm to an individual "for constitutional purposes if information about her telephone calls sits on two computers instead of one." Claims of

107 *Jewel v Nat'l Sec Agency*, 810 F3d 622, 625 (9th Cir 2015) (discussing district's ruling on standing and dismissing the appeal for lack of jurisdiction).

108 *Veronica School Dist. 47J v Acton*, 515 US 646, 652 (1995); *United States v Knights*, 534 US 112, 118–119 (2001) (internal quotation omitted).

109 *Board of Education v Earls*, 536 US 822, 830–834 (2002).

110 Donohue, *Section 702 and the collection of international telephone and internet content*, 253 (cited in note 48).

harm focus on speculation about what the government *could* do with the data, rather than what it *did* do, and in addition they focus on the chilling effect this hypothetical activity might produce.[111]

This argument overlooks the chilling effect the *very collection* of the data may have, as argued by Laura Donohue. Robert Litt's argument is antithetical to the analysis of Judge Leon in *Klayman v Obama*, in which the plaintiffs sought a preliminary injunction to block FISA §215.[112] Judge Leon, after concluding that there was a search and that the plaintiffs did have standing, turned to whether a preliminary injunction should be issued. To answer that he had to assess whether the plaintiffs were likely ultimately to succeed on their Fourth Amendment claim. Was the program likely to be found reasonable or unreasonable?

He used the three-pronged test noted above balancing privacy against the government's interest. Regarding the first two parts of the test, he wrote:

> I find that plaintiffs have a very significant expectation of privacy in an aggregated collection of their telephony metadata covering the last five years, and the NSA's Bulk Telephony Metadata Program significantly intrudes on that expectation. Whether the program violates the Fourth Amendment will therefore turn on "the nature and immediacy of the government's concerns and the efficacy of the [search] in meeting them."[113]

He took note of the "almost-Orwellian technology" of the government to store and analyze the data. Then he turned to the third prong and the efficacy of the §215 program. He began by noting "the Government does *not* cite a single instance in which analysis of the NSA's bulk metadata collection actually stopped an imminent attack, or otherwise aided the Government in achieving any objective that was time-sensitive in nature. . . . Given the limited record before me at this point in the litigation – most notably, the utter lack of evidence that a terrorist attack has even been prevented because searching the NSA database was faster than other investigative tactics – I have serious doubts about the efficacy of the metadata collection program as a means of conducting time-sensitive investigations in cases involving imminent threats of terrorism."[114] He concluded with additional findings necessary for the issuance of a preliminary injunction, and thus issued the injunction. However, in a per curiam opinion the D.C. Circuit reversed the grant of the preliminary injunction.

Collecting bulk Internet content – upstream

The Fourth Amendment based challenge in *Jewel v NSA* focused on the absence of a warrant, and a decision on its merits was not reached. Were the court to agree that a warrant was not required, the issue of the program's reasonableness or unreasonableness

111 Litt, *The Fourth Amendment in the information age*, at 14 (cited in note 85).

112 *Klayman v Obama*, at 39 (cited in note 83).

113 Id at 39.

114 Id at 41.

would have to be addressed. The arguments presented to a court would most likely address the following topics.[115] The focus here is on privacy, not free speech: (i) How serious is the privacy interest; (ii) Whether an automated transfer of data from the cable to an NSA computer amounts to a "seizure" or a search; (iii) What harm, if any, is done to the privacy interest when only a very small percentage of communications is seen by human eyes; (iv) Are the minimization procedures such that privacy is well protected as to the retention, use, and dissemination of the data; (v) To measure the value attributed to the government's interest, must the government's program actual increase safety, or does this analogy apply: "You do not get rid of a fire insurance policy that has never paid off because your house has never burned down."

Regarding incidental collection under §702, the Privacy and Civil Liberties Oversight Board (PCLOB) ended up making this observation:

> The present lack of knowledge about the range of incidental collection under Section 702 therefore hampers attempts to gauge whether the program appropriately balances national security interests with the privacy of U.S. persons.[116]

Jamshid Muhtorov, charged with providing material support to a terrorist organization (Chapter 7), argued that §702-acquired evidence could not be used because §702 was unconstitutional.[117] He argued that §702, by permitting "the generalized [incidental] acquisition of U.S. person's communications without any particularized show or demonstration of cause," was not reasonable. After balancing Muhtorov's privacy interest against the government's interest in prosecuting crime, the federal district court decided for the government, and upheld §702.

The Ninth Circuit Court of Appeals reached the conclusion that the incidental collection of the email communications of a criminal defendant – communications the defendant Mohamud wanted excluded from his criminal trial on the grounds that they were acquired in violation of the Fourth Amendment – had been constitutionally acquired.[118] The court said that the government's interest in combating terrorism was "an urgent objective of the highest order," and then that Mohamud's privacy interest in his emails was reduced somewhat because he sent them to a third party, a conclusion that of course means everybody's privacy interests are reduced. The court wound up its opinion by finding the government's targeting and minimization procedures "adequately protected Mohamud's diminished privacy interest."

115 See Litt, *The Fourth Amendment in the information age* (cited in note 85), and Cindy Cohn, *Protecting the Fourth Amendment in the information age: A response to Robert Litt*, 126 Yale L J f 107 (2016), archived at https://www.yalelawjournal.org/forum/protecting-the-fourth-amendment-in-the-information-age.

116 Privacy and Civil Liberties Oversight Board, *Report on the surveillance program operated pursuant to Section 702 of the Foreign Intelligence Surveillance Act*, 116 (cited in note 10).

117 *United States v Muhtorov*, 187 FSupp 3d 1240 (D Colo 2015).

118 *United States v Mohamud*, 843 F3d 420 (9th Cir 2016), cert denied, January 8, 2018. See, also, *In re Directives*, at 1015 (cited in note 67) (incidental collection upheld in context of an applied challenge to FISA brought by Yahoo challenging the PRISM program).

The collection of Mohamud's email did not involve an upstream program such as that in *Jewel v NSA*, so the question remains of whether Internet upstream collection under E.O. 12333 or under §702 can meet the test of reasonableness (putting aside issues of "about" communications and MCTs.)

When "about" collection was still going forward prior to April 2017, the PCLOB expressed its serious Fourth Amendment concerns with the policy, comparing what was happening under upstream collection to surveillance of more traditional forms of communication. "From a legal standpoint, under the Fourth Amendment the government may not, without a warrant, open and read letters sent through the mail in order to acquire those that contain particular information."[119]

As previously noted, the NSA has stopped "about" collection, but if it were renewed, it would have to comply with new FISA requirements.[120] If the Director of National Intelligence and the Attorney General wanted to reinstate "about" collections, Congress would have to be informed, and that notice must include a FISA court order approving the program and "a summary of the protections in place to detect any material breach." A FISA court considering a first certification for an "about" collection would have to deal with it as presenting a novel or significant interpretation of the law, thus triggering the appointment of an amicus curiae. Collection could not start until 30 days after notice to Congress, unless the two officials determined that there were "exigent" circumstances. These new rules are likely to mean FISA "about" collections would be found to be reasonable.

Collecting bulk Internet content – PRISM

The FISA review court concluded that the important PRISM collection program satisfied the Fourth Amendment's reasonableness requirement. The court said it would look at the nature of the government's intrusion into privacy and how the intrusion was implemented. It asserted that: "The more important the government's interest, the greater the intrusion may be constitutionally tolerated." Then the court stated the governmental interest involved was "of the highest order of magnitude."[121] Given this starting point, it was not surprising that the court brushed aside all the concerns of the plaintiff.

Remember under PRISM the NSA presents companies with lists of targeted emails, etc. that it wants collected. Yahoo said the program was unreasonable because there was no judicial review for determining probable cause that the target was a foreign power or agent of a foreign power. There were thus risks of error and abuse

119 Privacy and Civil Liberties Oversight Board, *Report on the surveillance program operated pursuant to Section 702 of the Foreign Intelligence Surveillance Act*, at 122 (cited in note 10).

120 FISA Amendments Reauthorization Act of 2017, Pub L 115–118, §103.

121 *In Re Directives*, at 1012 (cited in note 67).

in PRISM. The FISCR listed several reasons it was not concerned that the judiciary was not involved:

1 The Attorney General had to make a determination that probable cause existed to believe that a target was a foreign power or an agent of one. Other "safeguards" were also pointed to.
2 A presumption of regularity should be used: given proven safeguards, there is no justification for assuming in the absence of evidence, that those prophylactic procedures were implemented in bad faith.
3 The plaintiffs presented no evidence of actual harm, an "egregious" risk of error, or any "broad" potential for abuse.
4 There were "effective" minimization procedures in place.[122]

B. Retention

The NSA's general guideline here – USSID SP0018, January 25, 2011 – allows the retention of communications to, from, or about U.S. persons for foreign intelligence purposes if the information is evidence that the individual may be involved in a crime that has been, is being, or is about to be committed. Generally speaking the communications the NSA collects are stored and retained for five years, with the exception that upstream collections are retained for two years, and encrypted data are retained indefinitely.[123] The NSA's minimization procedures regarding §702 acquired information follows the policy of allowing the retention of information concerning U.S. persons if the information contains foreign intelligence or evidence of a crime.[124] The NSA's minimization procedures do require the "destruction of irrelevant communications of or concerning U.S. persons," but this only happens at the earliest practical point in the processing cycle and only "where the communication can be identified as 'clearly' not relevant to the purpose [foreign intelligence] under which it was acquired or containing evidence of a crime."[125] The reality is there is no routine deletion by the NSA of information involving U.S. persons, and it rarely happens.[126]

These retention policies have not been challenged in court, but it seems unlikely that they would fail the reasonableness test.

122 Id at 1013–1015.

123 Jeff Sessions, Attorney General of the United States, *Minimization procedures used by the National Security Agency in connection with acquisitions of foreign intelligence information pursuant to Section 702 of the Foreign Intelligence Surveillance Act of 1978* (cited in note 61); Marshall Erwin, *The latest rules on how long NSA can keep Americans' encrypted data look too familiar* (Just Security, January 22, 2015), archived at https://www.justsecurity.org/19308/ congress-latest-rules-long-spies-hold-encrypted-data-familiar.

124 Sessions, Attorney General of the United States, *Minimization procedures used by the National Security Agency in connection with acquisitions of foreign intelligence information pursuant to Section 702 of the Foreign Intelligence Surveillance Act of 1978, as amended* (cited in note 61).

125 Privacy and Civil Liberties Oversight Board, *Report on the surveillance program operated pursuant to Section 702 of the Foreign Intelligence Surveillance Act 128* (cited in note 10).

126 Id at 129.

Remember that the NSA disseminates data, even raw data, to the FBI and the NCTC. Thus data collected outside the strictures of the Fourth Amendment applicable in criminal prosecutions can find their way into the hands of the FBI in aid of its investigations. (See Chapter 6.) The legal issues regarding the introduction of FISA-acquired information in a criminal trial are taken up in Chapter 7.

C. *Querying*

A retention policy that permits that retention of information regarding U.S. persons and domestic communications means an extensive database is available for "queries," i.e., searches for information regarding U.S. persons and domestic communications. At one point the NSA policy regarding queries differentiated between Internet communications collected upstream and all other §702-acquired information. Unlike with other databases, NSA agents were forbidden by the NSA to use identifiers identifiable to U.S. persons to query upstream-acquired communications. When the acquisition of "about" communications was dropped in April 2017, the NSA sought approval from a FISA court to use the identifiers on the acquired upstream communications. The FISA court approved the use of the identifiers, allowing them to be run against the now more limited form of upstream Internet collection, subject to the same internal restrictions that apply to the querying of other forms of §702-acquired data.[127]

The NCTC may also undertake queries on §702 data in its possession that are reasonably designed to return foreign intelligence information.[128] The FISA court cited in footnote 63 said the NCTC's policy requiring queries of §702 data to be reasonably designed to return foreign intelligence information was compatible with the Fourth Amendment. In 2016 the NSA used 5288 search terms (email addresses, telephone numbers) connected with a known U.S. person to retrieve the contents of unminimized §702 communications.[129]

The FBI and its querying of NSA data is addressed in Chapter 6.

D. *Contact chaining, social networking analysis, and FBI assessments*

Recall that the NSA has multiple sources of data collected both within and without the U.S. The availability of these bulk database sets enhances the capacity of the government to uncover threats by means of a sophisticated data analysis operation by two offices within the NSA, one that works with metadata and the other with content.[130] A *New York Times* article reports that the NSA augments the data it

127 Memorandum opinion and order, 27–29 (cited in note 63).

128 Id at 63, n. 52.

129 *Transparency report*, at 8 (cited in note 45).

130 The materials in this section draw on Volume I at 20–21, 28–30 (cited in note 46); Working draft at 11–16 (cited in note 28).

has collected with data from "public, commercial and other sources, including bank codes, insurance information, Facebook profiles, passenger manifests, voter registration rolls and GPS location information, as well as property records and unspecified tax data, according to the documents."[131] Additionally location data from GPS companies such as TomTom, social networks, billing records, and bank codes are available. The NSA might also collect bulk cell phone tower records of Americans.

The data are used to conduct contact chaining, to create social network diagrams/graphs, and community of interest profiles, e.g., who travels with whom, who employs whom, who one's father is.

> Phone and email logs, for example, allow analysts to identify people's friends and associates, detect where they were at a certain time, acquire clues to religious or political affiliations, and pick up sensitive information like regular calls to a psychiatrist's office, late-night messages to an extramarital partner or exchanges with a fellow plotter.[132]

The analysis was assumed to be legal because of the Supreme Court's ruling in *Smith v Maryland* that said the Fourth Amendment did not protect the metadata the NSA was analyzing. The NSA also said its data queries had to have a foreign intelligence justification.

With the collapse of "the wall" (noted above) and because of the information sharing environment authorized and required by various statutes and policies, NSA raw data and analysis is shared with the FBI.[133] NCTC also retains and shares evidence of crime with the FBI.[134] After receiving these "tippers" (e.g., phone numbers), the central office can then disseminate the data to field offices for further investigation, which could become an "assessment" and lead the FBI to issue National Security Letters to obtain yet more information. (See Chapter 6.)

131 James Risen and Laura Poitras, *N.S.A. gathers data on social connections of U.S. citizens* (New York Times, September 28, 2013), archived at https://www.nytimes.com/2013/09/29/us/nsa-examines-social-networks-of-us-citizens.html.

132 Id.

133 *In Re Sealed Case* (cited in note 98); USSID SP0018 (cited in note 82); E.O.13888 70 Fed Reg No. 207 (Oct 27, 2005); Raw Sigint Availability Procedures (cited in note 18); Jane Chong, *E.O. 12333 raw SIGNIT availability procedures: A quick and dirty summary* (Lawfare, January 12, 2017), archived at https://lawfareblog.com/eo-12333-raw-sigint-availability-procedures-quick-and-dirty-summary;
Richard A. Best Jr., *Intelligence information: Need-to-know vs need-to-share* (Congressional Research Service, June 6, 2011, R41848). See, also, https://www.dni.gov/index.php/ic-legal-reference-book/intelligence-sharing-procedures-for-foreign-intelligence-and-foreign-counterintelligence-investigations-conducted-by-the-fbi.

134 Memorandum opinion and order, at 44 (cited in note 63).

4

SECURING THE BORDERS

Because the 9/11 attacks were carried out by terrorists who were U.S. residents, intense attention was drawn to the need to protect the domestic territory of the United States from terrorists entering the country from abroad. The government's authority in this area is subject to few constitutional constraints. The Preamble to the Constitution states it was created to, among other things, "insure domestic tranquility" and "provide for the common defense." Article 1, Section 8 authorizes Congress to regulate commerce with foreign nations, and to establish uniform rules of naturalization. The Supreme Court, based on these passages and on a general understanding of sovereignty, has said that the "power of exclusion of foreigners" is an incident of sovereignty and part of "those sovereign powers delegated by the Constitution" to the federal government. Thus the authority of the government to exclude immigrants based on race has been upheld.[1] In fact, the Supreme Court has recognized the authority of Congress to be so sweeping that Congress may exclude people based on their political views, even despite the fact that citizens in the U.S. may want to meet with the visitor in order to hear their views in person.[2] This decision suggests that if Congress so chose it could exclude immigrants based solely on their being Muslim.[3] [What the President may do pursuant to federal statutes and the Constitution is another

1 *Chae Chan Ping v United States*, 130 US 581 (1889) (the Chinese Exclusion Case). See, also, Immigration Act of 1917 imposing literacy tests on immigrants as a way of excluding immigrants from eastern and southern Europe. Jerome Karabel, *The chosen*, 78 (Houghton-Mifflin Company 2005).

2 *Kleindienst v Mandel*, 408 US 753 (1972).

3 David A. Martin, *Why immigration's plenary power doctrine endures*, 68 Okla L Rev 29, note 2 (2015).

question.[4] For example, the executive might try to avoid compliance with the statutes by claiming they were an unconstitutional invasion of his or her Article II authority.]

I. Security between ports of entry

Securing the border against terrorists who try to sneak into the country unnoticed is a daunting task given that the U.S. coastline is 12,497 miles in length, the border with Canada including Alaska is 5525 miles, and the Mexican–U.S. border is 1933 miles.[5] [As of this writing, the fence along the Mexican–U.S. border extends in separate pieces for 700 miles.[6]]

Primary responsibility for preventing terrorists and the instruments of terror from entering the United States has been assigned to the Secretary of the Department of Homeland Security (DHS).[7] Housed within the DHS is the Customs and Border Patrol (CBP) that employs 60,000 people; Immigration and Customs Enforcement (ICE) about 20,000; Transportation Security Administration (TSA) 60,000; and the Coast Guard 40,000. Pursuant to 6 USC §211, the CBP has the "primary responsibility for interdicting persons attempting to illegally enter or exit the United States with goods being illegally imported or exported from the United States at a place other than a designated port of entry." CBP agents have the authority to interrogate, arrest and search.[8] Customs officers, similarly, may arrest and search persons, baggage, vehicles, and vessels.[9] Aliens who enter the U.S. illegally without inspection and not through designated ports of entry commit a crime, may be detained, and are removable.[10]

The Fourth Amendment's search/seizure rules at the border are an exception to the usual rules. A number of federal courts have held that this exception applies to individuals either entering or exiting the U.S.[11] "That searches/seizures made at the border, pursuant to the longstanding right of the sovereign to protect itself by stopping and examining persons and property crossing into this country, are reasonable simply by virtue of the fact that they occur at the border, should, by now, require no extended demonstration."[12] Accordingly, a warrant is not required for (routine) searches at the border, known as the "border search exception."

4 See *Trump v Hawaii*, No. 17-965 (U.S. June 26, 2018) (slip opinion). See, also, Kate M. Manuel, *Executive authority to exclude aliens: In brief* (Congressional Research Service, January 23, 2017, R44743).

5 Janice Cheryl Beaver, *US international borders: Brief facts* (Congressional Research Office, November 9, 2006, RS21729).

6 http://www.fairus.org/issue/national-security/current-state-border-fence; https://www.usatoday.com/border-wall/us-mexico-interactive-border-map/.

7 6 USC §202.

8 8 CFR 1.2 (definition of immigration officer); 8 USC §1357.

9 19 USC §1581, §1582, §1583, §1589a, §1595.

10 8 USC §1325; 8 USC §1231; 8 USC §1227. See, also, 8 USC §1182(a)(7)(B).

11 *United States v Oriakhi*, 57 F3d 1290 (4th Cir 1995); *United States v Ezeiruaku*, 936 F2d 136 (3d Cir 1991).

12 *United States v Ramsey*, 431 US 606, 616 (1977).

Two questions arise here: Does a particular search or seizure in fact fall within the border search exception to the warrant requirement,[13] and if it does, did the search or seizure satisfy the basic requirement of the Fourth Amendment that the search be reasonable? Whether the border search exception applies depends on whether the search occurs at the border. Two doctrines are used in this connection: one doctrine – the functional equivalent doctrine – holds that a search at a port of entry is a border search even *if the port of entry is not literally* at the official border.[14] The second doctrine is the "extended border doctrine."

The extended border doctrine "provides that non-routine border searches that occur near the border are deemed constitutionally permissible if they are reasonable under the Fourth Amendment."[15] A federal statute authorizes the CBP to carry out warrantless arrests and searches within a "reasonable distance" of any U.S. external boundary.[16] A companion federal regulation interprets the phrase "reasonable distance" to mean 100 miles from the border.[17] CBP agents may also enter private lands within 25 miles from the border, but may not enter dwellings, for the purpose of patrolling.[18] Customs officials are also authorized by statute and the Constitution to search for unlawfully imported materials on board sea vessels, vehicles, and persons.[19] ICE officials may, without warrant, interrogate aliens in order to inquire into their right to be in the country.[20] A federal statute further empowers immigration officers to search without a warrant a person and his personal possessions when the officer has reasonable cause to suspect the search would turn up grounds for denying admission.[21] ICE officials have the authority to arrest, without warrant, people who in his presence are attempting to enter the U.S.[22] But that same law does not allow officials to enter dwellings such as a home or church; for that a warrant is necessary. (Also see Section VI, Removal of Aliens.)

The regulation that allows warrantless border searches 100 miles from the border, tests the limits of this doctrine. [The ACLU has noted that the 100-mile regulation from any U.S. "external boundary" means that CBP operations cover 200 million people, with many of the largest metropolitan areas within the 100-mile band running around the edge of the continent. Thus if the 100-mile regulation is permissible, a huge proportion of the U.S. population would be exposed to the warrant exception of the border search.]

13 Id.

14 *United States v Hill*, 939 F2d 934 (11th Cir 1991).

15 *United States v Yang*, 286 F3d. 940, 945 (7th Cir 2002). See *Almeida-Sanchez v United States*, 413 US 266(1973).

16 8 USC §1357(a)(3).

17 8 CFR §287.1.

18 8 USC 1357(a)(2) and (3); 8 CFR §287.1.

19 19 USC §482; *United States v Rivera*, 595 F2d 1095 (5th Cir 1979); *United States v Bilir*, 592 F2d 735 (4th Cir 1979); *United States v Glaziou*, 402 F2d 8 (2d Cir 1968); *United States v Berard*, 281 F Supp 328 (D Mass 1968).

20 8 USC §1357(a)(3).

21 8 USC §1357(c).

22 8 USC §1357(a)(2); 8 CFR §§287.3, 287.5.

To determine whether an extended border search or seizure doctrine is available, courts consider whether: (1) there is reasonable certainty that a border crossing has occurred; (2) there is reasonable certainty that no change in the condition of the luggage has occurred since the border crossing; and (3) there is reasonable suspicion that criminal activity has occurred.[23] Note the difference between an extended border search and a search occurring at the border or its functional equivalent. An extended border search always requires a showing of "reasonable suspicion of criminal activity" before undertaking the search, whereas a search at the border or functional equivalent *may not* require any degree of suspicion, depending in part on the intrusiveness of the search.[24] (See Section VI below.)

The lower courts have given the extended border doctrine a broad interpretation; that doctrine has been applied to planes and vehicles tracked as having crossed the border as many as 142 hours later and over 100 miles from the border.[25]

Checkpoints: The Supreme Court said that brief warrantless and suspicionless *checkpoint stops* 66 miles from the border were consistent with the Fourth Amendment.[26] In that case, the stops were three to five minutes in length, which the Court characterized as a "brief detention." The Court did not lay down any guidelines regarding when detentions for a longer period became constitutionally impermissible in the absence of mere suspicion or a warrant.

Roving patrols: The Supreme Court has said that Border Patrol officers may temporarily detain vehicles for investigation only if they are "aware of specific articulable facts, together with rational inferences from those facts, that reasonably warrant suspicion that the vehicle was involved in illegal activities."[27] "[I]f we approved the Government's position in this case, Border Patrol officers could stop motorists at random for questioning, day or night, anywhere within 100 air miles of the 2,000-mile border, on a city street, a busy highway, or a desert road, without any reason to suspect that they have violated any law." In another case the Supreme Court ruled that stopping and searching a vehicle over 20 miles from the border in the absence of probable cause was a violation of the Fourth Amendment.[28] The seriousness of the Court's concern is highlighted by the ACLU observation noted earlier.

Determining the reasonableness of a roving patrol involves taking into account a number of factors: proximity to the border, the characteristics of the area, information about recent illegal trafficking of aliens, and the experience of the border patrol

23 *United States v Yang*, at 946 (cited in note 15).

24 Yule Kim, *Protecting the US perimeter: Border searches under the Fourth Amendment*, 8 (Congressional Research Service, June 29, 2009 RL31826).

25 *United States v Caicedo-Guarnizo*, 723 F2d 1420 (9th Cir 1984); *United States v Garcia*, 672 F2d 1349 (11th Cir 1982). See, also, *United States v Fogelman*, 586 F2d 337 (5th Cir 1978); *United States v Martinez*, 481 F2d 214 (5th Cir 1973). But see *United States v Venzor-Castillo*, 991 F2d 634 (10th Cir 1993).

26 *United States v Martinez-Fuerte*, 428 US 543 (1976).

27 *United States v Brignoni-Ponce*, 442 US 873 (1975).

28 *Almeida-Sanchez v United States*, at 273 (cited in note 15).

agents.[29] There is also the question of the ethnicity or race of the individual stopped or searched. Given a hypothetical reasonable officer, might race or ethnicity warrant an articulable suspicion supporting a stop and/or search? Here a distinction arises in the law between checkpoints and roving patrols. When it comes to checkpoint stops, which the Supreme Court considers minimally intrusive, the Court said that officers must have wide discretion in selecting motorists for diversion to a secondary screening. In particular at the southern border of the U.S., a Mexican appearance was a relevant factor that could often be taken into account; such referrals could be made "largely on the basis of apparent Mexican ancestry."[30]

The law under both the Fourth and Fourteenth Amendments is different when it comes to ethnicity and race used by roving patrols. Under the Fourth Amendment, the Supreme Court has said that by itself ethnicity or race does not support reasonable suspicion necessary for even a brief roving stop.[31] In dictum, however, the Court did suggest Mexican appearance could be a *relevant* factor along with many other factors such as erratic driving. Thereafter the Ninth Circuit said that the race of an individual could not be considered in determining if an officer had reasonable suspicion under the Fourth Amendment to make the stop.[32]

Adjudicating the constitutionality of these stops under the Fourteenth Amendment's Equal Protection clause is different. In the case of roving stops, there are two categories of cases, Category 1: the intentional use of ethnicity or race to target individuals either by an individual officer or by a law enforcement agency as a matter of policy; Category 2: selective enforcement of law(s). In a Category 1 case, the plaintiff must establish an intent by the officer or agency to use a racial criterion, a proof not easily accomplished;[33] but if proof is available that ethnicity or race was the sole basis for the stop or investigation, then the Equal Protection Clause has been violated.[34] However, if race or ethnicity was "but one factor" for a stop detention, then the Equal Protection Clause may not have been violated.[35] [One reason that may be true is that proving that a racial criterion was used may only mean that the government must convince the court that the use of the "protected characteristic" (race or ethnicity) was *necessary* to achieve a compelling state interest. This is a difficult burden for the government to meet, but not impossible.[36]]

29 *United States v Inocencio*, 40 F3d 716, 722 (5th cir 1995).

30 *United States v Martinez-Fuerte*, at 563, 564 (cited in note 26).

31 *United States v Brignoni-Ponce*, at 885–887 (cited in note 27).

32 *United States v Montero-Camargo*, 208 F3d 1122 (9th Cir 2000).

33 *Washington v Davis*, 426 US 229, 235 (1976); *United States v Travis*, 62 F3d 170 (6th Cir 1995). See, also, *Brown v City of Oneonta*, 221 F3d 329 (2d Cir 2000), reh'g en banc denied, 235 F3d 769 (2d Cir 2000), cert denied, 534 US 816 (2001).

34 Jody Feder, *Racial profiling: Legal and constitutional issues*, 4–5 (Congressional Research Service, April 16, 2012, RL31130). See, also, *Ortega Melendres v Arpaio*, 989 F Supp2d 822 (D Ariz 2013).

35 Id at 5–6.

36 See, for example, *Fisher v University of Texas*, 570 US 297 (2013).

In the Category 2 case, the plaintiffs in some jurisdictions have to meet the very difficult burden of showing specifically and precisely that similarly situated individuals of another race were treated differently.[37] But some lower courts have ruled differently, creating confusion, with some courts saying a "similarly situated" showing is not necessary, and another ruling that it was neither necessary nor sufficient to prove discriminatory purpose.[38]

II. Passports

The U.S. passport serves several functions. It identifies the owner as an American citizen; it is an authorization to leave the U.S.; and it is a request to other countries that the bearer of it be allowed to pass safely and freely.[39] *By law* a citizen may not depart from or enter the U.S. without a passport.[40] However, importantly, denial or revocation of a passport is not a denial or revocation of citizenship.

The Code of Federal Regulations lists many grounds for denying a passport, including if the Secretary of State "determines that the applicant's activities abroad are causing or are likely to cause serious damage to the national security or foreign policy of the United States."[41] A federal statute provides: A passport may not be denied issuance, revoked, restricted, or otherwise limited because of any speech, activity, belief, affiliation, or membership, within or outside the United States, which, if held or conducted within the United States, would be protected by the First Amendment to the Constitution of the United States.[42] Hence an administration that wants to deny a passport to someone suspected of having an interest in terrorist activities may only do so based on that person's actual behavior – not based merely on their beliefs, memberships, or speech activities. [A complication arises if the speech activity is deemed to be material support for a terrorist organization in violation of 18 USC §2339A or §2339B.] The passport regulation noted above seems only to apply to "activities abroad," thus raising the question of the revocation of a passport of someone outside the country, a topic taken up below. It may be possible to deny a passport to a wannabe terrorist on any number of other grounds such as an outstanding felony arrest warrant issued by federal, state, local, or foreign authorities.[43]

As is the case with denying a passport in the first place, revocation is possible if the applicant's activities abroad are causing or are likely to cause serious damage to the national security or foreign policy of the United States.[44] But again the same

37 Id at 7 citing *United States v Armstrong*, 571 US 456 (1996).

38 Id at 7–8.

39 Patrick Weil, *Citizenship, passports, and the legal identity of Americans: Edward Snowden and others have a case in the courts*, 123 Yale L J 565, 568–569 (2014).

40 8 USC §1185(b).

41 22 CFR §51.60(c)(4). See, also, *Haig v Agee*, 453 US 280 (1981).

42 22 USC §2721. See, also, *Aptheker v Secretary of State*, 378 US 500 (1964).

43 22 CFR §51.60.

44 22 CFR §51.62.

"free speech" limitation applies. Of course, an individual whose passport has been revoked may not wish to return to the U.S., but as a U.S. citizen they continue to have the right to return, a right that cannot be denied a citizen.[45] A citizen located abroad whose passport has been revoked may obtain a passport from the Department of State "for direct return to the United States."[46] Incidentally, revoking citizenship itself is not a constitutionally available option.[47]

At the time of this writing, a complex case is before a federal court, a case in which an individual with dual U.S.–Saudi Arabian citizenship is being held by the U.S. in Iraq incognito and without charges as an unprivileged enemy belligerent, not allowed to consult with an attorney, and may be facing transfer to Saudi Arabia.[48]

Placement on the No Fly List serves as another potential obstacle to returning to the U.S. via air transport. (See Chapter 5.)

III. Visas, immigrants and refugees

Whether an applicant seeking legal entry is seeking a non-immigrant entry (e.g., student, pleasure, foreign press etc.), a permanent immigrant status, a refugee status, or asylum, the law sets up criteria and procedures. Determining if a visa applicant qualifies for a particular visa is largely in the hands of consular officers in the Department of State who have the authority to deny visas subject only to administrative supervisory review.[49] The consular officers conduct a personal interview, review all the documents the applicant must submit (fingerprints, photograph, birth certificate, marriage license), and check numerous large databases of suspected terrorists. Consular officers use the Consular Consolidated Database, a biometric and biographic database, for screening. This database is, in turn, linked to several databases in the Department of Homeland Security and the FBI. An additional crosscheck is made with the Terrorist Screening Center.[50]

Consular officers look for engagement in "terrorist activity," membership in a terrorist organization, the endorsement or espousal of terrorist activity or persuading others to do the same, military training from a terrorist organization, or being the spouse or child of such a person.[51] [These terms are discussed at greater length in the last section of the chapter.]

Immigrant visas (held by lawful permanent residents or LPRs) face both augmented eligibility requirements and augmented screening. To be eligible for an immigrant

45 *Newton v INS*, 736 F2d 336 (6th Cir 1984); *Mohame v Holder*, 995 F Supp2d 520 (ED Vir 2014).

46 22 CFR §51.60.

47 *Vance v Terrazas*, 444 US 252 (1980); *Afroyim v Rusk*, 387 US 253 (1967).

48 http://www.kansascity.com/news/nation-world/article209391944.html;https://www.yahoo.com/news/judge-rule-test-case-us-enemy-combatant-184652087.html.

49 22 CFR §41.121 and §42.81. See, also, *Kleindienst v Mandel*, 408 US 753 (1972).

50 Ruth Ellen Wasem, *Immigration: Visa security policies*, 5–6 (Congressional Research Office, November 18, 2015, R43589).

51 8 USC §1182(a)(3)(A) and (B).

visa the applicant must fit within one of several categories that sharply tilt toward the admission of people with family links to people already in the U.S., and employment.[52] Others may gain visas by winning the "diversity lottery," open to aliens from foreign nations with low admission levels.[53] And, of course, applicants for permanent immigration face the same disqualifications related to terrorism as do nonimmigrant entrants.

United States policy regarding immigration has always been politically charged, no less so today as people seek escape from the turmoil in the Mideast and Central America.[54] The number of refugees admitted to the country is determined each year by the President after consultation with Congress. There is a default cap, which can be exceeded, set by statute at 50,000 per year.[55] President Trump has lowered the refugee cap to 45,000. Refugees are inadmissible on the same grounds as those who apply for visas, e.g., engagement in terrorist activities, endorsement of terrorism, membership or support of a terrorist organization.[56]

Screening refugees is jointly undertaken by the Department of State and the Department of Homeland Security. It is a multistep process that includes biometric screening and checking various government databases.[57] Final approval for admission of a refugee is made by the U.S. Citizenship and Immigration Services in the Department of Homeland Security.[58]

A separate set of statutes deals with those seeking asylum.[59]

IV. Pre-departure databased screening

Airplane safety screening, e.g., x-rays, passenger pat-downs, and the No Fly List are taken up in Chapter 5. Addressed here is a different aspect of screening faced by travelers. Databased preflight screening at foreign (and U.S. airports) is carried out by Customs and Border Patrol agents who are located in foreign airports.[60] Databases such as the Terrorist Screening Database (TSDB) are checked and "rule-based targeting" is used, which might also be called "rule-based evaluation," to identify people who are not already in the database but who, based on an algorithm, fit the profile of a high-risk

52 8 USC §1153.
53 8 USC §1153(c).
54 See http://www.pewresearch.org/fact-tank/2017/01/30/key-facts-about-refugees-to-the-u-s/.
55 8 USC §1157.
56 8 USC §1182; 8 USC §1227.
57 https://www.state.gov/j/prm/releases/factsheets/2017/266447.html. For more information, see https://www.uscis.gov/ refugeescreening.
58 6 USC §271(b); 8 CFR §207.4.
59 8 USC §1158. See, also, Ruth Ellen Wasem, *US immigration policy on asylum seekers* (Congressional Research Service, May 5, 2005, RL32621); 8 USC §1225; 8 USC 1227; 8 USC 1182; 8 CFR §1208.13(a).
60 8 USC §1103 (a)(7); 19 USC §1629; US Government Accountability Office, Border Security, *Report to congressional requesters*, January, 2017, p.7.; https://www.tsa.gov/travel/security-screening.

traveler and thus warrant a further look. Airlines flying to the U.S. must provide U.S. passenger and crew manifests for each fight that include names, birth dates, citizenship, gender, passport number, visa number and other information U.S. officials may determine is reasonably necessary to ensure aviation safety.[61] Travelers may also go through a prescreening security clearance to speed up the preboarding screening process.[62] In the future biometric screening may be used for both international and domestic flights.[63]

In addition to the No Fly List taken up in Chapter 5, the Department of Homeland Security and CBP use the Automated Targeting System (ATS), a "decision support tool that compares traveler, cargo, and conveyance information against law enforcement, intelligence, and other enforcement data using risk-based scenarios and assessments."[64] ATS compares information about individuals (defined as passengers, travelers, crew members, or persons appearing on documents supporting the movement of cargo) against the Terrorist Screening Database (TSDB) as well as data regarding outstanding warrants.[65] The ATS allows for searching multiple databases to obtain a consolidated view of a person. An important starting point for this analysis are the departure manifests each commercial vessel or airline must supply; such manifests list each passenger, crew member, and other occupants being transported.[66]

A principal purpose for the database screening by the CBP is to find aliens whose "departure [from the U.S.] would be prejudicial to the interests of the United States."[67] The list of such aliens is long and includes aliens with national defense secrets, ones who are likely to engage in activities that counteract the effectiveness of the national defense, and ones whose circumstances might render "the alien's departure prejudicial to the interests of the United States." Another reason for screening those exiting the country is to identify aliens who have overstayed their visas, a concern, given the possibility of terrorist activity while in the U.S. People who overstay are, of course, removable and, if they have been removed involuntarily or even if they have exited voluntarily, they may be prohibited from returning for periods of five and 10 years, after which they may be eligible to obtain a visa to return to the U.S.[68]

U.S. citizens planning to depart the U.S. who are at ports of entry/exit must, as noted earlier, have a passport. Departure to avoid prosecution is a crime under 18 USC §1073.

Note that the Customs and Border Patrol claims the authority to search electronic devices and look at the information on them pre-departure. The general policy regarding the conduct of these searches is discussed below in sections V.C. and V.D.

61 49 USC §44909.

62 https://www.cbp.gov/travel/trusted-traveler-programs/global-entry/tsa-precheck.

63 8 USC §1365b; https://www.eff.org/deeplinks/2017/11/tsa-plans-use-face-recognition-track-americans-through-airports.

64 https://www.dhs.gov/publication/automated-targeting-system-ats-update.

65 Department of Homeland Security, *Privacy impact assessment update for the automated targeting system*, January 13, 2017, DHS/CBP/PIA-006(e), p.1, archived at https://www.dhs.gov/sites/default/files/publications/privacy-pia-cbp-006-e-ats-january2017.pdf.

66 8 USC §1221.

67 8 CFR §215.2.

68 8 USC §1227; 8 USC §1202(g); 8 USC §1182(a)(6)(G) and §1182(a)(9)(A).

V. Arrival screening at ports of entry

People disembarking from domestic flights may be targets of ordinary law enforcement agents, such as dog-sniffs of luggage, operating within the rules of the Fourth Amendment and Fourteenth Amendment (equal protection) applicable to ordinary criminal law enforcement.[69] This topic is beyond the scope of this book. We turn here to the screening of passengers arriving on international flights at ports of entry.

CBP officers interview arriving passengers and examine travel documents to determine admissibility into the U.S. The traveler is checked against TECS (not an acronym) and Automated Targeting System data; and new data is added to the TECS database, e.g., name, date, and location of arrival.[70] (See Chapter 1.)

Arriving passengers are also searched. What the Supreme Court has called "routine" (a vague term) border searches may be conducted without first obtaining a warrant and without individualized suspicion, much less individualized suspicion based on probable cause. The issue was raised in one case, but not finally settled, as to whether the border search exception has an outer limit and no longer applies. Were that so, a warrant would be necessary when the search became one inspired by a general interest in law enforcement instead of being tied to the rationale for having the border search exception in the first place.[71]

The following discussion is broken down into five sections: (A) Who enjoys the protections of the Fourth Amendment at the border?; (B) Terminology and principles; (C) Routine searches; (D) Nonroutine searches; and (E) Exclusion following arrival.

A. Who enjoys the protections of the Fourth Amendment at the border?

No one questions that U.S. citizens entering or departing the country enjoy whatever protections the Fourth Amendment may provide. [Exactly what that means is a vexing question and is taken up shortly.] Searches by U.S. officials of U.S. citizens that occur outside the country are rare.[72]

Aliens entering or departing from the U.S. are also covered by the Fourth Amendment. However, aliens outside the country searched by U.S. agents are not generally protected by the Fourth Amendment, unless – according to four justices – that person has a "substantial connection" with the country.[73] This amorphous phrase arguably

69 See, for example, *Farag v United States*, 587 F Supp2d 436 (ED NY 2008), discussed in Chapter 5.

70 Lisa Seghetti, *Border security: Immigration inspections at port of entry*, 10 (Congressional Research Service, January 26, 2015, R43356).

71 *United States v Kolsuz*, No. 16-4687 *14 (4th Cir 2018).

72 See, for example, *Reid v Covert*, 354 US 1 (1957).

73 *United States v Verdugo-Urquidez*, 494 US 259 (1990).

means that an alien with a visa arriving at a U.S. port of entry does have a substantial connection.[74]

B. Terminology and principles

While the Fourth Amendment does apply to searches at the border, the Supreme Court has said that the expectation of privacy is lower at the border than it is in the interior. (The search of luggage and passengers following a domestic flight is subject to normal Fourth Amendment rules.[75]) On international flights, the Fourth Amendment balance between the interests of the government and the privacy right of the individual is loaded much more favorably toward the government at the border.[76] Furthermore, the Court has embraced a distinction between "routine" and "nonroutine" border searches. In the Court's words: "Routine searches of persons and effects of entrants are not subject to any requirement of reasonable suspicion, probable cause, or warrant."[77] The Court underscored what it meant by elaborating: "[W]e suggest no view on what level of suspicion, if any, is required for nonroutine border searches such as strip, body cavity, or involuntary x-ray searches." The Seventh Circuit Court of Appeals draws the line between, on the one hand, searches that do not pose a serious invasion of privacy and which do not embarrass of offend the "average" traveler (as with luggage), and, on the other, a body cavity or strip search.[78] Note the distinction being made between searches of a person's body and the search of personal effects, a distinction of importance addressed below.

The duration of the border stop has not been determinative of whether or not a search is nonroutine. Searches of four to six hours in duration have been held to be routine searches.[79]

C. Routine searches

In *US v Flores-Montano*, the Supreme Court concluded that the search of the gas tank of a station wagon was a routine search, hence the government could without suspicion remove, disassemble, and reassemble the vehicle's fuel tank.[80] Naturally

74 ACLU Complaint to Acting Officer for Civil Rights and Civil Liberties and Acting Inspector General, Department of Homeland Security, Complaint and request for investigation of abuse of power, excessive force, coercion, and unlawful confiscation of property by Customs and Border Protection at ports of entry along the US–Mexico border, May 9, 2012, archived at https://www.aclu.org/files/assets/aclu_2012_cbp_abuse_complaint_2.pdf.

75 *United States v Place*, 462 US 696 (1983).

76 *United States v Montoya De Hernandez*, 473 US 531 (1985).

77 Id.

78 *United States v Johnson*, 991 F2d 1287, 1291–1292 (7th Cir 1993).

79 *Tabba v Chertoff*, 509 F3d 89 (2d Cir 2007); *United States v Feiten*, No. 15-20631 (ED Mich 2016).

80 541 US 149 (2004).

enough, routine searches also include the emptying of pockets and the inspection of luggage.[81] Whether this case also applies to the search of computers and cell phones is addressed below.

The suspicionless border search doctrine has also been applied to the reading of a letter, which, in this case, involved soliciting sex from a child in the Philippines.[82] The decision, cited as *United States v Ramsey*, 431 US 606 (1977), applied the border search exception to the opening of international mail by customs officials.

D. Nonroutine searches and reasonable suspicion

Using the reasonable suspicion standard, courts have upheld the following nonroutine searches: strip searches, alimentary canal searches involving the forced ingestion of laxatives, and x-rays.[83] The Ninth Circuit has even upheld under the Fourth Amendment a forced rectal examination. The court wrote: "We believe a previously convicted and registered user of narcotics (18 USC §1407), coming across the border under the influence of narcotics readily shown by his eyes, disclosing thirty 'recent' needle marks on one arm, and 'recent' needle marks on the other, who acts 'in an extremely nervous manner,' may be searched, as one reasonably portraying a 'clear indication' he may be smuggling contraband."[84] Another case upheld the detainment of the defendant for approximately four days as customs inspectors waited for the defendant to defecate drug balloons she had swallowed. Here, customs officials had a particularized and objective basis for suspecting her of alimentary canal smuggling, and while the length of detention was especially long, it was still reasonable, since she had to be detained long enough to confirm suspicions, lest she be released into the U.S. carrying the reasonably suspected drugs.[85]

E. Computers and cell phones and non-forensic searches

A non-forensic search of a device (turning it on, and manually scrolling) is permissible without suspicion.[86] The Ninth Circuit even upheld the manual opening of folders on the desktop of the computer.[87] The next cases represent a gray area. A federal district court ruled that the use of the Cellebrite device to obtain information from a cell phone that was not password protected, encrypted, or deleted was a routine search.[88] Another federal district court upheld as routine a search that used OS Triage

81 Kim, *Protecting the US perimeter: Border searches under the Fourth Amendment*, at 9 (cited in note 24).

82 *United States v Seljan*, 547 F3d 993 (9th Cir 2008).

83 *United States v Montoya de Hernandez* (cited in note 76); *United States v Adekunle*, 980 F2d 985, 987–88 (5th Cir 1992); *US v Afanador*, 567 F2d 1325 (5th Cir 1978).

84 *Rivas v United States*, 368 F2d 703, 710 (9th Cir 1966).

85 *United States v Montoya de Hernandez* (cited in note 76).

86 *United States v Ickes*, 393 F3d 501 (4th Cir 2005).

87 *United States v Arnold*, 533 F3d 1003(9th Cir 2008).

88 *United States v Lopez*, No. 13CR2092 WQH (SD Cal 2016).

to identify whether pictures or videos on a computer were child pornography.[89] In doing so, the court also rejected the applicability of *Riley v California*, 134 S Ct 2473 (2014), which had prohibited the search of a cell phone incident to an arrest.

Turning now to the policy of the CBP. CBP wants to be able to inspect devices; thus passcodes must be provided. Devices that cannot readily be inspected may be excluded or seized for off-site investigation for a "reasonable period of time."[90] Information may be copied and then shared with law enforcement if there is probable cause to believe the device contains evidence of a violation of law. The CBP will not use the passenger's device to access the passenger's cloud-stored information.[91] Regarding foreign visitors, the Secretary of the Department of Homeland Security said he would like a policy that would require them to provide passwords to sites visited online. He also said that the department is considering looking at an applicant's social media use, financial information, and cell phone contacts.[92]

The Electronic Frontier Foundation (EFF) opposes these policies, relying in part on *Riley v California* (noted above).[93] A lawsuit is pending against CBP and its policies.[94]

F. Computers and cell phones and forensic searches

Turning now to forensic searches of electronic devices, a search that requires attaching a device to a cell phone or computer either by a wire or wirelessly. Although not a circuit court opinion, the opinion in *United States v Saboonchi* is worth looking at because of the care Judge Grimm took to explain the unique nature of a forensic search, one that he felt warranted being classified as a nonroutine search.

89 *United States v Feiten* (cited in note 79).

90 CBP Directive No. 3340-049, 6 (Jan 4, 2018), archived at https://www.dhs.gov/sites/default/files/publications/CBP% 20Directive%203340-049A_Border-Search-of-Electronic-Media.pdf.

91 Id at 4. In a case regarding searching of cell phones incident to an arrest (not allowed), the Supreme Court said allowing the searching of files in the cloud "would be like finding a key in a suspect's pocket and arguing that it allowed law enforcement to unlock and search a house." *Riley v California*, 134 S Ct 2473, 2491 (2014).

92 https://www.npr.org/templates/transcript/transcript.php?storyId=514175464; https://www.nbcnews.com/news/us-news/us-visitors-may-have-hand-over-social-media-passwords-kelly-n718216.

93 Sophia Cope, Amul Kalia, Seth Schoen, and Adam Schwartz, *Digital privacy at the U.S. border: Protecting the data on your devices*, archived at https://www.eff.org/wp/digital-privacy-us-border-2017#searches-digital-devices. See, also, ACLU Complaint to Acting Officer for Civil Rights and Civil Liberties and Acting Inspector General, Department of Homeland Security, Complaint and request for investigation of abuse of power, excessive force, coercion, and unlawful confiscation of property by Customs and Border Protection at ports of entry along the US–Mexico border, May 9, 2012, archived at https://www.aclu.org/files/assets/aclu_2012_cbp_abuse_complaint_2.pdf.

94 Complaint for Injunction and Declaratory Relief, *Alasaad v Duke* No 1:17-cv-11730-DJC (DC D MA filed September 13, 2017), archived at https://www.eff.org/files/2017/09/13/7._amended_complaint.pdf.

After commenting on how much information these devices may contain he turned to the nature of a forensic search: (a) An image of the drive is made and saved for use at a later time. This may take far more time than it takes to execute a luggage search. (b) A forensic search can obtain data that the owner of the device had thought he or she had deleted. Even reformatting a hard drive often erases less than a tenth of 1% of the data on the disk. (c) Even if the user never saves any data in the first place, a forensic search may still obtain unsaved data. Thus thoughts written in a document that was never saved to the disk may yet wind up in the hands of the government. (d) The search can collect tracking data from a cell phone, revealing much about a person's day-to-day life. (e) Metadata regarding when and how a computer was used becomes available to the government. (f) Word processing files store data about who created the file, and its history. (g) Browsers used to surf the web hold information about the user's interests, webpages visited, search terms used, habits, identity, and online whereabouts. In fact, in this case the forensic search recovered contacts, call logs, calendar entries, text messages, email, chat logs, web browser information, photos, documents, and video files.

Judge Grimm thus concluded that "there is no doubt that such a search results in the exposure of intimate details and abrogates a traveler's reasonable expectations of privacy in his or her most personal and confidential affairs – including information that, from the user's perspective, no longer even exists."[95] Hence before a forensic search is undertaken a customs officers must have "reasonable suspicion," i.e., a particularized and objective basis for suspecting that a particular device contains contraband or evidence of criminal activity.[96]

There is a division among the circuit courts whether or not border agents may conduct forensic searches of mobile devices without reasonable suspicion. The Fourth and Ninth Circuits have said the Fourth Amendment requires at least reasonable suspicion for a forensic search given the search implicates significant privacy interests.[97] The Eleventh Circuit has ruled a forensic search does not require any amount of suspicion because only property is being searched (not a person's body), a person's expectation of privacy at the border is diminished, and the government's interest in preventing the entry of unwanted persons is at its zenith at the border.[98]

The Customs and Border Patrol calls a forensic search an "advanced search." Its policy requires there be a reasonable suspicion of activity in violation of a law or in which "there is a national security concern."[99] An individual on the Selectee List (Chapter 5) would be subject to a forensic search.

95 Id at 568.

96 Id at 570.

97 *United States v Kolsuz* (cited in note 71); *United States v Cotterman*, 709 F3d 952, 963 (9th Cir 2013). Compare *United States v Romm*, 455 F3d 990 (9th Cir 2006) (upholding forensic search of a computer, but the issue on appeal was whether the search was a border search); *House v Napolitano*, No. 11–10852–DJC, 2012 WL 1038816 (D Mass, March 28, 2012) (the search was akin to the search of luggage).

98 *United States v Touset*, No. 17-11561 (11th Cir 2018).

99 CBP Directive No. 3340-049 at 5 (cited in note 90).

A doctrine that further opens the door to the use at trial of evidence actually obtained in violation of the Fourth Amendment is the "good faith" exception allowing the use of evidence obtained by law enforcement in reasonable reliance on a warrant that is ultimately found to be defective. This doctrine has been extended to border searches executed without reliance on a warrant when the border agents reasonably relied on the expansive authority of the government to search persons and effects at the border.[100]

G. *Other border issues*

What else happens at the border is legally unsettled territory. Free speech activities of travelers have also triggered extra scrutiny at the border, for example when U.S. citizens returning to the U.S. were detained for hours for interviews and searches after attending an Islamic meeting in Canada.[101] The Second Circuit held that the significant penalty suffered by the plaintiffs solely because of their attendance at the conference was nevertheless justified. The length of time the plaintiffs were detained – four to six hours. During those hours the plaintiffs were subjected to various "searches" including intrusive questioning, being photographed and fingerprinted, having to spread their legs, and being patted down. The court noted that the detainment was certainly more than the more typical delay of one or two hours, but the court went on to say that common sense and experience suggests it may take up to six hours to complete the kind of investigation that took place here, an investigation the court also noted was constitutionally permissible.

Complaints have been filed by Muslim U.S. citizens regarding the questions being asked of them when they return to the country. These questions have covered social media information, asking if they are devout, and their views of the U.S. and jihad.[102]

The American Civil Liberties Union has raised the alarm over allegations by travelers crossing the southern U.S. border of physical abuse at the hands of CBP agents, abuse consisting of twisted arms, slamming into walls, painful handcuffing, chaining to benches and walls, as well as verbal abuse, all potential violations of the Fourth and Fifth Amendments.[103] Also the use of racial profiling, especially

100 The following two cases from the 4th and 5th Circuits extend the application of United States v Leon, 468 US 897 (1984) *United States v Kolsuz*, No. 16-4687 *14 (4th Cir 2018), *United States v Molina-Isidoro*, 884 F3d 287 (5th Cir 2018).

101 *Tabba v Chertoff*, 509 F3d 89 (2d Cir 2007).

102 Murtaza Hussain, *Complaints describe border agents interrogating Muslim Americans, asking for social media accounts* (The Intercept, January 14, 2017), archived at https://theintercept.com/2017/01/14/complaints-describes-border-agents-interrogating-muslim-americans-asking-for-social-media-accounts/.

103 ACLU Complaint to Acting Officer for Civil Rights and Civil Liberties and Acting Inspector General, Department of Homeland Security, Complaint and request for investigation of abuse of

at the southern border, continues to be suspected. (The complex and somewhat unsettled law of profiling is returned to both in Chapter 5 in the context of airline safety and in Chapter 6 regarding FBI investigations.) The CBP and the TSA are both exempt from the Attorney General's guidance regarding racial, ethnic, gender, national origin, religion, sexual orientation, and gender identity guidance. In addition, this guidance does not apply to interdiction activities in the vicinity of the border, or to protective, inspection, or screening activities. All such activities must be conducted in a manner consistent with the Constitution and applicable federal law and policy, in a manner that respects privacy, civil rights, and civil liberties, and is subject to appropriate oversight.[104] In fact the following question has been raised: Since routine border searches do not require even reasonable suspicion, does that mean government agents may use race or ethnicity to subject arrivals to extra screening? At least when it comes to law enforcement relying on drug courier profiles, the courts have upheld their use as long as the profiles incorporated are more than an individual's race or ethnicity in determining reasonable suspicion.[105]

VI. Exclusion following arrival

When an alien with a visa arrives from outside the U.S. the possibility remains, despite the visa, that the alien will not be admitted into the country. Section 8 USC §1185(d) underscores that point when it declares that even though an alien may have a visa to enter the U.S., the alien may nevertheless be found to be inadmissible on arrival. As noted above, a U.S. citizen retains the right of return. The CBP has the authority to interrogate any alien as to his right to be in the United States, and to arrest any alien who is entering or attempting to enter "in violation of any law or regulation made in pursuance of law regulating the admission, exclusion, expulsion, or removal of aliens."[106] Both aliens and U.S. citizens will be examined at the port of entry.[107]

Screening may lead an immigration officer to conclude that the traveler is inadmissible as a suspected terrorist.[108] Acting on that suspicion, the officer "shall" order the alien removed and report the order of removal to the Attorney General. At that

---

power, excessive force, coercion, and unlawful confiscation of property by Customs and Border Protection at ports of entry along the US–Mexico border, May 9, 2012, archived at https://www.aclu.org/files/assets/aclu_2012_cbp_abuse_complaint_2.pdf.

104 United States Department of Justice, *Guidance for federal law enforcement agencies regarding the use of race, ethnicity, gender, national origin, religion, sexual orientation, or gender identity*, 2 fn.2 (December 2014), archived at https://www.justice.gov/sites/default/files/ag/pages/attachments/2014/12/08/use-of-race-policy.pdf.

105 Sharon L. Davies, *Profiling terror*, 1 Ohio St J Crim L 45, 60–61 (2003).

106 8 USC 1357(a); 8 CFR §1235.1.

107 8 CFR §1235.1.

108 8 USC §1225(c).

point, any further inquiry or hearings stop until ordered by the Attorney General. The Attorney General may order the removal of the alien forthwith, or order a further inquiry or hearing by an immigration judge.

VII. Removal of aliens

Section 1227 of Title 8 says that "any alien in and admitted to the United States" may be removed in accordance with required procedures on order of the Attorney General if they fall into any of a number of listed categories.[109] This applies both to aliens who were, in fact, inadmissible at the time of entry (i.e., were erroneously admitted), and to aliens whose behavior after admission placed them in a deportable category. In either case, an alien may be removed on security and related grounds, which cover activities relating to espionage, sabotage, and criminal activity that endangers public safety or national security. In addition, the following are grounds for removal: *terrorism activities*, being a *representative* of a terrorist organization or of *a group* that endorses or espouses terrorist activity, being a member of a *terrorist organization* endorsing or espousing terrorist activity, persuading others to endorse or espouse terrorist activity, supporting a terrorist organization, or perhaps even being a spouse or a child of a person who fits these categories.[110] [Not addressed here is the authority of ICE officials to arrest undocumented aliens and enter homes, schools, and churches to conduct searches and make arrests.[111]]

The statute goes on to provide definitions of the terms "terrorist activity," "engage in terrorist activity," "representative," and "terrorist organization." These terms are defined in a way that they are simultaneously inclusive, ambiguous, and vague. The definition of "terrorist activity" covers any activity that is unlawful and that involves:

> highjacking; sabotage; detaining and threatening to kill or injure or continue to detain another individual to compel someone else or the government to do or abstain from doing something; a violated attack on an internationally protected person (defined by law); assassination; use of biological, chemical or nuclear agent, explosive, firearm or other weapon with intent to endanger; conspiracy to do any of the above.

109 8 USC §1227. Detention, expedited removal, and removal proceedings are covered by: 8 USC §1225(b), §1226, §1229, and §1229a. DHS limits application of expedited removal to noncitizens inadmissible who either arrive at a port of entry or are apprehended within 14 days of their arrival and within 100 miles of an international land border. Designating Aliens for Expedited Removal, 69 FR 4887, August 11, 2004.

110 8 USC §1182.

111 8 CFR §287.5. See, also, https://www.ice.gov/ero/enforcement/sensitive-loc; https://www.nilc.org/get-involved/community-education-resources/know-your-rights/imm_enfrcmt_homework_rts_2008-05-2/.

To "engage in terrorist activity" includes: committing, inciting, preparing for, gathering information on targets, soliciting funds for, and knowing membership in a terrorist organization. Also included is knowingly providing material support (e.g., funding) for the commission of a terrorist activity. Being a "representative" of a terrorist organization includes not just officers and officials but also a spokesman, and "any person who directs, counsels, commands, or induces an organization or its members to engage in terrorist activity." This provision is further broadened by the definition of "terrorist organization" that includes not just those listed by the Department of State but also "two or more individuals, whether organized or not, which engages in, or has a subgroup which engages in, the activities" listed above.

[Removal is only one option. The government also may seek to criminally prosecute. See Chapter 7.]

Besides covering actual engagement in criminal and violent behavior, these definitions include many activities that would fall within the protections of the First Amendment, including the right of freedom of speech and freedom of association. For one example, two people who exchange emails could constitute a group discussing jihad and be dubbed "representatives" of a terrorist organization. To suggest another example: Could an alien lawfully in the country be targeted for removal for writing a letter to the editor saying he supports Hamas's activities, and hopes that Hamas prevails in the struggle with Israel? Under the statute these voiced opinions could be construed as endorsing or espousing terrorist activity. Or, what if that same person sent money (money is speech)[112] to a charity of Hamas? Presumably this would be construed as "material support" under the statute, and, hence, grounds for removal if not conviction for violating 18 USC §§2339A and 2339B. Or perhaps an alien who translates statements of an ISIS spokesman for publication on a website could be singled out for deportation.

It is doubtful that a legal alien within the U.S. could rely on the First Amendment to block removal as violating his or her right of free speech. The history of affording First Amendment rights to illegal and lawful aliens was a complex one even before the Supreme Court's decision in *Reno v American-Arab Anti-Discrimination Committee*, 525 US 471 (1999).[113] In this case the respondents sued the Immigration and Naturalization Service (INS) for allegedly targeting them for deportation because of their membership in the Popular Front for the Liberation of Palestine (PFLP), which the government deemed to be an international terrorist and communist organization. The respondents were comprised of both temporary (individuals who had overstayed their visas) and permanent residents. As to whether the INS could constitutionally single out the respondents for removal because of their membership in the PFLP, Justice Scalia wrote: "As a general

112 *Buckley v Valeo*, 424 US 1 (1976).

113 See. Maryann Kamali Miyamoto, *The First Amendment after* Reno v American-Arab Anti-Discrimination Committee: *A different bill of rights for aliens?* 35 Harv CR-CL L Rev 183 (2000).

matter – and assuredly in the context of claims such as those put forward in the present case – an alien unlawfully in this country has no constitutional right to assert selective enforcement as a defense against his deportation."[114] He then said: "[W]e need not rule out the possibility of a rare case in which the alleged basis of discrimination is so outrageous that the foregoing considerations can be overcome. Whether or not there be such exceptions, the general rule certainly applies here. When an alien's continuing presence in this country is in violation of the immigration laws, the Government does not offend the Constitution by deporting him for the additional reason that it believes him to be a member of an organization that supports terrorist activity."[115]

Whether the opinion could be read as also applying to *legal* aliens is possible – despite Scalia's language focusing on those in violation of the immigration laws, since several of the respondents in *Reno v American-Arab Anti-Discrimination Committee* were legally within the country. Commenting on the case, David Cole and James X. Dempsey wrote that the Court ruling had cut off access to the courts for such claims, and that:

> [F]oreign nationals have no constitutional right to object to being targeted for deportation based on activities that would clearly be protected by the First Amendment if engaged in by United States citizens. In effect, the Court put immigrants on notice that if they engage in political activity which the government disapproves, they are vulnerable to selective retaliatory enforcement of the immigration laws.[116]

This result is sharply in conflict with earlier precedent that recognized that lawful aliens, like citizens, enjoyed the protection of the First Amendment.[117] Some argue that denying aliens First Amendment rights violates the following proposition: "Prohibited, too, are restrictions distinguishing among different speakers, allowing speech by some but not others. . . . Quite apart from the purpose or effect of regulating content, moreover, the Government may commit a constitutional wrong when by law it identifies certain preferred speakers."[118]

President Trump's Executive Order of January 25, 2017 needs to be looked at in this context. In that order, he listed his administration's enforcement priorities when it came to enforcing the immigration laws. Among those targeted are people who have "committed acts that constitute a chargeable criminal offense" but who have not yet in fact been charged. The federal statutes that authorize removal do not

114 *Reno v American-Arab Anti-Discrimination Com*, 525 US 471, 488–489 (1999).

115 Id at 491.

116 David Cole and James X. Dempsey, *Terrorism and the Constitution*, 4 (New Press 2006).

117 *Bridge v Wixon*, 326 US 135 (1945). See, also, *Chew v Colding*, 344 US 590, 598 n.5 (1953).

118 *Citizens United v FEC*, 558 US 310, 340 (2010). *See* Michael Kagen, *Do immigrants have freedom of speech?* 6 Cal L Rev 84, 93–95 (2015).

include this as a basis for removal. Thus the question is does President Trump have Article II authority to control which aliens, including legal aliens, may be removed, and, even if he has such authority, is he constitutionally constrained to follow the statutes in this area? Federal law 8 USC §1182(f) gives the President authority to suspend the entry of "any aliens or any class of aliens into the United States" who would be detrimental to the interests of the U.S. Whether this statutory provision can be interpreted as amending the law regarding those who are removable, is another unanswered question.

Section 1226a says that the Attorney General "may" certify an alien as a person engaged in terrorism or as someone "engaged in any other activity that endangers the national security of the United States."[119] Once this authority is invoked, the Attorney General is required to take that person into custody. The statute in effect opens the door to indefinite detention by providing that an alien who has not been removed from the U.S. "may be detained for additional periods of up to six months only if the release of the alien will threaten the national security of the United States or the safety of the community or any person." Certification is to be reviewed in six-month increments. The alien detained under this authority may seek habeas corpus in a federal court. Significantly, the Supreme Court in *Zadvydas v Davis* placed a six-month limit on detaining immigrants who no other country will accept.[120]

A detailed look at removable proceedings is beyond the scope of this book, but a few observations are in order. The government must prove by a preponderance of the evidence that the alien is subject to removal as an alien terrorist.[121] [In an exclusion case – not a removal case – the burden is on the alien who is trying to enter the country.[122]] The rights afforded the alien in removal proceedings are less extensive than would be available in a criminal trial, e.g., the Fourth Amendment exclusionary rule does not apply to immigration proceedings.[123] And the alien in a removal proceeding is afforded only a "reasonable opportunity" to examine the evidence against him and to cross-examine any witnesses.[124] This means the prohibition against reliance on hearsay evidence would not be applicable since the federal rules of evidence do not apply.[125] Also, federal regulations permit the introduction of classified or secret evidence that the alien may not see.[126] Detainees do not have a right under federal statutory law to a periodic bond hearing during their detention, but the question remains open as to whether or not the possibly indefinite detention without bond of noncitizens while waiting for a decision on removal is constitutional.[127]

119 8 USC §1226a (a)(3).
120 533 US 678 (2001).
121 8 USC §1534(g). See, also, 8 USC §1533.
122 8 USC §1361.
123 8 USC §1534(e). *INS v Lopez-Mendoza*, 468 US 1032 (1984).
124 8 USC §1534(c).
125 8 USC §1534(h).
126 8 USC §1534.
127 *Jennings v Rodriquez*, Supreme Court Docket No.15-1204 (February 27, 2018).

5

AIRLINE SECURITY AND THE NO FLY LIST

The pretravel screening of a traveler to protect the safety of the airplane (and ships) involves both a physical search of the person and luggage, and a check against electronic databases, significantly the No Fly and the Selectee Lists. This chapter discusses the law regarding both kinds of preflight checks that have had a significant and visible effect on the lives of many people. Besides their importance for the security of air transportation, the two lists represent something somewhat novel in American policy and law. People who find themselves on the No Fly or Selectee Lists experience a significant limitation on their lives at the hands of the government, a loss of liberty, without their ever having been formally adjudicated by a court to have violated any law. Another unresolved question is the possibility that there is bias in the listing of people on the two lists with more Muslims being listed than non-Muslim domestic extremists.

I. Preflight air safety searches by the Transportation Security Administration (TSA)

The most visible and talked about aspect of travel is the physical search at international and domestic airports. These searches take the form of full body scans, pat-downs by human hands, the examination of luggage, and the x-raying and forensic examination of portable electronic devices. They are directed toward enforcing the laws against smuggling as well as, of course, assuring the safety of the airline or ship, as the case may be.[1] The task of screening passengers is

1 19 USC §482. The authority of customs officials extends to searching for merchandise that has been "introduced into the United States in any manner contrary to law." This authority includes the search of vehicles for aliens as well as contraband, and in exercising this authority customs officials at the border do not need a warrant and may search when they have reasonable cause to suspect there is merchandise imported contrary to law. Yule Kim, *Protecting the US perimeter: Border searches under the Fourth Amendment*, 2 (Congressional Research Office, June 29, 2009, RL31826).

enormous given that approximately 2 million people board flights in the U.S. each day.[2]

TSA officials screen luggage, carry-ons, and the boarding passengers themselves for weapons and explosives.[3] The agents are of two sorts – those whose authority is limited to screening for weapons and explosives, and those who are designated law enforcement officers who have the authority to arrest with a warrant and to conduct searches for criminal evidence to "seek and execute warrants for arrest or seizure of evidence issued under the authority of the United States upon probable cause that a violation has been committed."[4] However, the primary mission of the TSA is not to uncover evidence of crimes broadly conceived, e.g., possession of child pornography. Instead, TSA agents focus on enforcing 49 USC §46505, which makes it a crime to carry a weapon or explosive on an aircraft.

A legitimate TSA search can be intrusive, as it can include a through-the-clothing pat-down of private areas.[5] (The backscatter x-ray scanner that has been described as a "virtual strip search" is no longer in use.) The TSA warrantless searches have been upheld under the Fourth Amendment by the judiciary relying on different legal rationales, including implied consent; by calling a search an "administrative search," which does not require the issuance of a warrant and may be conducted as long as it satisfies the Fourth Amendment's standard of reasonableness; and by claiming a "special need."[6] (See Chapter 4's discussion of border searches and the Fourth Amendment.)

In *United States v Aukai*, the defendant passed through the initial screening without triggering an alarm but was subjected to a secondary screening because he presented a boarding pass on which "No ID" had been written.[7] This secondary screening used a wand that alarmed, which led to a pat-down and the detection of a lump in the defendant's pocket, which was ultimately proved to be a package. A law enforcement officer was called over, and the TSA agent, fearing it was a weapon, unwrapped it to discover a glass pipe used to smoke methamphetamine. This then led to a further search and a discovery of drugs. The court upheld the constitutionality of the TSA procedures, although the TSA was not a drug enforcement

2 https://www.transtats.bts.gov/.

3 49 USC §114; 49 USC §44901.

4 49 USC §114(p). See, also, Declaration of William Switzer III, *Bierfeldt v Napolitano*, Docket No 09-cv-01117 (DCDC), Attachment 2, TSA Management Directive 100.4, September 1, 2009, archived at https://s.ai/tsa/legal/evidence/2009-09-04%20Bierfeldt%20v%20Napolitano%20US%20Dist.%20Ct.%20DC%20No.%2009-cv-01117%20-%20Declaration%20of%20William%20Switzer%20III%20and%20attachments.pdf.

5 Tobias W. Mock, *The TSA's new x-ray vision: The Fourth Amendment implications of body-scan searches at domestic airport security checkpoints* 49 Santa Clara L Rev 213 (2009). The backscatter X-ray scanner that can provide detailed body images are no longer in use.

6 See, for example, *United States v Wehrli*, 637 F.2d 408 (5th Cir. 1981); *United States v Davis*, 482 F2d 893 (9th Cir 1973); *United States v Figueroa Cruz*, 822 F. Supp. 853 (D.P.R. 1993). The special need doctrine is cited to justify waiver of the requirement for obtaining a warrant. See *New Jersey v T.L.O*, 469 US 325 (1985).

7 497 F3d 955 (9th Cir 2007).

agency. Important here is the fact that the search program included an escalating set of searches, each one more intrusive than the next, in order to definitively resolve the question of whether or not the passenger was attempting to carry a weapon or explosives onboard. In this case, the search was upheld as having satisfied the following test: An airport security screening process satisfies the reasonable requirement of the Fourth Amendment provided: "that [it] is no more extensive nor intensive than necessary, in the light of current technology, to detect the presence of weapons or explosives, that it is confined in good faith to that purpose, and that potential passengers may avoid the search by electing not to fly."[8]

In another case, a passenger was carrying Arabic vocabulary cards, among which were the Arabic words for "bomb," "terrorist," "explosion," "attack," "battle," "kill," "to target," "to kidnap," and "to wound" as well as words such as "fat," "thin," "sad," "friendly," etc., this was sufficient to lead to a five-hour search.[9] Let's look more closely at the passenger's screening experience. As part of routine screening he had to empty his pockets, which led to the discovery of 80 Arabic flashcards. This led to his being swabbed for explosives, and extensive questioning by TSA agents. Next came an arrest by Philadelphia police and detainment for four hours. The FBI then arrived and questioned him for 30 minutes. The plaintiff filed suit for damages against three TSA and two FBI agents in a so-called *Bivens action*[10] for violation of his Fourth and First Amendment rights. [The four-hour detention by the Philadelphia police involved another issue not relevant here.]

The Third Circuit Court of Appeals concluded that the Fourth Amendment had not been violated by the TSA who held the plaintiff for perhaps a half hour. Once the TSA officials were satisfied that the plaintiff was not armed and not carrying explosives, much of the concern that satisfied his detention dissipated, but in a world where the TSA has to worry about underwear and shoe bombs, the detention by the TSA following the initial screening was reasonable. The 30-minute questioning by the FBI also was permissible. As for the First Amendment claim, the court agreed that the plaintiff enjoyed a First Amendment right to carry the cards, but here the search was not initiated in "retaliation" of his exercise of his First Amendment right.

There are circumstances when a departing traveler's cell phone may be searched forensically.[11] (See the discussion of searches of electronic devices in Chapter 4, Section V.)

Two additional points. TSA search must be confined "in good faith" to the purpose of finding weapons and explosives.[12] TSA agents have the authority to look for weapons and explosives without suspicion; this means they many not impermissibly

8 Id at 962.

9 *George v Rehiel*, 738 F3d 562 (3d Cir 2013).

10 *Bivens v Six Unknown Fed. Narcotics Agents*, 403 US 388 (1971).

11 *United States v Kolsuz*, No. 16-6687 (4th Cir May 9, 2018); *United States v Oriakhi*, 57 F3d 1290 (4th Cir 1995).

12 *Torbet v United Airlines, Inc.*, 298 F3d 1087, 1089 (9th Cir 2002); *United States v Maldonado-Espinosa*, 767 FSupp. 1176, 1187 (D PR 1991).

use this authority as a pretext for searching without suspicion for evidence of other crimes in order to avoid the usual strictures of the Fourth Amendment.

Yet if the agent is executing the required procedures when searching for weapons, and in the course of that search develops reason to believe the traveler is transporting, for example, child pornography, the TSA agent may coincidentally search for the pornography. Once, however, the agent is satisfied there are no weapons or explosives, his or her authority to search comes to an end, and the agent may not continue the search beyond what was necessary to detect a weapon or explosives.[13]

Second, passengers facing escalating searches of their persons and luggage may not midway through the search truncate it by saying they have decided not to board the plane. To rule otherwise would encourage terrorism by assuring the terrorist a secure exit when discovery was threatened.[14]

II. Behavior and profiling

Travelers who have exhibited certain behavioral characteristics are placed on a TSA-created list that can impel extra scrutiny. Passengers who have loitered near security checkpoints, who have appeared unruly or swatted away a screener's hands can end up the "95 list." The guidelines do prohibit profiling based on race, religion, or gender.[15]

As discussed in Chapter 4, singling out individuals for extra scrutiny or perhaps even arrest based on race or ethnicity raises constitutional issues under both the Fourth Amendment and the Fourteenth Amendment's Equal Protection clause. To simplify this discussion, it is assumed here that the extra scrutiny or arrest did not result in a criminal conviction. Instead, it is assumed here that the aggrieved party is suing the TSA agents for monetary damages for the violation of their constitutional rights either under 42 USC §1983 or in a *Bivens action.*

When race or ethnicity in fact was a factor for subjecting someone to a secondary screening, it is possible the courts will allow the screening under the Fourth Amendment, saying officers need the discretion, especially when the secondary screening is of short duration.[16]

However, if race or ethnicity were an important factor leading to a full-fledged arrest lasting for hours, the judicial analysis of the constitutionality of the seizure under the Fourth Amendment is likely to be quite different. (Under the Fourth Amendment probable cause for an arrest depends on whether a hypothetical "reasonable person," given the facts and circumstances of the arrest, would have warrant to believe that a crime had been committed, and that this person had committed

13 *United States v McCarty*, 648 F3d 820, 831 (9th Cir 2011).

14 *United States v Pulido-Baquerizo*, 800 F.2d 899, 902 (9th Cir 1986).

15 Ron Nixon, *Watch list shields T.S.A. screeners from threatening, and unruly, travelers* (New York Times, May 27, 2018), archived at https://www.nytimes.com/2018/05/17/us/politics/new-watch-list-tsa-screeners-.html.

16 Compare *United States v Martinez-Fuerte*, 428 US 543 (1976).

the crime.[17]) The decision in *Farag v United States* is instructive.[18] In that case, two law enforcement officers on board an aircraft observed two men during the flight, who among other things, despite sitting on opposite sides of the aisle, spoke over the heads of other passengers in Arabic; made an unusual seat change to be nearer each other; one looked at his watch when the plane took off and landed; moved to the back of the plane to converse; and one deleted information from his cell phone. After they disembarked from the plane they were frisked, handcuffed, arrested, taken to a police station, and held for four hours in jail while undergoing interrogation. The court concluded that the non-ethnic behaviors noted above were insufficient to establish probable cause of the arrest. Changing seats, moving about the cabin, deleting information from a cell phone, speaking loudly, nervousness on being arrested, did not establish probable cause. When the court asked whether Arab ethnicity and speaking Arabic were relevant factors in determining probable cause, the answer was "no," the court saying that "the likelihood that *any given airline passenger* of Arab ethnicity is a terrorist is so negligible that Arab ethnicity has no probative value in a particularized reasonable-suspicion or probable cause determination." Furthermore, there was a significant body of pre-9/11 precedent "concluding that race is not indicative of criminal propensity."[19]

For challenges to discriminatory screening under the Fourteenth Amendment, recall the discussion of profiling in Chapter 4.

III. The No Fly and Selectee Lists

A. *An overview*

The creation of the No Fly List started on September 16, 2003 when President Bush issued Homeland Security Presidential Directive 6 (HSPD-6). Today the list is the product of a variety of data flowing into the National Counterterrorism Center (NCTC) from the NSA and FBI and other parts of the Intelligence Community. (Both the NSA and FBI in turn have multiple sources of data.) The NCTC's Terrorist Identities Datamart Environment (TIDE) according to the NCTC in February 2017 had the names of 1.6 million people, of whom 16,000 were citizens and permanent residents. Although the NCTC is authorized to received information related to domestic terrorism (50 USC §3056(e)), it does not integrate and analyze information that is exclusively related to domestic terrorism.

HSPD-6 also led to the creation of the Terrorist Screening Center (TSC) administered by the FBI.[20] (See Chapter 1.) This Center uses the TIDE list and

17 *Beck v Ohio*, 379 US 89, 96 (1964).
18 587 F Supp 2d 436 (D ED NY 2008).
19 Id at 464, 466.
20 https://fas.org/irp/offdocs/nspd/hspd-6.html; https://www.fbi.gov/about/leadership-and-structure/national-security-branch/tsc; 49 CFR §1540.3.

nominations from the FBI to create a Terrorist Screening Database (TSDB), aka the terrorist Watchlist, components of which are the No Fly and Selectee Lists. TSC, in turn, determines whether to add a name to the TSDB.[21] The TSDB has information on both international and domestic terrorists.[22] United States citizenship does not prevent someone from being nominated for the Watchlist; white supremacists and other domestic extremists can be included on the list as well as suspected unprivileged enemy belligerents (Chapter 8). The No Fly List, according to the Department of Homeland Security (DHS), is a list of individuals who are prohibited from boarding an aircraft. The No Fly List can include names of people linked to either foreign or domestic terrorism. The Selectee List is a list of individuals who must undergo additional security screening before being permitted to board an aircraft.[23] No Fly and Selectee Lists are subsets of the TSDB. The Watchlist itself is used in connection with applications for passports and visas, and during federal domestic law enforcement encounters.

Whether a nominated person satisfies the substantive derogatory criteria necessary to be placed in the TSDB is generally based on whether there is reasonable suspicion to believe that a person is a known or suspected terrorist. What goes into the decision to place someone on either the No Fly or Selectee List is taken up below. It has been reported that as of June 2016 the Watchlist contained approximately 1 million identifier records, of which about 5000 have names of U.S. citizens and legal permanent residents.[24] The No Fly List is estimated to have 81,000 names, among whom are 1000 U.S. persons. The Selectee List contains 28,000 records, of which 1700 are citizens or permanent residents.[25]

Incidentally, individuals may also be barred under 49 USC §44939 from obtaining flight training on the grounds that they are a threat to national security.

B. Consequences

The obvious immediate consequence of being placed on the No Fly List is that someone may not board an airplane even if a physical screening revealed nothing. It may be extreme to say it, but people on the No Fly List are deemed to be too

21 Jared P. Cole, *Terrorist databases and the no fly list: Procedural due process and hurdles to litigation*, 2–3 (Congressional Research Service, April 2, 2015, R46730). See, also, *Counterterrorism policy directive and policy guide*, 77–99 (FBI April 1, 2015, review April 1, 2018), archived at https://archive.org/details/Counterterrorism PolicyDirectiveAndPolicyGuide.

22 National Counterterrorism Center, *Watchlisting guidance*, 15, 51 (March 2013); Office of the Inspector General, U.S. Department of Justice, *Review of the Terrorist Screening Center*, 12, 24, 59 (Audit Report 05-27, June 2005), (hereafter Guidance), archived at https://oig.justice.gov/reports/FBI/a0527/final.pdf.

23 Maureen Cooney, *Report assessing the impact of the automatic selectee and no fly lists on privacy and civil liberties as required under Section 4012(b) of the Intelligence Reform and Terrorism Prevention Act of 2004*, Public Law 108-458, i (US Department of Homeland Security, April 27, 2006), archived at https://www.dhs.gov/xlibrary/assets/privacy/ privacy_rpt_nofly.pdf.

24 Jerome H. Kahan, *Quis custodiet ipsos custodes?: Who watches the watchlisters?*, Harv L Sch Natl Security J, February 1, 2017, archived at http://harvardnsj.org/2017/02/who-watches-the-watchlisters/.

25 Id.

dangerous to fly even if they were to board the plane naked and even if they cannot be arrested or detained.[26] Not being able to reach one's destination in a timely fashion can generate a cascade of consequences including but not limited to: missed doctor's appointments, a missed wedding or funeral, an inability to carry out one's occupation, a loss of federal benefits for having missed a required appointment, disruption of one's education, etc. There is also potential damage to one's reputation, denial of a professional license, and suspicions aroused among family, friends, and community. People on the Selectee List are routinely exposed to greater scrutiny at the airport even if they are eventually permitted to board the airplane. Encounters with local police can become more onerous if the police are aware that the person is on the Watchlist. And being on the Watchlist exposes one to an increased likelihood that an FBI assessment or even a preliminary investigation will be triggered. In short, it is no exaggeration to say that being placed on the Watchlist can transform one's life.

False-positive listings have occurred. Rahinah Ibrahim's life as a Ph.D. student in the U.S. was totally disrupted for eight years (she was excluded from flying back to the U.S. from a visit to her home) until the government confessed its error, saying that an FBI agent had made a clerical error when filling out a form regarding her.[27] In the case of Asif Iqbal, a Rochester, NY management consultant and University of Texas graduate who flew regularly for business, was delayed and subjected to extra scrutiny at airports because he had the same name as a suspect on the No Fly List; this was in spite of the fact that he had letter from the TSA establishing his identity as not that of the suspected terrorist.[28]

C. Substantive standard for listing a name

There are two preconditions for a person to be listed on the No Fly or Selectee List: (i) there must be satisfaction of minimum identifying criteria (first name, last name, date of birth) and (ii) satisfaction of the minimum substantive derogatory criteria.[29]

A federal district court described the minimum substantive derogatory criterion as follows:

> The TSC determines whether to place individuals in the TSDB based on "nominations" received from the National Counterterrorism Center (NCTC)

26 *Mohamed v Holder*, 995 F Supp 2d 520, 532 (ED Vir 2014), No. 1:11-cv-50 (AJT/MSN) (ED Va July 16, 2015), No. 1:11cv0050 (AJT/MSN) (E.D. Va. July 20, 2017).

27 John Silver, *After seven years, exactly one person gets off the gov't no fly list* (Ars Technica, March 27, 2014), archived at https://arstechnica.com/tech-policy/2014/03/after-seven-years-exactly-one-person-gets-off-the-govt-No Fly-list/.

28 New York Civil Liberties Unions, *NYCLU call for relief New York man in mistaken identity "no fly" dilemma* (March 29, 2004), archived at https://www.nyclu.org/en/press-releases/nyclu-calls-relief-new-york-man-mistaken-identity-No Fly-dilemma.

29 Guidance, at 12, 50 (cited in note 21).

> and the FBI. The TSC places a nominated individual on the TSDB if the nomination is supported by "minimum substantive derogatory criteria." Whether an individual satisfies the substantive derogatory criteria necessary to be placed in the TSDB is "generally based on whether there is reasonable suspicion to believe that a person is a known or *suspected terrorist* [italics added]." In order to meet this standard, "the nominator, based on the totality of the circumstances, must rely upon 'articulable' intelligence or information which, taken together with rational inferences from those facts, creates a *reasonable suspicion* [italics added] that the individual is a known or suspected terrorist." By contrast, "[m]ere guesses or 'hunches,' or the reporting of suspicious activity alone are not enough to constitute a reasonable suspicion and are not sufficient bases to watchlist an individual." Likewise, "nominations must not be *solely* [italics added] based on race, ethnicity, national origin, religious affiliation, or First Amendment protected activities." "TSC personnel" make the decision of whether to place an individual in the TSDB, and "TSA employees assigned to and stationed at the TSC serve as subject matter experts regarding those individuals nominated to the No-Fly and Selectee Lists."[30]

The term "suspected terrorist" is defined by the NCTC as "an individual who is reasonably suspected to be, or has been, engaged in conduct constituting, in preparation for, in aid of, or related to terrorism and/or terrorist activities based on an articulable and reasonable suspicion." First, the minimum substantive criteria do include domestic terrorism, not just foreign-connected terrorism. Second, the emphasis on engaging in conduct seems to rule out being placed on the list simply because of beliefs. But note that in this formulation there is a double suspicion at work – suspicion of being a suspected terrorist, i.e., a suspicion regarding a suspicion. As one court put it, "an American citizen can find himself a suspected terrorist because of a 'reasonable suspicion' based on a 'reasonable suspicion.'"[31]

Next, as noted, speech activities may be taken into account, albeit they may not be the "sole" basis for being listed. This rule leaves considerable leeway for the consideration of free speech activities as figuring into being listed. One may be deemed a suspected terrorist if one incites others to commit acts of terrorism, and engages in speech "advocating a violent or dangerous terrorist activity is incitement if such advocacy is directed toward inciting or producing imminent lawless action and is likely to incite or produce such action."[32] Sympathizers and supporters of "designated terrorist organizations" (DTO) may be watchlisted when the "reasonable suspicion standard is met, and the nomination includes particularized derogatory information concerning how the individual's activities warrant watchlisting, as opposed to information about why the organization is a DTO." The sympathizer

30 *Mohamed v Holder*, at 525–526 (cited in note 25).

31 Id at 532.

32 Guidance, at 40 (cited in note 21). See, also, *Brandenburg v Ohio*, 395 US 444, 447–448 (1969).

should be nominated if the support is "operational" and not merely ideological.[33] One should not be listed "solely based on" race, ethnicity, national origin, or religious affiliation. But then there is this further guidance: Two behavioral indicators that would support a reasonable suspicion conclusion include attendance at a school that teaches "an ideology that includes the justification of unlawful use of violence or violent extremism; and repeated contact with individuals identified by the [Intelligence Community] as teaching or espousing an ideology that includes the justification of the unlawful use of violence or violent extremism."[34]

Someone identified as an associate or affiliate of a suspected terrorist or terrorist cell may also be listed, although "[n]eutral associations such as janitorial, repair, or delivery services of commercial goods are not sufficient." Yet the door is open to being considered an affiliate if one is the business partner, spouse, or child of a suspected terrorist. In fact, one commentator noted that a DHS official said that one might end up on the Watchlist if one had the misfortune of bumping into a suspected terrorist at a restaurant and an FBI agent happened to observe the encounter.[35]

The Watchlisting Guidance also permits watchlisting someone "who [merely] represents" either "a threat of committing an act of domestic terrorism" or "a threat of engaging in or conducting a violent act of terrorism and who is operationally capable of doing so."[36] The phrasing "represents a threat" seems broader and vaguer than the "minimum substantive derogatory criteria" discussed above.

More probing of the Watchlisting Guidance reveals how truly broad the criteria are. Someone who is acquitted or whose charges are dismissed may nevertheless meet the reasonable suspicion standard. The court quoted above had this observation about the standard being used.

> What constitutes conduct sufficiently "related to" or "in aid of" terrorism is not explained, but it is not difficult to imagine completely innocent conduct serving as the starting point for a string of subjective, speculative inferences that result in a person's inclusion on the No Fly List. For example, is the academic study of terrorism or the investigative reporting of terrorist activities "related to terrorism and terrorist activities"? Is providing financial support to a charitable organization enough, even without knowledge that some of the organization's activities are "in aid of . . . terrorist activities"? Is it enough to be a member of a lawfully operating social or religious organization whose membership may include other persons suspected of terrorism? Is studying Arabic abroad, as Mohamud concedes he did, conduct "in preparation for . . . terrorist activities"? A showing of past or ongoing unlawful conduct does not

33 Id.

34 Id at 35.

35 Shirin Sinnar, *Rule of law tropes in national security*, 129 Harv L Rev 1566, 1592 (2016).

36 Guidance, at 51 (cited in note 21).

> seem to be required, and the level of proof required for inclusion on the No Fly List appears to be far less than that required to obtain such law enforcement tools as a search or arrest warrant or a thirty-day wiretap. *See* U.S. Const, amend. IV; 50 USC §1805(a)(2). But the Court has little, if any, ability to articulate what information is viewed by the TSC as sufficiently "derogatory" beyond the labels it has provided the Court.[37]

As broad and vague as the substantive derogatory criteria are, the Watchlisting Guidance also opens the door to listing people without reliance on an individualized determination under the reasonable suspicion criteria. Whole "categories of individuals" may be temporarily upgraded based on current and credible intelligence information or a particular threat stream that indicates a certain category of individuals may be used to conduct an act of domestic or international terrorism. This upgrade must be made by the Assistant to the President for Homeland Security and may be renewed at 30-day intervals.[38]

Another exception to individualized determination occurs when a person is "associated with a terrorist group," which is a group identified as a terrorist group by departments or agencies of the federal government other than the NCTC. The Watchlisting Guidance states:

> While members or active participants of such groups may be nominated without PARTICULARIZED DEROGATORY INFORMATION, the watchlisting of an individual pursuant to this clause must be based on the determination by a Department or Agency's internal processes that the group is engaging in TERRORISM and/or TERRORIST ACTIVITIES. Neutral associations like janitorial, repair, or delivery services of commercial goods do not meet the REASONABLE SUSPICION standard. [capitalization in the original][39]

This phrasing leaves open the possibility that an individual could be listed because of membership in a domestic terrorist group. And the government may presume that an individual identified by certain foreign governments with whom the U.S. has agreements also meet the reasonable suspicion standard without the government checking on the accuracy of the information supporting this designation.[40]

Finally, it is important to note another exception related to the granting of temporary and permanent visas. The Watchlisting Guidance makes a broad explicit exception to reasonable suspicion for an alien spouse or child of an alien inadmissible under the Immigration and Naturalization Act. In addition, other aliens who

37 *Mohamed v Holder*, at 532 (cited in note 25).

38 Guidance, at 26–27 (cited in note 21).

39 Id at 38.

40 Id.

endorse or espouse terrorist activities, or who persuade others to endorse, or espouse should be nominated to the No Fly List.[41]

The procedures and quality control mechanisms used by the nominating agencies, the NCTC, and the TCS are only roughly outlined in the Watchlisting Guidance. What seems clear is that *except as regards U.S. persons*, the Guidance does not require that identified individual employees of the agencies take personal responsibility for nominating someone or double-checking that the criteria have been satisfied.[42]

D. Redress

Federal law requires that there be established a way for a traveler who has been delayed or prohibited from boarding an aircraft to seek redress.[43] The redress system has been under constitutional attack as violating the Fifth Amendment's due process clause; these cases are taken up below.

Problematical, too, is the situation of those on the Selectee List. First, they may not even realize they are on the list until they cannot obtain a renewal of a passport, or are denied a professional license. Meanwhile, they may be under extra scrutiny by local law enforcement.[44] And there is no formally established process for them to obtain redress. What process is available is lengthy and can lead to controversial results or to no final conclusion.[45]

IV. The Constitution and the watchlist[46]

Recall that placement on the Selectee or No Fly List has different consequences for a traveler. Those on the Selectee List are not prohibited from flying but are singled out for more extensive screening, and accordingly before being permitted to board face embarrassment and more inconveniences and delays than does the ordinary traveler. Being on the No Fly List, of course, means one may not board the plane. Placement on these lists has been challenged on both "substantive due process" and on "procedural due process" grounds.

A substantive due process challenge to the No Fly List would go something like this: one has lost a protected interest (liberty to fly) without adequate justification either because the purpose of the No Fly List is not legitimate (a claim that without doubt would fail) and/or that the No Fly List was an irrational way of achieving the purpose.[47] An argument such as this was rejected by a federal district court.

41 Id at 44. There are other categories of alien that also should be nominated.

42 Guidance, at 19 (cited in note 21). Nominations of U.S. persons are to be reviewed by the nominating agency's legal counsel or a designated reviewer.

43 49 USC §44903(j)(2)(C)(iii)(I); 49 CFR §1560.205.

44 Kahan, *Quis custodiet ipsos custodes?l* (cited in note 23).

45 Id.

46 See Cole, *Terrorist databases and the no fly list: Procedural due process and hurdles to Litigation* (cited in note 20).

47 *Williamson v Lee Optical Co.*, 348 US 483 (1955).

The court was convinced no workable alternative would prevent terrorist attacks against commercial aviation, and that the No Fly system was rational in that it did have a way to avoid "false positives" because of the built-in redress system (discussed below).[48] A substantive due process attack on the Selectee List also failed, but this time the court rejected the claim because a delay in boarding caused by extra screening was not sufficient to trigger a substantive due process inquiry.[49]

A substantive due process challenge has also been brought against the Selectee List on the grounds that the extra security hurdles the plaintiffs had to endure unconstitutionally impinged upon their liberty to fly.[50] The Sixth Circuit rejected the claim, noting that the plaintiffs had not been prevented from flying and the plaintiffs could not cite any authority that a delay of 10, 30 minutes or even an hour violated their fundamental right to travel. The court took note of a Second Circuit opinion that rejected a similar claim even though the traveler had been delayed for an entire day.[51]

The due process clause of the Fifth Amendment is also a fountainhead for a different line of attack, the claim that the two lists violate a right to *procedural* due process. The idea here is that plaintiffs have a liberty interest (flying by airplane) at risk and that before the government may deprive them of that liberty, plaintiffs should be provided with an individualized evidentiary hearing to assure a fair and non-erroneous decision that would adversely affect their liberty to fly.

The courts have dealt differently with this line of argument in challenges to the Selectee List and the No Fly List. In the Selectee cases, plaintiffs have not even been able to get to first base because the courts did not see that a delay in boarding because of extra screening was a loss of liberty sufficient to trigger any procedural due process procedure. Neither was there enough proof of damage to reputation to otherwise trigger a right to due process procedures.[52]

But in *Latiff v Holder*, the plaintiffs challenged the adequacy of the government's redress procedures available for getting off the No Fly List.[53] The court concluded that although the government's interest in combating terrorism was indeed compelling, the plaintiff's interest was also important, and the redress procedures the government was using fell far short of satisfying the requirements of due process. The plaintiffs received no notice of the reasons for their placement on the list, or

48 *Mohamed v Holder*, Civil Action No 1:11cv0050 *18 (ED Va July 20, 2017).

49 *Kadura v Lynch*, Case No 14-13128 (ED Mich March 8, 2017).

50 *Beydoun v Sessions*, 871 F3d 459, 468 (6th Cir 2017).

51 *Torraco v Port Auth of NY & NJ*, 615 F3d 129 (2d Cir 2010).

52 Id at 469; *Bazzi v Lynch*, No 16-10123 (ED Mich August 30, 2016); *Beydoun v Lynch*, Case No 14-cv-13812 (ED Mich July 14, 2016).

53 28 F Supp 3d 1134 (D Oregon 2014). See, also, *Mohamed v Holder* (cited in note 25). One court ruled that even though the plaintiff might have suffered a stigma by being placed on the no fly list, this was insufficient to trigger a due process claim; the loss of the opportunity to make use of one mode of transportation was not a sufficient additional harm to trigger a due process claim. *Green v Transportation Security Administration*, 351 F Supp 2d 1119 (WD Wash 2005).

any evidence to support their inclusion on the list. With no notice or opportunity to be heard, "an individual could be doomed to indefinite placement on the No Fly List." Hence the plaintiff's due process rights were violated.

In the aftermath of this decision the DHS revised its redress system.

> Under the revised redress process now in place, a U.S. person who applies for redress from an allegedly erroneous inclusion on the No Fly List would receive an initial response letter indicating whether he or she is in fact on the No Fly List. If so, this letter would also notify the individual that he or she may elect to receive or submit additional information. These processes generally do not apply to foreign citizens as such individuals have no specific legal rights to redress under current law.
>
> If the individual requests further information, DHS TRIP [Traveler Redress Inquiry Program] will forward the details of the case to the TSC Redress Office, which in turn would notify NCTC and the relevant nominating agencies that a redress submittal has included a request for additional information concerning an individual's placement on the No Fly List. The TSC Redress Office would then request an unclassified summary of information supporting an individual's placement on the No Fly List. Upon receipt of this information, the TSC would forward it to DHS TRIP, which would typically provide a second response to the redress seeker that would include details of the unclassified summary provided by the TSC. This second letter informs recipients that they may seek further review of their status and that they may submit any information supporting the position that their placement on the No Fly List is not warranted.
>
> The TSC Redress Office will review the relevant materials provided by federal agencies and the redress seeker and provide a recommendation to the TSA Administrator regarding whether or not the individual should remain on the No Fly List. The TSA Administrator would review that recommendation and issue a final decision to remove the individual from the No Fly List, maintain the individual on the list, or remand the case to TSC for further information. This final order would be sent to the individual petitioner and TSC. If the order removes the individual from the No Fly List, the TSC would update the relevant information in the TSDB.[54]

The plaintiffs then challenged the revised redress procedures on multiple grounds, but the federal district court upheld the procedures, reaching the following conclusions:[55] It was permissible for the government to use a "reasonable suspicion"

54 Jerme P. Bjelopera, Bart Elias, and Alison Siskin, *The terrorist screening database and preventing terrorist travel*, 19 (Congressional Research Office, November 7, 2016, R44678).

55 *Latif v Lynch*, 3:10-cv-00750-BR (D Or 2016), dismissed; *Latiff v Sessions* 3:10-cv-00750-BR (D Or Apr 21, 2017).

standard in deciding whether to include an individual on the list, thus refusing to impose a "clear and convincing" standard. The government need not afford those listed with a redress procedure that included a live hearing where they could confront and cross-examine live witnesses. The notice to those placed on the list need only be a summary of the reasons and need only include a summary of the evidence. It was possible to withhold evidence from those placed on the list; but a decision to withhold "material evidence" must be subject to judicial review, and the government must minimize the amount of material information withheld. The government must provide those seeking redress "with sufficient information to permit them to respond meaningfully" to the reasons the government was able to disclose. And it was permissible for the government to make its judgment based on "predictive judgments" about those listed.

A Congressional Research Service report outlines looming hurdles to suits challenging the constitutionality of the No Fly List. The government has used the state secrets privilege, the law enforcement privilege, and the deliberative process, seeking to have cases dismissed in their entirety. The privileges exist to protect government national security and law enforcement secrets, as well as to assure that governmental deliberations will be candid. Litigation concerning the applicability of these privileges to No Fly challenges is ongoing.[56]

56 Cole, *Terrorist databases and the no fly list: Procedural due process and hurdles to litigation*, at 19–21 (cited in note 20).

6

INVESTIGATING INDIVIDUAL SUSPECTS

This chapter looks at the methods of targeted investigations conducted in the U.S. and directed at domestic terrorists such as militia extremists, foreign-connected terrorists who may (or may not) be U.S. citizens, and unprivileged enemy belligerents who also may (or may not) be U.S. citizens. The criminal laws at the heart of these investigations are addressed in Chapter 7. An investigation designed to build a case against an individual would have to pay close attention to the substantive requirements of these laws. For example, if the goal were to convict a person for providing material support for terrorism (18 USC §2339A), the investigation would have to obtain evidence that the individual had provided the support with an intent to abet the crime of terrorism.

The investigative agency most centrally involved in these focused investigations is the Federal Bureau of Investigation (FBI).[1] (But, as outlined below, the FBI and the National Security Agency (NSA) are closely entwined in criminal investigations even though the NSA does not have to adhere to the Fourth Amendment rules applicable to the investigation of ordinary crimes.) The Director of the FBI made it clear that, when it came to counterterrorism, the FBI's top priority was dealing with foreign-connected terrorism. The statement, in fact, made no mention of domestic terrorism.[2] Nevertheless, as of September 2017 the FBI was conducting about 1000 domestic terrorism cases and about 1000 foreign-connected

1 28 USC §533; 28 USC §509; 21 USC §871; 18 USC §3052; 28 CFR §§ 0.85(1), §0.85a. Under 18 USC §2332b(f), the Attorney General (hence the FBI) has the primary investigative responsibility for Federal crimes of terrorism – defined in the statute.

2 James B. Comey, *Statement before the house appropriations committee, subcommittee on commerce, justice, science and related agencies*, February 26, 2016, archived at https://www.fbi.gov/news/testimony/fbi-budget-request-for-fiscal-year-2017.

terrorism cases.[3] (See the Introduction for definitions of domestic and foreign-connected terrorism.)

I. An initial alert

The attention of the FBI regarding a particular person may be triggered a number of ways even before a crime has been committed. The NSA may tip the FBI as well might foreign partners. Other federal agencies such as the Customs and Border Patrol, or the Treasury Department may also alert the FBI. State and local law enforcement agencies can provide tips and suspicious activity reports. The FBI's trolling of social media may lead to domestic terrorists, domestic jihadist terrorists, and foreign-connected terrorists. The FBI and the NSA may also team up to collect information pursuant to §702 (50 USC §1881a) that could involve "incidental" collection of the communication of a person in the U.S. involved in a crime.[4] Reports suggest the FBI engages in a significant data mining effort that can produce additional leads and targets (42 USC §2000ee-3).[5]

Once an individual or group is on the FBI's radar screen the FBI may start an assessment (see Section II). In turn, the assessment may escalate into a preliminary investigation and ultimately into a full investigation. As the FBI moves from stage to stage its investigative techniques expand in number and in invasiveness. Likewise, law regulating the techniques gets more demanding as the techniques become more invasive. As reviewed below the most invasive techniques like wiretapping may only be used in a full investigation.

> Prosecution of a suspect is only one outcome of an FBI investigation. In addition the FBI may disrupt suspected terrorist activity by seeking deportations, interviews, providing disinformation, mounting a media campaign to publicize activities, by seeking deportation and revocation of an immigration visa, and seizing financial assets. The subjects of investigation may be placed on the Terrorist Screening Database maintained by the Terrorist Screening Center. Even people who are the subject of a non-predicated assessment (discussed below) may be watchlisted, and also end up on the No-Fly List.[6]

Before looking at the methods of investigation used by the FBI it is useful to see how complex an undertaking an investigation of even a single person can be. Daniel

3 Devlin Barrett, *FBI investigating 1,000 white supremacist, domestic terrorism cases* (Washington Post, September 27, 2017), archived at https://www.washingtonpost.com/world/national-security/fbi-investigating-1000-white-supremacist-domestic-terrorism-cases/2017/09/27/95abff24-a38b-11e7-ade1-76d061d56efa_story.html?utm_term=.64c4a3286938.

4 See, also, 50 USC §1861 (aka §215).

5 Ryan Singel, *Newly declassified files detail massive FBI data-mining projects* (Wired, September 23, 2009), archived at https://www.wired.com/2009/09/fbi-nsac/; Office of the Inspector General, U.S. Department of Justice, *The Federal Bureau of Investigation's foreign terrorist tracking task force*, 9–10 (Audit Report 13–18, March 2013), archived at https://oig.justice.gov/reports/2013/a1318r.pdf.

6 *Counterterrorism policy directive and policy guide*, 23–24, 95 (FBI, April 1, 2015, reviewed April 1, 2018), archived at https://commons.wikimedia.org/wiki/File:Counterterrorism_Policy_Directive_and_Policy_Guide_(redacted).pdf.

Rigmaiden was convicted for filing more than 1200 fraudulent tax returns, claiming more than $3,000,000 in tax refunds.[7] To gather the evidence against Rigmaiden the Internal Revenue Service (IRS) and the FBI used the following investigative techniques: several subpoenas; a confidential agent; collection of historical (stored) cell site data; a mobile tracking device; court authorization to use pen register/trap and trace; information from an apartment building owner; information from an alarm company; an undercover deception; physical surveillance of the suspect; a search incident to his arrest; and a search warrant for his apartment. The investigation ran from June 2007 until August 2012. To mount an investigation such as this the IRS and FBI agents needed a strategic plan informed by a detailed understanding of the law regarding the predicates required for each type of search, e.g., probable cause in order to obtain a search warrant.

II. The stages of a terrorist investigation

The FBI investigates domestic terrorism, domestic jihadist terrorism, and foreign-connected terrorism, as well as ordinary crimes that can be dubbed precursor terrorism crimes. (The term "terrorism" is discussed in the Introduction and in Chapters 1 and 7.) To deal with domestic and foreign-connected terrorism, the FBI has shifted from only investigating and solving crimes after they have occurred, to a forward leaning prevention posture used in combination with its traditional capture-the-culprits posture. (This seems to be especially true regarding foreign-connected terrorism.) As of 2008 the hallmark of the FBI's new posture is the use of a first-stage investigation called an "assessment" followed by subsequent stages as justified by the evidence.[8] These different stages are distinguished by their purpose and scope, the predicate required to undertake the investigation, and the authorized investigative methods.

The assessment: according to the FBI's Domestic Investigations and Operations Guide (DIOG), an assessment, whether its purpose is related to ordinary crime, to domestic terrorism, or to foreign-connected terrorism, does not require a particular factual predication, but cannot be arbitrary or based on groundless speculation; neither can it be based solely on the exercise of First Amendment-protected activities, or on the race, ethnicity, national origin, or religion of the subject.[9]

> [A]n Assessment may be conducted when: (i) there is reason to collect information or facts to determine whether there is a criminal or national security threat; and (ii) there is a rational and articulable relationship between the

7 *United States v Rigmaiden*, Docket No. CR 08-814-PHX-DGC (D Ariz 2013).

8 Emily Berman, *FBI: Fact or fiction?* (Brennan Center for Justice, July 27, 2011), archived at https://www.brennancenter.org/analysis/fbi-fact-or-fiction.

9 Federal Bureau of Investigation, *Domestic investigations and operations guide* 5-1 (October 16, 2013), (hereinafter DIOG), archived at https://vault.fbi.gov/FBI%20Domestic%20Investigations%20and%20Operations%20Guide%20%28DIOG%29/fbi-domestic-investigations-and-operations-guide-diog-2013-version/FBI%20Domestic%20Investigations%20and%20Operations%20Guide%20%28DIOG%29%202013%20Version%20Part%2001%20of%2001/view.

> stated authorized purpose of the Assessment, on the one hand, and the information sought and the proposed means to obtain that information, on the other. An FBI employee must be able to explain the authorized purpose and the clearly defined objective(s), and the reason the particular investigative methods were used to conduct the Assessment.

An individual FBI agent can launch an assessment without a supervisor's approval, but after starting the assessment the agent must report to his or her supervisor. The assessment is renewable every 30 days.[10] Online speech activities can lead to an assessment.[11]

Despite the "limitations" noted above, the American Civil Liberties Union has asserted that with the creation of the "assessment" the FBI has authorized itself to conduct investigations without a factual basis to suspect that the target had engaged in wrongdoing or posed a threat to national security.[12] It appears that participants in an online activity may be subject to an assessment.

The preliminary investigation: a preliminary investigation may only be opened on the basis of "information or an allegation" indicating "an activity constituting a federal crime or a threat to national security has or may have occurred, is or may be occurring, or will or may occur." Similarly, it may be launched when there is an indication that: "An individual, group, organization, entity, information, property, or activity is or may be a target of attack, victimization, acquisition, infiltration, or recruitment in connection with criminal activity in violation of federal law or a threat to the national security."[13]

The full investigation: a full investigation may be opened not just because there is information or an allegation, but only if there is an "articulable factual basis" that reasonably indicates the kind of circumstance just noted. The DIOG offers the following examples that illustrate sufficient predication to open a full investigation:

A Corroborated information from an intelligence agency [NSA] states that an individual is a member of a terrorist group.

B An analyst discovers on a blog a threat to a specific home builder and additional information connects the blogger to a known terrorist group.

C FBI [Directorate of Intelligence] has posted an authorized [Positive Foreign Intelligence] requirement for collection.[14]

Preliminary and full investigations require supervisory approval.

10 *Counterterrorism policy directive and policy guide*, 29, 52-53 (FBI, April 1, 2015, reviewed April 1, 2018), archived at https://commons.wikimedia.org/wiki/File:Counterterrorism_Policy_Directive_and_Policy_Guide_(redacted).pdf.

11 Id at 74–75.

12 https://www.aclu.org/other/expanded-fbi-authority.

13 DIOG, at 6-3 (cited in note 9).

14 Id at 7-3.

The enterprise investigation: Enterprise investigations must be opened and operated as full investigations; thus they may not be conducted as an assessment or as a preliminary investigation.

> The purpose of an Enterprise Investigation is to examine the structure, scope, and nature of the group or organization including: its relationship, if any, to a foreign power; the identity and relationship of its members, employees, or other persons who may be acting in furtherance of its objectives; its finances and resources; its geographical dimensions; its past and future activities and goals; and its capacity for harm.[15]

An enterprise investigation of a group or organization may be opened if there is an "articulable factual basis . . . that reasonably indicates the group or organization may have engaged, or may be engaged in, or may have or may be engaged in planning or preparation or provision of support for" a racketeering activity or domestic/foreign-connected terrorism.

The evidence to support a finding of an "articulable factual basis" for opening an enterprise investigation may *in part* be the speech activities of the organization.[16] Also, when the activities of one individual are deemed to fit the definition of domestic terrorism (18 USC §2331(5)), that may provide the necessary predicate to undertake an enterprise investigation of groups and organizations of which the suspect is part.[17]

Being aware of the civil rights and civil liberties interests at stake when it undertakes an investigation, the DIOG provides that:

> No investigative activity, including Assessments, may be taken solely on the basis of activities that are protected by the First Amendment or on the race, ethnicity, national origin or religion of the subject, or a combination of only such factors.[18]

Nevertheless, as discussed in Chapter 7, speech activities have been among the activities that have been the basis of charges and convictions under the statutes criminalizing material support of terrorism. And as noted below, federal statutes expressly permit targeting people based *in part* on the First Amendment activities of the target.

Investigative methods: Let us now turn to the investigative methods that may be used in assessments, preliminary investigations, and full investigations. Unless

15 Id at 8-1.

16 Id at 8-3.

17 The Attorney General's guidelines for domestic FBI operations, 23 (2008), archived at https://www.dni.gov/files/documents/1118/CLEANED116%20AG%20Guidelines.pdf.

18 Id at 5–7.

otherwise specified the methods discussed may be used in investigating both domestic and foreign-connection terrorism cases.

The assessment is limited to the following sources of information and investigatory methods:

- Public information.
- The FBI's and Department of Justice's own records and databases.
- Other governmental records [e.g., data from the NSA].
- Online services and resources (including social media, e.g., Facebook).
- Information voluntarily provided by governmental or private entities.
- Use of alias or false identification.
- Confidential human resources.
- Interviews (of the target, friends, family, associates).
- Information voluntarily provided by government or private entities.
- Physical surveillance not requiring a court order (including physical surveillance of person, home office, car).
- Grand jury subpoenas for telephone and email subscriber information only.

In addition, assessments can involve identifying locations of concentrated ethnic communities, computer based mapping of ethnic/racial demographics, and pattern-based data mining.

Information collected regarding a subject includes: criminal history, contacts of the subject with subjects of other FBI investigations, special licenses/permits, data held by the Intelligence Community on the subject, travel history, purchase of firearms, military training, and similar information regarding the subject's associates.[19]

The preliminary investigation can use all the above, and in addition the following:

- Consensual monitoring of communications.
- Intercepting the communications of a computer trespasser.
- Closed-circuit television/video surveillance, direction finders, and other monitoring devices.
- Administrative subpoenas.
- Grand jury subpoenas.
- National Security Letters.
- Pen Register and Trap and Trace.
- Stored wire or electronic communications and transactional records.
- Foreign Intelligence Surveillance Act Order for Business Records.
- Mail covers.
- Trash covers that do not require a warrant.

19 FBI, *Counterterrorism program guidance baseline collection plan, administrative and operational guidance*, September 24, 2009, archived at https://www.aclu.org/files/fbimappingfoia/20111019/ACLURM004887.pdf.

- Polygraph examinations.
- Undercover operations.

When it comes to the full investigation, all the sources of information and investigatory techniques listed above may be used, and in addition: physical searches requiring a warrant and electronic surveillance (wiretapping) requiring either a judicially ordered warrant or a court order pursuant to the Wiretap Act or Foreign Intelligence Surveillance Act.

When approaching an assessment, preliminary investigation, or a full investigation, the DIOG notes that the Attorney General requires that the "least intrusive" means or method available for that investigation be considered, and if reasonable, used.[20]

The leeway the FBI has granted itself despite the professed limitations is clear in the guidelines. Investigative activities may not be based *solely* on the subject's exercise of First Amendment rights or *solely* on the basis of race, ethnicity, national origin or religion of the subjects.[21] This point is underscored and elaborated on in the DIOG when it notes: "This is not to say that any diminution of First Amendment rights is unconstitutional."[22] "Despite the high standard for interfering with free speech or punishing those engaged in it, the law does not preclude FBI employees from observing and collecting any of the forms of protected speech and considering its content – as long as those activities are done for a valid law enforcement or national security purpose and are conducted in a manner that does not unduly infringe upon the ability of the speaker to deliver his or her message."[23]

As for taking religion and ethnicity into account, the DIOG says that religious practitioners and facilities may be examined and the role of religion may be taken into account regarding motivation of a criminal or terrorism enterprise.[24]

Charges of ethnic discrimination in conducting terrorism investigations have arisen in New York City and California. A parallel claim arose in Arizona, where it was claimed that the local sheriff used ethnicity and race in a program used to enforce immigration laws.[25] The program in question used ethnicity and race to target people for pretextual traffic stops as a way to identify illegal immigrants. A federal district court found the program violated both the Equal Protection Clause and the Fourth Amendment. Noting that the great majority of Hispanic persons in the area were citizens or legal residents, the fact that a person was Hispanic was not a "narrowly-tailored basis" [quoting the relevant constitutional test] on which to conclude the person was an unauthorized alien. Rulings such as this of course have implications for terrorism investigations.

20 Id at 4-15.
21 Id at 3-4; 4-1; 5-7.
22 Id at 4-5.
23 Id at 4-7.
24 Id at 4-8, 4-12, 4-13.
25 *Manual De Jesus Ortega Melendres v Arpaio*, 989 F Supp2d 822 (D Ariz 2013).

Other constitutional issues regarding each of the different sources of information and methods of investigation will be taken up in the sections that follow.

III. Public information and the third party doctrine

An FBI assessment or preliminary investigation presumably would begin by first collecting low-hanging fruit that is not private and not protected by the Fourth Amendment. Stated legally, the FBI collection of information available to members of the general public is not a "search" for Fourth Amendment purposes.[26] For example, the Supreme Court has ruled that people have no reasonable expectation of privacy regarding their movements on public roadways.[27] [The police use of GPS tracking devices has created legal complications discussed below. Approaching people on the street and then stopping and frisking them does implicate the Fourth Amendment.[28]] Thus FBI/police reliance on the videos taken by surveillance cameras posted in the city is not a constitutional problem. (Surveillance videos from private businesses involves obtaining a subpoena and other issues such as is the video "evidence" of a crime.) Also not a problem is public information obtained by visiting any place or attending an event that is open to the public, or that which is "observed, heard, smelled, detected, or obtained by any casual observer or member of the public."[29] Items left on the curb for trash pickup have effectively been made available to the public, and hence do not enjoy Fourth Amendment protection.[30] Accordingly the FBI lists "trash covers" as an investigative technique that does not require a warrant.[31] In an old case, the Supreme Court ruled that although the Fourth Amendment protected the contents of letters and sealed packages, the Fourth Amendment did not protect their "outward form and weight."[32] Thus the DIOG lists as an investigative technique the examination of mail covers, and federal regulations specify that a nonconsensual record may be made of data appearing on the outside cover of mail in order to protect national security and to obtain evidence of commission or attempted commission of a crime.[33] [Recall the discussion of *Smith v Maryland*[34] and metadata in Chapter III.V.A, and see Section V below.]

The DIOG also specifies that FBI employees may use any publicly available online "service or resource including those that the FBI has obtained by subscription or

26 Stephen A. Saltzburg and Daniel J. Capra, *American criminal procedure: Investigative*, 8th ed., 49 (Thomson-West 2007).

27 *United States v Knotts*, 460 US 276 (1983). See, also, Christopher Slobogin, *Privacy at risk*, 79–117 (University of Chicago 2007).

28 *Terry v Ohio*, 392 US 1 (1968).

29 DIOG, at 18-7 (cited in note 9).

30 *California v Greenwood*, 486 US 35 (1988).

31 DIOG, at 18-7 (cited in note 9).

32 *Ex Parte Jackson*, 96 US 727 (1877); *United States v Choate*, 576 F 2d 165 (9th Cir 1978).

33 39 CFR §233.3; DIOG, at 18-145 (cited in note 9).

34 442 US 735 (1979).

purchase."[35] The DIOG states that public information includes information accessible online (social media, blogs) or otherwise available to the public by subscription or purchase.[36] Information published or broadcast for public consumption is also deemed to be public information.

An FBI policy directive includes extensive guidelines regarding online investigations. Such an investigation may include focusing on the online activity of extremists, the targeting of administrators of chat rooms, bulletin boards, blogs, servers, and websites, targeting "virtual couriers" of extremist messages, using undercover agents, and confidential human resources (discussed below) carried out under a program called Net Talon.[37]

The Supreme Court also held that a criminal defendant had no justifiable expectation of privacy regarding conversations he voluntarily had and which were overheard by a law enforcement agent because of a transmitter voluntarily worn by the agent; the defendant took the risk that the other party would divulge the conversation.[38] The next section continues this line of cases with a discussion of human intelligence.

IV. Human intelligence

Anyone who follows TV crime shows or reads police procedural mysteries has a sense of the range of human intelligence relied on by law enforcement – eyewitnesses, victims, the suspects themselves, and informants including confidential ones. People become witnesses when they see and make suspicious activity reports (SARS) such as a citizen reporting someone photographing a bridge. Confidential informants are injected into wholly peaceful organizations in order to keep an eye out on behalf of the FBI, and to provide a forewarning of possible terrorist planning. Observers are posted at public events to gather bits of ostensibly "innocent" information that may at a future time be part of a mosaic in building a case. Talk picked up in a café about, for example, a chemical plant, may be useful in assessing the vulnerability of the plant (risk analysis). More generally, the collection of multiple bits and pieces of human information, along with electronic information, provide the basis for further analysis, the drawing of links and inferences. The DIOG specifically talks of "pattern-based data mining," which it describes as:

> [Q]ueries or other analysis of electronic databases using two or more search criteria designed to discover or locate a predictive pattern or anomaly indicative of terrorist or criminal activity on the part of any individual or individuals. . . . Any

35 DIOG, at 18-13 (cited in note 9).

36 Id at 18-7.

37 *Counterterrorism policy directive and policy guide*, at 126 (cited in note 10).

38 *United States v White*, 401 US 745 (1971).

> such analysis based solely on racial, ethnic, national origin or religious characteristics is strictly prohibited.[39]

An important investigative starting point for the FBI is the interview. The DIOG informs agents they may not obtain statements by force, threats, or improper promises, e.g., promises of leniency or immunity from prosecution. The Attorney General's Guidelines for Domestic FBI Operations – the fundamental guide for the FBI – says FBI interviews and requests for information may extend broadly to members of the public and private entities. [Finding, validating and protecting human resources is an inevitable necessity for the FBI.[40]]

The guidelines regarding confidential human sources (CHS) say that they can be used for "undisclosed participation" (UDP) and to engage in "otherwise illegal activity."[41] As noted above, CHSs are used in online social networks. One of the most sensitive and aggressive uses of CHSs and UDPs occurs when these people engage in an "otherwise illegal activity" such as supplying the targeted suspect with illegal drugs, explosives, or arms. These sting operations, when the suspect is brought to trial, may trigger "entrapment" defenses or "overinvolvement" by the government in the criminal activity (discussed in Chapter 7). The claim has been raised that the FBI has created terrorists out of law-abiding citizens.[42]

Undisclosed participation might also take the form of undercover surveillance. Undercover activities can include the attendance of religious services.[43] The CHS (or FBI agent) may, in addition, engage in what the DIOG calls "consensual monitoring of communications," which DIOG describes as the "monitoring of wire, oral or electronic communications based on the consent of *one party* [italics added] to the communication."[44] This mode of investigation has proved to be very controversial in New York City and California.

The FBI's "Operation Flex" operated for a year in southern California. It entailed the FBI placing a confidential informant equipped with monitoring equipment (audio and video) inside 10 mosques where the informant interacted with members of the Muslim community in a "dragnet" surveillance program.[45] The CHS was instructed to gather "as much information on as many people in the Muslim community as possible." The CHS was told to gather information on the travel plans of Muslims, attend lectures by Muslim scholars, attend classes and prayer sessions, track followers of extremist websites, elicit people's views of extremist scholars and

39 DIOG, at 18–19 (cited in note 9).

40 Id at 19–20.

41 Id at 16-1, 17-3. See Jerome P. Bjelopera, *The Federal Bureau of Investigation and terrorism investigation*, 21–22 (Congressional Research Service, April 24, 2013, R41780).

42 https://www.theguardian.com/world/2014/jul/21/government-agents-directly-involved-us-terror-plots-report.

43 Id at 18-8.

44 Id at 18-49.

45 *Fazaga et al. v Federal Bureau of Investigation*, 885 F Supp 2d 978 (CD Cal 2012).

thinkers, and to gather information that could be used against Muslims so as to persuade them to become informants. Also collected by the FBI were hundreds of phone numbers, thousands of addresses; video recordings of the interior of buildings, homes, and businesses. Operation Flex, the FBI, and specific agents were sued by Muslim plaintiffs alleging violations of the First Amendment's establishment and free exercise clauses, violation of the Fifth Amendment's implied equal protection clause, violation of the Fourth Amendment's unreasonable search and seizure clause, and, in addition, violation of various statutes. The government moved for dismissal on grounds that the suit would risk disclosure of information properly protected by the state secrets privilege. The federal district court agreed with the government and dismissed the complaint, except those involving specific FBI employees.

A similar surveillance program was undertaken in New York City.[46] This surveillance program was more comprehensive. One component involved taking pictures, collecting license plate numbers of mosque attendees, and mounting surveillance cameras aimed at mosques. Using officers from the community, the New York Police Department went to restaurants, bookstores, nightclubs, markets, and cafés. Student groups at colleges and universities were monitored and, of course, mosques. Undercover agents went into 20 mosques, 14 restaurants, 11 retail stores, two grade schools, and more. Another aspect of the program was "mapping" the city in terms of 28 "ancestries of interest," almost all of which were immigrant communities with the exception of "American Black Muslims." Extensive data were assembled, including the names of converts and scholars and students associated with Muslim student associations. After this program was reported in the press, it stirred considerable criticism, and the program was disbanded.

The constitutionality of these surveillance programs involves a number of intertwining issues that have not yet been adjudicated by the courts. One set of issues has to do with the methods of surveillance, apart from any claim of discrimination. The second set claims that discrimination is and has been at the heart of the programs.

As noted above, using a CHS who reports on what s/he has heard or who wears a wire has been found to be constitutionally permissible. In *Hoffa v United States*, a CHS regularly reported his conversations with James Hoffa (reports that could be used against Hoffa); a sting operation involving an FBI agent purchasing drugs from the defendant was upheld; and the communications of a wired CHS was allowed into evidence.[47] [The FBI, of course, had to carry out these operations so that an entrapment defense would not succeed, as discussed in Chapter 7.] However, the idea that one's communications may be divulged by another communicant because one assumes the risk that his or her communications could be divulged smacks of being quite circular.

46 *Hassan v The City of New York*, 804 F 3d 277 (3d Cir 2015); Wadie E. Said, *Crimes of terror*, 23 (Oxford 2015). See, also, Matthew A. Wasserman, *First Amendment limitations on police surveillance: The case of the Muslim surveillance program*, 90 NYU L Rev 1786 (2015).

47 385 US 293 (1966); *Lewis v United States*, 385 US 206 (1966); *Lopez v United States*, 373 US 427 (1963); *United States v White*, 401 US 745 (1971). Compare *Maine v Moulton*, 474 US 159 (1985).

In *United States v Osmakac*, the FBI operated a sting operation that involved a CHS who put the defendant in contact with one Amir who was an undercover FBI agent.[48] Amir then consulted with Osmakac about his terrorist plans, provided him with the guns and bomb necessary for the plot, all of which were inoperable. Osmakac was arrested as he was about to drive off to commit his plot with the inoperable guns and bomb. He was ultimately charged and convicted of attempting to use weapons of mass destruction (18 USC §2332a(a)(2)) and being in possession of an unregistered firearm (26 USC §§5861(d) and 5871).

The decision in *Laird v Tatum*, 408 US 1 (1972) poses a different obstacle for plaintiffs attacking surveillance programs based on the First Amendment's free speech clause. According to the dissent in that case the plaintiffs alleged that:

> [T]he Army maintains files on the membership, ideology, programs, and practices of virtually every activist political group in the country, including groups such as the Southern Christian Leadership Conference, Clergy and Laymen United Against the War in Vietnam, the American Civil Liberties Union, Women's Strike for Peace, and the National Association for the Advancement of Colored People. The Army uses undercover agents to infiltrate these civilian groups and to reach into confidential files of students and other groups. The Army moves as a secret group among civilian audiences, using cameras and electronic ears for surveillance. The data it collects are distributed to civilian officials in state, federal, and local governments and to each military intelligence unit and troop command under the Army's jurisdiction (both here and abroad); and these data are stored in one or more data banks.[49]

The plaintiffs lost their suit challenging the program on the grounds of lack of standing, with Chief Justice Burger writing that an allegation of a subjective "chill" was insufficient.[50] (The involvement of the military raises a question whether the Posse Comitatus Act (18 USC §1385), which prohibits the use of the military to "execute laws," was violated.[51])

The *Laird* case can be distinguished on the facts from the New York and California surveillance programs. The surveillance in those programs targeted Muslims, and thus arguably violated both the equal protection clause of the Fourteenth Amendment and the free exercise clause of the First Amendment. Both lines of that argument were raised by the plaintiffs in *Hassan v City of New York*, a suit seeking monetary damages and an injunction because of the surveillance program described above.[52] The federal district court dismissed the suit for lack of standing, and for failure to state a legal claim that the law recognizes. On appeal the Third Circuit

48 868 F3d 937 (11th Cir 2017).

49 408 US 1, 25 (1972) (Douglas, dissenting).

50 Id at 14.

51 Compare *Bissonette v Haig*, 776 F2d 1384 (8th Cir 1985), aff'd 800 F2d 812 (8th Cir 1986) (en banc).

52 *Hassan v The City of New York* (cited in note 46).

Court of Appeals reversed and remanded on both counts. Central to the reversal on the standing issue was the conclusion of the Third Circuit that unequal treatment was a personal injury that has been judicially cognizable and provides a basis for standing. The court then turned to whether the complaint, stated a claim on which relief could be granted.

Here the court concluded that those facts, assuming they were true, did raise a case of intentional discrimination based on religious affiliation, and on remand the government would have to establish that its discriminatory policy *at least* served an important governmental interest and that the means used were substantially related to the purpose. The possibility was left open that the government would have to meet an even tougher test, namely, that the policy was necessary to achieve a compelling state interest. The court also let the First Amendment claim go forward in the district court.

V. Obtaining stored information

Methods of obtaining stored information discussed below are not always available, hence the FBI may have to rely on legally more difficult routes to obtain that information. The most difficult method entails going to a judge to obtain a search warrant based on probable cause, a higher standard than what is required by any of the techniques listed below.[53]

Grand jury subpoenas can be used to demand documents, records, and the testimony of witnesses prior to indictment.[54] Subpoenas may also be issued by federal courts in the course of a trial (FRCP Rule 17).

A defendant may seek to quash a subpoena on the grounds that the information is privileged, compliance is burdensome, or on the grounds of the irrelevance of the evidence. These challenges are usually unavailing.[55] In addition, a subpoena that compelled the production of information of scope and nature analogous to the data collected in *Carpenter v United States*, discussed below, may be claimed to have violated the Fourth Amendment. Chapter 7 takes up efforts *at trial* to suppress on evidence obtained by means of a subpoena.

The Stored Communications Act (SCA), 18 USC §§2701-2712, provides another legal route to obtain stored wire or electronic communications, emails, IP addresses, session logs, toll billing records, service agreements, and subscriber information.[56] The government can use SCA provisions to obtain data from Google, Yahoo, Facebook,

53 FRCP 41.

54 US Department of Justice, Office of Legal Policy, *Report to Congress on the use of administrative subpoena authorities by executive branch agencies and entities*, archived at https://www.justice.gov/archive/olp/rpt_to_congress.htm#appd_b.

55 Slobogin, *Privacy at risk*, at 140–141 (cited in note 27). See, also, FRCP Rule 17(c). These objections have their root in the Fourth Amendment. Wayne R. LaFave, Jerold H. Israel, Nancy J. King, and Orin S. Kerr, *Principles of criminal procedure: Investigation*, 2nd ed., 389–395 (West 2009).

56 DIOG, at 18-86, 18-98, 18-113, 18-117 (cited in note 9).

perhaps even Amazon, and companies that make gadgets that are part of the "Internet of Things" that send data from the gadget to the company.[57] SCA can be used in both domestic and foreign-connected terrorist cases. The SCA does not apply to a target's private computer.

Without delving too deeply into the complexities of this statute, several observations are pertinent. The SCA requires the government to jump through ever more demanding hoops the greater the assumed sensitivity of the information. The most demanding requirements are imposed on obtaining the content of communications, e.g., email.[58] Subpoenas and National Security Letters (NSLs) may be used to acquire non-content information such as IP addresses; special court orders are needed for acquiring logs kept by the network server of email addresses sent from or received by the target; and warrants must be used for unopened emails in storage for fewer than 180 days. One provision of the SCA specifically references terrorism investigations. Under 18 USC §2709, the FBI can use National Security Letters to obtain subscriber information, toll billing records, and service agreements (transactional records). In the last case, the information must be "relevant" to a criminal, counterterrorism, or counterintelligence investigation. In making the request, the FBI must specifically identify a person, entity, telephone number, or account as the basis of the request. A library is covered by 18 USC §2709(g) if the library provides an electronic communication service, a service that gives users the ability to send or receive wire or electronic communications, which, in turn, covers the Internet and email. It can be used for both foreign-connected and domestic terrorism investigations.

In 2018 the Supreme Court in a 5-4 decision, *Carpenter v United States*, ruled that a wireless carrier violated the Fourth Amendment when it relied on SCA 18 USC §2703(d) and obtained a court order to get seven days of a suspected criminal's cell site location information (CSLI). Wireless carriers collect cell site location information when a cell phone is used or turned on near their towers.

CSLI provided an accounting of Carpenter's physical movements and was used by the government to establish that he was located where various robberies occurred, at the time the robberies occurred. A lower court under §2703(d) compelled the disclosure of CSLI after the government offered "specific and articulable facts showing that there [were] reasonable grounds to believe" the records were "relevant and material to an ongoing criminal investigation." But the Supreme Court ruled that by not obtaining a warrant for the CSLI, the Fourth Amendment was violated. The Court refused, given the data's "unique nature," to extend the "third party

57 *Ehling v Monmouth-Ocean Hosp Serv Co*, 961 FSupp 2d 659 (D NJ 2013) (concluding the SCA applies to Facebook). See. Kaveh Waddell, *The government might subpoena your toaster* (The Atlantic, February 3, 2016), archived at https://www.theatlantic.com/technology/archive/2016/02/why-the-government-might-subpoena-your-toaster/459696/.

58 See Orin S. Kerr, *A user's guide to the Stored Communications Act, as a legislator's guide to amending it*, 72 Geo Wash L Rev 1208 (2004).

doctrine" to these data (see Chapter III.V.A). Using the data would be akin to the government's attaching "an ankle monitor to the phone's user."[59] Since individuals have a "legitimate expectation of privacy in the recording of [their] physical movements," collecting the data was a search, and therefore the government had to obtain a warrant supported by probable cause before it could obtain the records.

Whether the opinion will be applied to the collection of data other than physical location data is a question to be answered in the future. A related additional question concerns the status of the third party doctrine, whose sweep has been at least limited by the decision. Will the opinion apply to URLs and IPs, or might these be collectable under the third party doctrine?[60] Might collecting one day's worth of CSLI count as a search? Will the opinion hinder law enforcement, as predicted by dissenting Justice Kennedy? The four dissenting opinions favored taking the interpretation of the Fourth Amendment in a different direction by arguing that the Fourth Amendment did not protect "privacy," it only protected "persons, houses, papers, and effects." This property-based approach could open the way to untrammeled wiretapping comparable to a case of wiretapping a telephone in 1928. In that case (which has now been overruled), the Court ruled there was no search or seizure because "the evidence was secured by the use of the sense of hearing and that only. There was no entry into the houses or offices of the defendants."[61]

One problem the government faces in the modern world of electronic communications is the issue of the SCA's extraterritorial reach. In today's world, the data regarding a particular person that the FBI is investigating may be moving about the world or stored outside of the United States. This creates a problem in obtaining a warrant for data since the Federal Rules of Criminal Procedure do not authorize a federal court to issue a warrant for items outside the U.S. or its territories.[62] In this situation, the government may turn to the SCA, as happened in *Microsoft Corporation v United States*,[63] where the government, in connection with a criminal investigation, obtained under 50 USC §2703(b)(1)(A) an SCA "warrant" for Microsoft to turn over to the government the contents of an account of a customer located in Ireland. Microsoft resisted, saying the SCA did not have extraterritorial application, and the Second Circuit Court sided with Microsoft. In another case involving Google, the government won, with the court concluding that the invasion of privacy that would occur when the government obtained the data would, in fact, happen inside the U.S. once Google had transferred it from outside the U.S. to inside. Hence there was no extraterritorial application of SCA.[64]

59 Id at 13.

60 See Mathew J. Tokson, *The content/envelope distinction in internet law*, 50 Wm & Mary L Rev 2105 (2009), archived at http://scholarship.law.wm.edu/cgi/viewcontent.cgi?article=1094&context=wmlr.

61 *Olmstead v United States*, 277 US 438, 464–465 (1928).

62 DIOG, Rule 41(b)(5) (cited in note 9).

63 829 F 3d 197 (2d Cir 2016), petition for rehearing denied October 13, 2016, appeal to Supreme Court, June 23, 2017.

64 *In Re Search Warrant No. 16-1061-M to Google*, 232 F Supp 3d 708 (ED PA 2017).

The FBI may send National Security Letters to telephone companies, Internet service providers, credit agencies, banks, and other financial institutions[65] in order to obtain a customer's name, address, length of service, and billing information. Like under the SCA, NSLs are not available to get execute a bulk collection from communication companies. Requests to financial institutions for financial records must specifically identify the customer, entity, or account, thus limiting the possibility of bulk collection (12 USC §3414(a)(2)).

The NSL has been a go-to tool of the FBI in important part because it does not require prior approval by a court. A former general counsel to the FBI said "virtually every significant national security investigation . . . requires the use of NSLs for at least some critical information [e.g., billing records, numbers dialed etc.]."[66] The FBI makes tens of thousands of NSL requests each year, in fact, in 2010 it made 54,000 such requests.[67]

A controversial aspect of older NSL laws has been the gag order that comes with an NSL.[68] But Congress amended the law to provide for the possibility of judicial review of the gag order and of the issuance of the NSL itself. It also allowed the recipient of the NSL to disclose it to those people to whom disclosure was necessary in order to comply with the request, such as an attorney in order to obtain legal advice or assistance regarding the request, and other persons as permitted by the FBI.[69] Under 18 USC §3511 an NSL recipient may, however, petition a district court "for an order modifying or setting aside the request" for records, and the court could do so if compliance would be unreasonable, oppressive, or otherwise unlawful. If the recipient of a NSL refused to comply, the Attorney General could go to a federal district court to seek an order of compliance, which if defied would expose the recipient to punishment for contempt. Recipients of NSLs may now publish aggregate data regarding the NLSs they have received, 50 USC §1874.

Now we ask whether NSLs are constitutionally permissible under the Fourth Amendment. A body of cases makes the success of such a challenge unlikely, unless the NSL seeks information of a nature and scope that the 2018 *Carpenter v United States* opinion, noted above, is applicable. In *United States v Miller*, 425 US 435 (1976) the Court refused to suppress a criminal defendant's subpoenaed bank records. The Court said: "This Court has held repeatedly that the Fourth Amendment does not prohibit the obtaining of information revealed to a third party and conveyed by him

65 Charles Doyle, *National security letters: Proposals in the 112th Congress*, 1 (Congressional Research Service, June 30, 2011, R41619); 18 USC §2709; 12 USC §3414; 15 USC §1681u; 15 USC §1681v; and 50 USC §436.

66 Quoted in Stephen Dycus, Arthur L. Berney, William C. Banks, Peter Raven-Hansen, and Stephen I. Vladeck, *National security law*, 6th ed., 713 (Wolter Kluwer 2016). See, also, Office of Inspector General, US Department of Justice, *A review of the Federal Bureau of Investigation's use of national security letters*, 65 (August 2014), archived at https://oig.justice.gov/reports/2014/s1408.pdf.

67 Id at 65.

68 See *Doe v Ashcroft*, 334 F Supp 2d 471 (SD NY 2004), vacated, 449 F 3d 415 (2d Cir 2006).

69 18 USC §2709(c)(2) and (d).

to Government authorities, even if the information is revealed on the assumption that it will be used only for a limited purpose and the confidence placed in the third party will not be betrayed." In other words, the Court concluded that the defendant did not have a legitimate expectation of privacy in the records, hence there was no Fourth Amendment search. The opinion was subsequently relied on by the Sixth Circuit in ruling that the plaintiff did not have a Fourth Amendment interest in his subscriber information found in the files of an Internet service provider.[70] Furthermore, NSLs directed to obtaining foreign intelligence fall within the more lenient Fourth Amendment rules applicable to national intelligence investigations.

Courts have not as yet addressed whether compelled disclosure of records violates the First Amendment by permitting the FBI to obtain without judicial authorization information possibly protected by the First Amendment, as when people are seeking to communicate or associate anonymously.[71]

Another way to obtain stored information is to turn to *FISA §215* (50 USC §1861) for use in foreign-connected terrorism investigations. (See Chapter 3.) This provision allows the FBI to collect a wide variety of tangible things (books, records, papers, customer lists, firearms sales, tax returns, library patron lists etc.). To use this authority, the FBI must file an application with a FISA judge. Alternatively, the Attorney General in an emergency can demand production of the "tangible things" basis without a preliminary judicial authorization, but subject to filing an authorization request with a court no later than seven days afterwards. The provision also includes a non-disclosure provision subject to the same kind of exceptions as are built into the NSL provision noted above.

FISA Sections 1881b and 1881c of Title 50 also permit the collection of stored electronic data of U.S. persons outside the U.S. whether the acquisition is in or outside of the U.S. There must be a significant purpose to obtain foreign intelligence, and the target must be believed to be a foreign power or agent of a foreign power.

VI. Stored information held by other governmental agencies

The FBI also has available data that have been collected by federal, state, and local governmental agencies. The FBI may request the CIA and the NSA to conduct a search of their records regarding a specific individual, but the NSA may not be asked to trace a U.S. person.[72] Also the FBI has its own database, eGuardian, which it uses and shares with other federal, state, local, tribal, and territorial agencies.[73]

The NSA-FBI linkage is broad and deep:

1 The primary purpose of the NSA's surveillance could be for investigating an ordinary domestic crime. (See Chapter 3 and "the wall.")

70 *Guest v Leis*, 255 F3d 325, 336 (6th Cir 2001).

71 https://www.eff.org/issues/national-security-letters/faq.

72 *Counterterrorism policy directive and policy guide*, at 100 (cited in note 10).

73 https://www.fbi.gov/resources/law-enforcement/eguardian.

2 The NSA and the FBI may coordinate investigations.[74] (50 USC §1806(k)).
3 The NSA may share raw data collected pursuant to E.O. 12333.[75]
4 The NSA may share communications collected under §702 (50 USC §1881a).[76]
5 The NSA may share telephony metadata collected under §215.
6 Based on the metadata NSA may "tip" the FBI regarding crime and provide information regarding it.[77]
7 The National Counterterrorism Center (which is a recipient of NSA data) may disseminate information regarding terrorism and/or crime to the FBI.[78]
8 The FBI may query NSA data in its possession using U.S. person information to find evidence of a crime/terrorism.[79]
9 NSA-derived evidence may be used in a criminal prosecution, 50 USC §1806. (See Chapter 7.)

Item 8 should be elaborated. The FBI has been permitted to query its FISA-acquired information using key words and telephone numbers reasonably likely to return foreign intelligence information or evidence of a crime. And there is no limitation on the use of querying terms that include information concerning

74 50 USC 1806(k); Bjelopera, *The Federal Bureau of Investigation and terrorism investigations*, at 4 (cited in note 41).

75 Procedures for the Availability or Dissemination of Raw Signals Intelligence Information by the National Security Agency Under Section 2.3 of Executive Order 12333 (RAW Availability Procedures), January 3, 2017, p.12, archived at https://www.documentcloud.org/documents/3283349-Raw-12333-surveillance-sharing-guidelines.html;Charlie Savage and Laura Poitras, *How a court secretly evolved, extending US spies reach* (New York Times, March 11, 2014), archived at https://www.nytimes.com/2014/03/12/us/how-a-courts-secret-evolution-extended-spies-reach.html.

76 Jeff Sessions, Attorney General of the United States, *Minimization procedures used by the National Security Agency in connection with acquisitions of foreign intelligence information pursuant to Section 702 of the Foreign Intelligence Surveillance Act of 1978, as amended*, 10, 12–13 (March 29, 2017), archived at https://www.dni.gov/files/documents/icotr/ 51117/2016-NSA-702-Minimization-Procedures_Mar_30_17.pdf; Privacy and Civil Liberties Oversight Board, *Report on the surveillance program operated pursuant to Section 702 of the Foreign Intelligence Surveillance Act*, 8, 12 (July 2, 2014), archived at https://www.pclob.gov/library/702-Report.pdf. See, also, Jake Laperrugue, *Closing Section 702 "backdoor search loophole." Also Companion reforms to use restrictions* (Lawfare, February 15, 2017), archived at https://www.lawfareblog.com/closing-section-702-backdoor-search-loophole-also-means-companion-reforms-use-restrictions.

77 Privacy and Civil Liberties Oversight Board, *Report on the telephone records program conducted under Section 215 of the USA Patriot Act and on the operations of the Foreign Intelligence Surveillance Court*, 18, 89 (January 23, 2014), archived at https://fas.org/irp/offdocs/pclob-215.pdf.

78 *Guidelines for access, retention, and dissemination by the National Counterterrorism Center and other agencies of information in databases containing non-terrorism information*, archived at https://fas.org/sgp/othergov/intel/ nctc_guidelines.pdf; Memorandum opinion and order, 44 (FISC April 26, 2017), archived at https://www.dni.gov/files/ documents/icotr/51117/2016_Cert_FISC_Memo_Opin_Order_Apr_2017.pdf.

79 Memorandum opinion and order, 39–44 (FISC November 6, 2015), archived at https://www.dni.gov/files/ documents/20151106-702Mem_Opinion_Order_for_Public_Release.pdf; *United States v Mohamud*, No. 3:10-CR-00475-KI-1, 2014 WL 2866749, at *1 (D. Or. June 24, 2014).

a United States person.[80] In fact, the 2016 minimization procedures for the FBI states:

> It is routine and encouraged practice for the FBI to query databases containing lawfully acquired information, including FISA-acquired information, in furtherance of the FBI's authorized intelligence and law enforcement activities, such as assessments, investigations and intelligence collection.[81]

The passage goes on to say the queries may be related to ongoing authorized investigations, or undertaken in order to make the initial decision to open an assessment regarding a threat to national security or to protect against a federal crime.

FBI querying of databases has been particularly sensitive because of Fourth Amendment concerns. Professor Donohue expressed her concern with the situation.

> The FBI stores unminimized Section 702 data together with information obtained from traditional FISA orders, allowing agents to search both caches of information simultaneously. FBI queries of Section 702 information may have nothing to do with threats to U.S. national security. . . . The use of §702 data, moreover, absent any of the protections otherwise present in Title III, traditional FISA . . . raises significant constitutional concerns.[82]

FBI querying, however, was approved by FISA and a federal district court that found no violation of the Fourth Amendment.[83]

In the Muhtorov case, the federal district court ruled that: "Accessing stored records in a database legitimately acquired is not a search . . . because there is no reasonable expectation of privacy in that information. Evidence obtained legally by one police agency may be shared with similar agencies without the need for obtaining a warrant, even if sought to be used for an entirely different purpose."[84] Thus §702 incidentally collected communications, even when the original collection was to obtain foreign intelligence, could be searched for purposes of prosecuting a crime.

80 Memorandum opinion and order, 26–28 (FISC November 6, 2015), archived at https://www.dni.gov/files/documents/ 20151106-702Mem_Opinion_Order_for_Public_Release.pdf.

81 Loretta E. Lynch, Attorney General, *Minimization procedures used by the Federal Bureau of Investigation in connection with the acquisition of foreign intelligence information pursuant to Section 702 of the Foreign Intelligence Surveillance Act of 1978, as amended* (September 21, 2016, p.11), archived at https://www.dni.gov/files/ documents/icotr/51117/2016_CIA_Section_702_Minimization_Procedures_Se_26_2016.pdf.

82 Id.

83 Memorandum opinion and order, 39–44 (FISC November 6, 2015), archived at https://www.dni.gov/files/documents/ 20151106-702Mem_Opinion_Order_for_Public_Release.pdf; *United States v Mohamud*, No. 3:10-CR-00475-KI-1, 2014 WL 2866749, at *1 (D. Or. June 24, 2014).

84 *United States v Muhtorov*, 187 FSupp 3d 1240, 1256 (D Colo 2015).

Then Congress, apparently seeking to assure no Fourth Amendment violations, imposed new querying procedures on the FBI in the FISA Amendments Reauthorization Act of 2017.[85] First, the Attorney General and the Director of National Intelligence had to adopt querying procedures consistent with the Fourth Amendment that were subject to judicial review. Second, the FBI was required to obtain a court order in order to access the contents of communications collected under §702 that were retrieved by a query using a U.S. person query term that was *not* designed to find foreign intelligence information, i.e., was designed to find evidence of a crime. Third, that court order had to find probable cause to believe the contents would provide evidence of a crime, contraband, or property related to committing a crime. Fourth, there was an exception to the court order requirement when the FBI had a reasonable belief that the contents would help preclude a threat to life or serious bodily injury. Fifth, the law restricted the use of U.S. person §702-acquired information as evidence in a criminal proceeding unless there was a court order, and unless the criminal proceeding involved one of an enumerated list of crimes including death, harm to critical infrastructure, and cybersecurity.

These new procedures would help assure that even if "abouts" collection were restarted and many U.S. persons were then included in the database, the query process would be found permissible under the Fourth Amendment.[86]

The FBI also has access to the Terrorist Identities Datamart Environment (TIDE) housed in the National Counterterrorism Center (NCTC). (See Chapter 1). TIDE is the U.S. government's central repository of information on international terrorist identities with 1.6 million people listed.[87] The NCTC is under an obligation under E.O. 12333, Section 1.6, to report to the Attorney General possible violations of federal criminal law. While the NCTC is itself not a law enforcement agency, it has access to raw NSA data that may contain evidence of a crime.

The fusion centers noted in Chapter 1 provide an additional source of information from state and local partners. And, of course, the FBI has access to its own databases, such as the National Crime Information Center.

VII. Physical searches

Television law enforcement programs inevitably seem to involve the police obtaining a warrant and then aggressively pushing their way into someone's living space to search for evidence like a piece of clothing or a weapon. These scenes are often preceded by a dramatic conflict between the police who want to conduct the search and, say, a district attorney who insists there is insufficient evidence for the warrant. In other words, the physical search of premises is a classic example of where the

85 FISA Amendments Reauthorization Act of 2017, Pub L. 115-118, §101 (amending 50 USC §1881a).
86 Compare Memorandum opinion and order, 27–29 (cited in note 81).
87 https://www.dni.gov/index.php/nctc-newsroom/nctc-resources/item/1718-terrorist-identities-datamart-environment-tide-fact-sheet-current-as-of-30-june-2016.

Fourth Amendment and the requirement for a judicially-authorized warrant apply.[88] Similarly, another large body of Fourth Amendment law has emerged regarding the confrontation between a law enforcement officer and an individual on the street. "Stop and frisk," a "search incident to an arrest," and "exigent circumstances" are terms that arise in this area of Fourth Amendment law.[89] Note police are also testing remote gun detection technology that can detect concealed weapons.

A. FISA physical searches

It is outside the scope of this book to review all Fourth Amendment doctrine applicable to ordinary law enforcement even if a terrorist precursor crime is involved. What follows is a look at obtaining FISA's authorization for a physical search in order to obtain foreign intelligence in a foreign-connection investigation, and at some of the unique Fourth Amendment issues regarding physical searches that have arisen in the course of the FBI's investigation of specific terrorist suspects. These FISA authorized searches must be used only for foreign-connected investigations.

FISA, 50 USC §1822, empowers the President, acting through the Attorney General, to authorize a physical search (see below) to acquire foreign intelligence information. Foreign intelligence is a broad term that includes information, roughly speaking, related to terrorism.[90] The certification to the court must only state that the search has as "a significant purpose" the collection of foreign intelligence, i.e., it need not be the search's primary purpose. (See Chapter 3 and "the wall.")

Recall that these FISA searches are not ordinary criminal searches. If the search does not have collecting foreign intelligence as "a significant purpose," the Fourth Amendment would require a warrant, a conclusion that the Department of Justice itself has reached.[91] (Constitutional challenges to FISA searches are addressed in Chapter 7.)

The law imposes several other requirements if a FISA physical search were to be authorized, one of which is probable cause that the target is a foreign power or an agent of a foreign power, i.e., a foreign connection. In finding probable cause that the target is a foreign power or an agent of a foreign power, the judge may take into account the free speech activities of the target. Those activities may not, however, be the sole basis for concluding that the target is a foreign power or an agent of a foreign power.[92] FISA also permits the Attorney General to authorize an emergency physical search. If the search is directed to premises used by a foreign power, and

88 See *Kyllo v United States*, 533 US 27 (2001); Slobogin, *Privacy at risk*, 51–78 (cited in note 27).

89 *Terry v Ohio*, 392 US 1 (1968) (stop and frisk); *Chimel v California*, 395 US 752 (1969) (incident to an arrest); *United States v Salava*, 978 F2d 320 (7th Cir 1992) (exigent circumstances).

90 50 USC §1801(e).

91 Office of Legal Education, *Searching and seizing computers and obtaining electronic evidence in criminal investigations*, 3 (Department of Justice), archived at https://www.justice.gov/sites/default/files/criminal-ccips/legacy/ 2015/01/14/ssmanual2009.pdf.

92 Id.

there is no substantial likelihood that the search would involve the property of a U.S. person, the search may be authorized without prior FISA court approval.

FISA has a surprisingly complex definition of what constitutes a "physical search."[93] The definition arguably is sufficiently broad to include the examination of someone's cell phone or computer in order to copy the information stored therein.[94]

B. Other (non-FISA) search authority

The FBI has also been authorized to conduct covert physical searches dubbed "sneak and peak" searches.[95] More technically, the law lets there be a delay in the notification to the target of the search. "Under a 'sneak and peek' warrant, FBI agents can secretly enter an apartment or home while the owner is asleep or away, take, alter, or copy things, and not tell the owner they were there for a 'reasonable period thereafter' [perhaps 90 days]."[96]

A further enhancement of the FBI's searching authority came with the amendment of Rule 41 of the Federal Rules of Criminal Procedure. Rule 41(b)(6) permits a judge, sitting in a district where activities related to a crime occurred, to issue a warrant, and assuming certain requirements are met, "to use remote access to search electronic storage media and to seize or copy electronically stored information located within or outside the district." One requirement is that the information has to have been concealed through technological means, for example, encryption or the use of Tor, software which serves to keep the user's location and Internet usage anonymous.

Because of the Supreme Court's ruling in *Riley v California*, it is now known that the old doctrine that allowed a warrantless search incident to an arrest *does not apply* to the arrestee's cell phone.[97] The Chief Justice said that comparing the search of a cell phone to a purse "is like saying a ride on horseback is materially indistinguishable from a flight to the moon. . . . Modern cell phones, as a category, implicate privacy concerns far beyond those implicated by the search of a cigarette pack, a wallet, or a purse. . . . [A]ny extension of that reasoning to digital data has to rest on its own bottom." Thus a warrant is now required to search cell phones, even those seized in connection to an arrest. (But see border searches, Chapter 4.) However, the Court also noted that the exigencies of the situation may make the needs of law enforcement so compelling that a search without a warrant is reasonable. Thus the Court said law enforcement should be able to act immediately if a suspect is texting an accomplice who, it is feared, is preparing to detonate a bomb.

93 50 USC §1821(5).
94 See, also, FRCP 41(e)((2)(B) (warrant seeking electronically stored information).
95 18 USC §3103a(b); FRCP 41.
96 David Cole and James X. Dempsey, *Terrorism and the Constitution*, 209 (New Press 2006).
97 573 US, 134 S Ct 2473 (2014).

The widely reported conflict between Apple Corporation and the government regarding unlocking the iPhone of a terrorist so that stored information on the phone could be read by the FBI does not raise the same Fourth Amendment problems discussed thus far. Apple's resistance to the FBI's claim for assistance, which was based on an old statute called the All Writs Act, was rooted in due process (arbitrary deprivation of liberty) and free speech claims, i.e., being forced to write new code to unlock the phone was arguably a form of compelled speech. The ultimate question of whether the government could under the All Writs Act compel Apple to unlock the phone was not resolved by the courts, since the government on its own was able to access the information stored on the phone. A timeline of events can be found on the web page cited in the footnote.[98]

We now turn to issues regarding the search of a computer or cell phone. (See also discussion of warrantless searches of electronic devices at the border in Chapter 4.) The law in this area is emerging regarding the authority of the government to look at every file on a suspect's computer, a very sensitive topic given the fact that a computer's hard drive might hold a library's worth of private documents and materials of the suspect that may have nothing to do with the specific crime that the target is suspected of having committed. The issue arises in the context of search warrants that authorize the search for documents related to a particular crime such as material support of terrorism. Law enforcement may seize a suspect's computer in order to conduct the search based on a search warrant authorizing search for evidence of material support. Does that mean the FBI may examine every file/document for proof of terrorism? What if then evidence of child pornography is discovered? May it be used as evidence in a prosecution for possession of child pornography? The courts have begun to write doctrines that open the door to an examination of all the files/documents, with the understanding that targets may camouflage documents, and hence law enforcement needs the leeway to cursorily view all the documents to determine if they are related to the crime under investigation.[99] When other incriminating documents are "inadvertently" found or are in "plain view," these may be used to prosecute for, say, possession of child pornography.

How long law enforcement may retain a complete copy of a computer following the completion of a search remains unclear.[100] Also unsettled is the Fourth Amendment and the situation in which law enforcement temporarily takes a computer, makes a copy of the contents that is not examined but retained for possible query at a later date.[101]

98 https://www.digitaltrends.com/mobile/apple-encryption-court-order-news/.

99 *United States v Stabile*, 633 F3d 219 (3d Cir 2011); *United States v Williams*, 592 F3d 511 (4th Cir. 2010. Compare *United States v Carey*, 172 F3d 1268 (10th Cir. 1999). Consider *Andresen v Maryland*, 427 US 463 (1976); Office of Legal Education, *Searching and seizing computers and obtaining electronic evidence in criminal investigations*, 4–5 (cited in note 92).

100 *United States v Ganias*, 824 F3d 199 (2d Cir 2016).

101 Orin S. Kerr, *Fourth Amendment seizures of computer data*, 119 Yale L J 700 (2010).

VIII. Real time surveillance[102]

Real time surveillance such as a car following another car, a police officer trailing a suspect on the street, or video footage from surveillance cameras posted in public spaces, does not usually raise legal problems under the Fourth Amendment because the subjects are being watched in public spaces where the law does not recognize them as enjoying an expectation of privacy protected by the Fourth Amendment. For example, the Ninth Circuit upheld the use of evidence from a video taken of defendants illegally cultivating marijuana in a public forest where a video camera had been installed. "Our holding on this issue is quite narrow. Illegal activities conducted on government land open to the public which may be viewed by any passing visitor or law enforcement officer are not protected by the Fourth Amendment because there can be no reasonable expectation of privacy under such circumstances."[103] However, real time *electronic* surveillance is another kettle of fish.

This section will focus on electronic surveillance that is covered by the Fourth Amendment (*Katz v United States*, 389 US 347 (1967)). Federal statutes authorizing and regulating the federal government's use of this investigative technique are carefully constructed to take the Fourth Amendment into account, all the while recognizing the important governmental interest in carrying out such surveillance in order to enforce ordinary criminal law and protect domestic and national security.

Four sets of statutory provisions are taken up here. Two of the sets regulate the use of pen register/trap and trace surveillance devices for investigations. One set is used for foreign-connected terrorism only, FISA's 50 USC §§1841-1866, and the other is used for all categories of terrorism investigations, 18 USC §§3121-3127. The other two sets regulate the use of "wiretapping," FISA's 50 USC §§1801-1812 (foreign-connected investigations only), and Title III of the Omnibus Crime Control and Safe Streets Act of 1968, 18 USC §§2510-2522 (all categories of investigation). (See also the Communications Assistance for Law Enforcement Act, 47 USC §1001 et. seq.)

A. *Pen register/trap and trace (P/T)*

The pen register device "records or decodes dialing, routing, addressing, or signaling information transmitted by an instrument or facility from which a wire or electronic communication is transmitted." The trap and trace device "captures the incoming electronic or other impulses which identify the originating number or other dialing, routing, addressing, and signaling information reasonably likely to

102 This discussion omits wiretapping with consent of a party to the conversation, surveillance by providers of electronic communication services, intrafamilial surveillance, a review of the FISA court system, and state laws regarding electronic surveillance. The use of evidence obtained by electronic surveillance in a trial will be taken up in a later chapter.

103 *United States v McIver*, 186 F3d 1119 (9th Cir 1999). See, also, *United States v Gonzalez*, 328 F3d 543 (9th Cir 2003).

identify the source of a wire or electronic communication."[104] Thus according to these statutory definitions, P/T applies to the telephone and to other forms of electronic communication.

The statutory provisions regulating the use of P/T began by first laying down prohibitions against its use. Subsequently the statute creates an exception to the prohibition, namely, allowing governmental law enforcement surveillance efforts to use the P/T by obtaining a court order authorizing its installation and use.[105] Use of the P/T has been deemed to be consistent with the Fourth Amendment because, as noted, the Supreme Court said people do not have a reasonable expectation of privacy in the kind of metadata collected by these devices.[106] (Recall from Chapter 3 the bulk collection of metadata under §215 came under constitutional attack, and §215 was also amended by Congress.)

The government's use of P/T must be relevant to an ongoing criminal investigation, and the order authorizing the P/T must specify the offense committed to which the information relates.[107] There is also an emergency P/T statutory provision for proceeding without a prior court order when there is an immediate danger of death or serious bodily injury, or an immediate threat to national security.[108] A judicial order needs to be obtained within 48 hours after installation of the P/T; if not, the surveillance must stop.

P/T authorization allows FBI agents to monitor from their offices a target's online activities on an Internet provider's network.[109] [Until 2005 the FBI used a tool called Carnivore, which they dropped in favor of commercial products for eavesdropping on a target's network traffic.[110]] P/T technology obtains metadata regarding a suspect's email and websites visited. Law enforcement has also relied on P/T to obtain a court order to install a "mirror port" on an Internet service provider that allows that government to learn the to/from addresses of the suspect's email messages, the IP addresses of websites visited, and the volume of information sent to and from the account.[111] Courts have rejected the Fourth Amendment claims of criminal defendants challenging the use of pen registers and the collection of their metadata stored in the computers of telecommunication companies.[112]

104 18 USC 3127(3) and (4).

105 18 USC 3122.

106 *Smith v Maryland* (cited in note 34).

107 18 USC §3122.

108 18 USC §3125.

109 http://computer.howstuffworks.com/carnivore1.html.

110 https://www.schneier.com/blog/archives/2005/01/fbi_retires_car.html.

111 The clear trend in the cases is to deny Fourth Amendment protection for IPs: *United States v Ulbricht*, 858 F3d 71 (2d Cir 2017); United *States v Caira*, 833 F3d 803 (7th Cir 2016); *United States v Wheelock*, 772 F3d 825, 829 (8th Cir 2014); *United States v Christie*, 624 F3d 558 (3d Cir 2010); *United States v Perrine*, 518 F3d 1196 (10th Cir. 2008); *United States v Forrester*, 495 F3d 1041 (9th Cir 2007).

112 See, for example, *United States v Moalin*, Crim. No. 10-4246, 2013 WL 6079518 *5-8 (SD Cal. Nov 18, 2013) (holding that bulk telephony metadata collection does not violate Fourth

These statutory provisions intersect with FISA provisions in so far as §3121 allows the use of P/T when it has been authorized under FISA. FISA 50 USC §1842 authorizes the Attorney General to apply to a FISA court for an application to institute P/T surveillance in order to obtain foreign intelligence information – not information concerning a U.S. person – and to protect against international terrorism (defined in 50 USC §1801(c)) or clandestine activities that U.S. persons could be engaged in. Again, this FISA provision opens the door to issuing the order relying, at least in part, on activities protected by the First Amendment.[113]

The two P/T laws have similarities and differences not reviewed here.

B. "Wiretapping"

Turning now to one of the most intrusive of all investigative techniques – electronic surveillance designed to acquire in real time the actual content of communications. A variety of techniques are covered by the law, old-fashioned telephone wiretapping, bugging a room, all without the consent of either party to the communication. The government remotely and surreptitiously can turn on a computer's webcam and microphone, and activate a cell phone in order to eavesdrop.[114] The two sets of statutes noted above (FISA's 50 USC §1801 and Title III) differ in greater respect from each other than the two sets of P/T laws, largely because of the different constitutional requirements applicable to criminal versus foreign intelligence investigations. Title III expressly notes the possibility of FBI agents using FISA.[115]

To use FISA the government must meet specific requirements (50 USC §§1804, 1805, 1881a, 1881b, 1881c). [The book cited in the footnote describes the FISA application process for obtaining authority to engage in electronic surveillance or a physical search.[116]] To obtain a surveillance order, a federal officer with the approval of the Attorney General must submit an application to a FISA court. If the target is a U.S. person the application must identify the target, provide facts to justify the belief *that the target is a foreign power or agent of a foreign power*, describe the facilities that will be used by the target, specify that the information sought is foreign intelligence, and that collecting *foreign intelligence* is "a significant purpose" of the surveillance. Although FISA must be used to collect foreign intelligence, it may also serve the primary purpose of obtaining evidence of ordinary crime. (See Chapter 3

Amendment); *United States v Forrester*, 512 F3d 500, 510 (9th Cir 2008) (no Fourth Amendment rights in IP addresses); *United States v Fregoso*, 60 F3d 1314, 1321 (8th Cir 1995) (stored telephone records and subscriber information not protected). But see *Carpenter v United States*, No. 16-402 (U.S. June 22, 2018) (slip opinion) (Fourth Amendment violated when seven days' cell site location information was collected without the issuance of warrant based on probable cause.)

113 50 USC §1842.

114 https://www.wired.com/2014/03/webcams-mics/; https://www.theverge.com/2013/8/1/4580718/fbi-can-remotely-activate-android-and-laptop-microphones-reports-wsj.

115 18 USC §2511(2)(e) and (f).

116 Dycus, Berney, Banks, Raven-Hansen, Vladeck, *National security law*, at 647–651 (cited in note 67).

and "the wall.") In fact, the evidence may be collected in a coordinated NSA and FBI investigation, and then with notice to the defendant, may be used in a criminal proceeding (50 USC §1806).

The two primary probable cause findings the court needs to make are that the target is an agent of or actually is a foreign power, and that the targeted facilities will be used by the target. The other claims by the government simply need be not clearly erroneous (50 USC §1805(e)).

FISA permits the targeting of lone wolves (individuals *who are not working* on behalf of a foreign power) only if they are not U.S. persons. The lone wolf must, however, be engaged in "international terrorism" (discussed below). The lone wolf not engaged in "international terrorism" would be covered by Title III, taken up below.

As noted, FISA can't be used to wiretap U.S. persons acting as lone wolves. To use FISA on a U.S. person, that person must, among other things, be acting *on behalf of* a foreign power, e.g., a group engaged in international terrorism. (See 50 USC §1801(a) and (b).) "On behalf of" is an important term not defined in FISA, but might mean at the order of, at the request of, or under the direction of the group. (See 22 USC §611(c)(1).)

The terms "foreign intelligence," "foreign agent," and "foreign power" refer to and rely on the concept of "international terrorism" defined as "violent acts or acts dangerous to human life that . . . appear to be intended . . . to influence the policy of a government by intimidation or coercion . . . and occur totally outside the United States, or transcend national boundaries in terms of the means by which they are accomplished."[117] Free speech activities may in part be the basis for the court's order if there is probable cause that the target is an agent of a foreign power or a foreign power.[118]

> Incidentally, FISA also authorizes the Attorney General to undertake without a prior court order electronic surveillance in an emergency (as does Title III) followed not later than 7 days later by a request for authorization.[119]

Although FISA has to serve a foreign intelligence purpose, if the surveillance turns up evidence of a crime, §1806 lays out the procedures for use of the information in a criminal trial. The Attorney General must authorize its use and the government must notify the defendant of the evidence that will be offered.

While turning to FISA may be an attractive option, it may not be legally available if the FISA requirements noted earlier cannot be satisfied. The only option then is to turn to the even more demanding Title III which can be used for domestic and foreign connected terrorism, lone wolves, and unprivileged enemy belligerents.

117 50 USC §1801(c).
118 50 USC §1805(a)(2)(A).
119 50 USC §1805(e) and (f).

When Title III is the applicable statutory scheme regarding the acquisition of the *contents* (18 USC §2510(8)) of a communication by means of a device in real time, what are the requirements the FBI must satisfy in order to obtain a Title III authorization? The purpose of the authorized interception must be to obtain evidence regarding a specific set of criminal offenses listed in the statute.[120] The list of items that the FBI must provide information about, and the findings that the judge must make in a Title III authorization, is long and includes the following: (i) finding probable cause for the belief that the target is committing, has committed, or is about to commit one of the relevant crimes; (ii) probable cause for the belief that the types of communication that have been identified for interception concerning the offense(s) will be obtained through interception at the identified facility; (iii) probable cause that the targeted facilities are used or will be used in connection with the crime; and (iv) other techniques were tried first and failed, or would have been likely to fail.[121] Furthermore, U.S. Attorneys are guided by this statement:

> In *United States v Donovan*, 429 US 413, 422-32 (1977), the Supreme Court held that 18 USC §2518(1)(b)(iv) requires the government to name all individuals whom it has probable cause to believe are engaged in the offenses under investigation, and whose conversations it expects to intercept over or from within the targeted facilities. It is the Criminal Division's policy to name as subjects *all* persons whose involvement in the alleged offenses is indicated, even if not all those persons are expected to be intercepted over the target facility or at the target location.[122]

Title III also has some serious "particularization" requirements.[123] The FBI must provide "details" regarding the crimes at stake; it must provide a "particular description" of the facilities where the interception will take place. A "particular" description of the communications to be intercepted also has to be provided. All previous applications for authorization have to be noted. The duration of the interception is limited to 30 days, and renewals basically require a new application and may also be only for 30 days. Title III requires that the interception be carried out in a way that minimizes the interception of communications not otherwise subject to interception.[124]

To underscore a point made above, a judge considering a Title III application must determine that there is probable cause for belief in the four items noted above,

120 18 USC §2516(1)(c). The relevant crimes are listed in the statute many of which could be crimes people motivated by a terrorist agenda may seek to commit.

121 18 USC §2518.

122 https://www.justice.gov/usam/criminal-resource-manual-28-electronic-surveillance-title-iii-applications.

123 18 USC §2518.

124 Id.

which is a far more demanding hurdle than under FISA. [Title III also has provision for an emergency wiretap without prior court approval.[125]]

1. *Roving surveillance*

A special problem the FBI has had to face is when the subject moves about using different phones owned by different people, or who uses disposable cell phones. To deal with this problem Title III (18 USC §2518(11) (a) and (b)) establishes an exception to the usual requirement that there be "a particular description of the nature and location of the facilities from which or the place where the communication is to be intercepted." To obtain this exception certain things have to be established, e.g., the target's actions have the effect of thwarting interception from a specified facility. In contrast to the ordinary Title III application, these roving applications place an emphasis on the identity of the person who is the target, as opposed to the facility to be targeted. A consequence of this exception is the FBI, in wiretapping the target, may "tap phones in the homes and offices of friends, relatives, and business associates visited by a suspect, despite the Fourth Amendment's requirement that the government specify with particularity the person or place to be searched."[126]

> FISA also authorizes the roving wiretap (50 USC §1805(c)(2)(B)) so as to allow continuous surveillance of the FISA target who moves from one phone to another. The requirements for getting a FISA roving wiretap are the same as for ordinary FISA surveillance, but when the roving wiretap is justified because the target may thwart identification, the FISA court can order assistance from various people.

2. *Computer hacking*

As noted in the P/T discussion, the FBI has been able to track Internet usage in real time. Monitoring real time computer usage also is possible with additional tools. Reports have leaked of the FBI remotely installing a key logger on a suspect's computer that records keystrokes, web browsing history, usernames, and passwords.[127] Another tool was able to collect a computer's IP and MAC address, a list of open ports, installed software, the last URL visited by the machine, and the usernames of people logged in. In an investigation of consumers of child pornography, the FBI used a technique called network investigative technique (NIT) that embedded malware in the computers of those people who visited a child pornography site

125 18 USC §2518(7).

126 Cole and Dempsey, *Terrorism and the Constitution*, at 169 (cited in note 97).

127 Kim Setter, *Everything we know about how the FBI hacks people* (Wired, May 15, 2016), archived at https://www.wired.com/2016/05/history-fbis-hacking.

thereby enabling the FBI to learn the IP the subscribers were attempting to keep private.[128]

IX. Real time tracking and cell phones

In 1983 the Supreme Court held in *United States v Knotts*, 460 US 276 (1983), that following a suspect by means of a beeper tracking device, without a warrant, was not a search under the Fourth Amendment. [Significantly, the beeper had been placed inside a drum of chemicals not owned by the defendant, which the defendant was transporting.] In reaching this conclusion Justice Blackmun said there was a lower expectation of privacy on public thoroughfares where both the vehicle and occupants were in plain view; thus there was no privacy to be protected as one moved from one place to another. The Court also significantly noted that the Fourth Amendment did not prohibit the technological enhancement of the police's natural sensory abilities.[129]

Not long after GPS tracking devices came into use, they inevitably came to be used by law enforcement to track suspects. In 2012 the Supreme Court ruled on the use of these devices in the absence of a warrant. A unanimous Court concluded that the use of a GPS device physically attached to the criminal defendant's vehicle for 28 days without a warrant was a violation of the Fourth Amendment.[130] While that much about the decision is clear, law enforcement and citizens alike are left with many unanswered questions regarding future applications of the case. These questions arise because of difficulty interpreting what is dubbed "the opinion of the Court," and the fact that a concurrence by four justices, while agreeing that the Fourth Amendment was violated, agreed for a very different reason than that expressed in the opinion of the Court. Furthermore, Justice Sotomayor authored her own concurring opinion, which, while not rejecting the analysis of the opinion of the Court, offered additional arguments and speculations.

Here are several questions not yet answered as of this writing. The opinion of the Court emphasized the point that there was a trespass when the GPS device was attached to a car the *defendant owned*; hence, under its view of the Fourth Amendment, this was a material fact in concluding there was a Fourth Amendment violation. But what if the GPS device were a factory-installed device on the vehicle that could be remotely turned on, allowing the suspect to be tailed for 28 days? The concurrence of Justice Alito would seem to suggest this would be a search,

128 See Orin Kerr, *Government "hacking" and the playpen search warrant* (Washington Post, September 27, 2016), archived at https://www.washingtonpost.com/news/volokh-conspiracy/wp/2016/09/27/government-hacking-and-the-playpen-search-warrant/?utm_term=.521c18; *United States v Matish*, 2016 WL 354776 (ED Va June 1, 2016). Compare *United States v Grubbs*, 547 US 90 (2006) (anticipatory warrant).

129 Compare *Kyllo v United States*, 533 US 27 (2001) (finding that the use of thermal imaging to detect heat lamps inside a house to be a search).

130 *United States v Jones*, 132 S Ct 945 (2012).

but only four Justices signed this opinion. Next, what if the vehicle the suspect was driving belonged to his spouse and s/he had consented to the attachment of the GPS, or perhaps did not consent, not being aware of what the FBI was up to? If the vehicle were jointly owned, could a spouse's consent avoid the Fourth Amendment problem?[131] Would there be a violation of the Fourth Amendment if the FBI remotely turned on the suspect's cell phone with its built-in GPS, thereby tracking the comings-and-goings of the suspect? Will it matter in the future how long the tracking went on? Justice Sotomayor suggested that even a short-term use of the GPS raised privacy problems because of the precision with which a person's travels could be pinned down.

> GPS monitoring generates a precise, comprehensive record of a person's public movements that reflects a wealth of detail about her familial, political, professional, religious, and sexual associations. See, e.g., *People v Weaver*, 12 N. Y. 3d 433, 441–442, 909 N. E. 2d 1195, 1199 (2009) ("Disclosed in [GPS] data . . . will be trips the indisputably private nature of which takes little imagination to conjure: trips to the psychiatrist, the plastic surgeon, the abortion clinic, the AIDS treatment center, the strip club, the criminal defense attorney, the by-the-hour motel, the union meeting, the mosque, synagogue or church, the gay bar and on and on.") The Government can store such records and efficiently mine them for information years into the future.[132]

The technologically-savvy law enforcement agency has more than GPS device with which to track suspects. There is also a cell site simulator, or IMSI catcher, also called a "StingRay," the product name of a particular company. ["Triggerfish" is another term used for these devices.] This is how they work:

> Wireless carriers provide coverage through a network of base stations, also called cell sites, that connect wireless devices to the regular telephone network. Cell phones periodically identify themselves to the base station that has the strongest radio signal, which is often, but not always, the nearest base station. A cell phone automatically transmits to the base station "signaling data," which includes the phone's unique numeric identifier, as well as its cell site code, which identifies its location. An IMSI catcher masquerades as a wireless carrier's base station, thereby prompting cell phones to communicate with it as though it were actually the carrier's base station. The equipment consists of "an antenna, an electronic device that processes the signals transmitted on cell phone frequencies, and a laptop computer that analyzes the signals and allows

131 Compare *United States v Matlock*, 415 US 164 (1974) (third party who shared a house with defendant consented to the search, which was held to be lawful).

132 *United States v Jones*, at 955 (Sotomayor, J. concurring) (cited in note 131).

> the agent to configure the collection of information." It "can be carried by hand or mounted on vehicles or even drones."[133]

Law enforcement on the streets or overhead in a helicopter with an IMSI catcher can, when it has the cell phone's unique numeric identifier, find its location, and track the user as he or she moves about making phone calls. Working the other way around, if the FBI knows the suspect's location the device can determine the unique numeric identifier. And the device can capture the content of both aural calls and text messages.[134]

If the StingRay were to be used for grabbing the content of cell phone communications, either approval pursuant to Title III or FISA would be required, a point that the Department of Justice concedes.[135] The remote turning on of cell phones to convert them into broadcasting devices triggers the same legal concerns.

A question that has roiled the courts is the use of the StingRay as a tracking device. There are two dimensions to the controversy – the prospective collection of location data (real time collection) and the collection of stored cell phone location data. The real time collection of location data of course leads back to the meaning of the Supreme Court's GPS decision just discussed and the 2018 decision of the Court regarding the collection of stored cell site location information discussed above.

The acquisition in real time of a subject's location based on his or her cell phone may or may not be obtainable by the government trying to get authorization to use P/T.[136] This authorization is not for the issuance of a warrant; hence the question arises as to whether collection under the P/T, or possibly collection even without any court authorization, violates the Fourth Amendment. There are two ways the question could be answered. One way is to say location data are a form of metadata voluntarily disclosed, and therefore the *Smith v Maryland* decision discussed above is applicable, i.e., the data do not enjoy Fourth Amendment protection. Then one would have to argue that the GPS case *United States v Jones* did not apply.[137] The Sixth Circuit Court of Appeals upheld the collection of real time location data.[138] Note the same issue arose in connection with the collection of historical (stored) cell site location data, discussed earlier.

133 Linda Lye, *Stingrays – The most common surveillance tool the government won't tell you about*, 2 (ACLU of Northern California, June 27, 2014), archived at https://www.aclunc.org/sites/default/files/StingRays_The_Most_ Common_Surveillance_Tool_the_Govt_Won%27t_Tell_You_About_0.pdf.

134 Id at 2–3.

135 *Electronic surveillance manual*, 41 (Department of Justice, Criminal Division June 2005), archived at http://www.justice.gov/criminal/foia/docs/elec-sur-manual.pdf.

136 *In re Application for Pen Register and Trap/Trace Device with Cell Site Location Authority*, 396 F Supp. 2d 747 (SD Tex 2005) (P/T may not be used); *United States v Espudo*, 954 F Supp 2d 1029 (SD Cal 2013) (P/T may be used).

137 *Tracey v Florida*, 152 So 3d 504, 529 (Fla. 2014) (Canady J., dissenting).

138 *United States v Skinner*, 690 F3d 772 (6th Cir 2012), cert. denied, 133 S. Ct. 2851 (2013).

The second way to answer the question is to rely heavily on the Supreme Court's decision in the GPS case *United States v Jones*, at the same time distinguishing it from *Smith v Maryland*. This was the approach taken by the majority in *Tracy v Florida*.

> Simply because the cell phone user knows or should know that his cell phone gives off signals that enable the service provider to detect its location for call routing purposes, and which enable cell phone applications to operate for navigation, weather reporting, and other purposes, does not mean that the user is consenting to use of that location information by third parties for any other unrelated purposes. While a person may voluntarily convey personal information to a business or other entity for personal purposes, such disclosure cannot reasonably be considered to be disclosure for all purposes to third parties not involved in that transaction. . . . It is true that a cell phone user can prevent locational signals from being used for tracking purposes by turning off the cell phone, thus concealing the signals and the location of the user. However, we do not find that such concealment is a necessary predicate to the Fourth Amendment claim presented under the facts of this case. We have previously recognized that in addition to using cell phones to make telephone calls, "a significant portion of our population relies upon cell phones for communications, text-messaging information, scheduling, and banking." . . . Requiring a cell phone user to turn off the cell phone just to assure privacy from governmental intrusion that can reveal a detailed and intimate picture of the user's life places an unreasonable burden on the user to forego necessary use of his cell phone, a device now considered essential by much of the populace.[139]

Also relevant in resolving the issue will be the Supreme Court's decision in *Carpenter v United States*, discussed earlier. Recall the Court ruled in that case that collecting a person's historical CSLI for a period of seven days or more is a Fourth Amendment search and therefore required a search warrant.

139 *Tracey v Florida*, at 522 (cited in note 138). See, also, *Jones v United States*, No. 15-CF-322, 1 (DC September 21, 2017).

7

THE TRIAL

Once the FBI has the information in hand the U.S. attorneys can begin the process of actually mounting a prosecution. This chapter turns to the prosecutorial effort, specifically, the trial. While reading, keep in mind that not all terrorism is carried out in the name of radical-political Islam; for example, in early 2018 Taylor Michael Wilson, a white supremacist, was charged with terrorist-related crimes directed toward a railroad carrier.[1] Accordingly, the crimes discussed here may be perpetrated domestic terrorists, foreign-connected terrorists, and those who might also be designated unprivileged enemy belligerents (see Chapter 8).

Prosecution may be undertaken for the usual reason that the accused committed a serious crime, but it may be pursued for two other reasons: as part of a disruption strategy to prevent the defendant from engaging in a more serious crime in the future, and also as an Al Capone strategy, i.e., prosecuting for lesser crime X in the face of an inability to prosecute for a much more serious crime that the individual is suspected of committing.

This chapter will not address some topics that are legally, politically, and morally important, for example, the decision of whether to prosecute or seek deportation; the indictment; pretrial detainment (including solitary confinement); plea bargaining; the details regarding sentencing and enhancement of sentences for a felony intended to promote terrorism;[2] the imposition of "special administrative measures,"[3] and

1 Bill Chappell, Alleged white supremacist is charged with terrorism after stopping Amtrak train (NPR January 5, 2018), archived at https://www.npr.org/sections/thetwo-way/2018/01/05/575960858/alleged-white-supremacist-is-charged-with-terrorism-after-stopping-amtrak-train.

2 18 USC §3553; USSG §3A1.4; *United States v Wright*, 747 F.3d 399 (6th Cir 2014); Wadie E. Said, *Sentencing terrorist crimes*, 75 Ohio S L J 477 (2014).

3 28 CFR §501.3.

conditions of the imprisonment. Chapters 8 and 9 however, will take up military detainment interrogation, forced feeding, and prosecution by a military commission.

I. Terrorism and federal crimes: a general overview

A wide range of criminal statutes are relevant to the prosecution of terrorists; some mention "terrorism" and some do not.[4] When the statute does not mention terrorism conviction under the statute does not require, for example, a need to prove an intent to intimidate or coerce the government. Ordinary murder is considered a state crime; however, Section 1111 of Title 18 gets close when it declares that murder in the first degree includes unlawful killing with malice aforethought, which is willful, malicious, and premeditated, or intending to commit treason, espionage, or sabotage. Other federal statutes touching on murder focus on murder directed at specific kinds of people (federal, state or local officials); murder conducted in the course of an activity such as aircraft hijacking; killing involved in the destruction of an aircraft, a railroad, or government property; murder in certain locations such as an international airport or in a government facility. These crimes are capital offenses.[5] Other statutes, too numerous to list, address, among other things, destruction of aircraft and other property, using weapons of mass destruction, and destruction of infrastructure.[6]

There are, of course, other ordinary crimes that may be committed as part of a terrorist agenda, such as robbing a bank, engaging in drug dealing to obtain money, illegally transporting explosives across state lines (18 USC §§842, 844), or other crimes involved in the transportation of firearms (18 USC §922). Add to these the crimes of money laundering, conspiracy, document fraud, illegal possession of a weapon, dealing with controlled substances, and extortion and ransom demands.

Domestic hate groups, anarchists, special interest extremists, or revolutionaries may be prosecuted for some of the crimes listed above in addition to hate crimes under 18 USC §249. Section 43 of Title 18 criminalizes damaging or interfering with an "animal enterprise," which is a law that is directed toward extreme animal liberation organizations. Eco-terrorists may end up being charged with arson, or, in the case of tree spiking, with the use of a hazardous device on federal land.[7] Other laws aim to thwart terrorism by regulating, for example, the sale and purchase of ammonium nitrate.[8] Bribery to commit terrorism related to port security is a

4 *Terrorist Trial Report Card*, Appendix-Table of Statutes 64 (Center on L and Security New York University, January 2010), archived at http://www.lawandsecurity.org/wp-content/uploads/2011/09/02_TTRCFinalJan1422009.pdf; 18 USC §2384, seditious conspiracy, was used in prosecuting Abdel Rahman, a blind Islamic scholar and cleric. *United States v Rahman*, 189 F3d 88 (2d Cir 1999).

5 41 federal capital offenses, archived at https://deathpenalty.procon.org/view.resource.php?resourceID=004927.

6 Federal terrorism charges, archived at https://www.harriscarmichael.com/federal-terrorism-charges. The items in the list in the text are taken from 18 USC 2332b(g)(5).

7 18 USC §844 and §1864.

8 6 USC §488a, 18 USC §1001, §1028.

crime. 18 USC §226 and §2331. And, of course, suspects can be charged with aiding and abetting, conspiracy, and providing false information. Witnesses are under legal pressure not to violate the federal statute criminalizing the failure to report a crime.[9]

The items listed above are not necessarily terrorism crimes, but if the prosecutor proves the commission of the crime and proves the accused "calculated to influence or affect the conduct of government by intimidation or coercion, or to retaliate against government conduct," then the crime is a "federal crime of terrorism."[10] When the crime falls into this category, the sentence on conviction may be enhanced beyond what it would have been had the crime been committed without the purpose of influencing the government.[11] Other crimes not officially classified as federal terrorist crimes might also involve enhanced sentencing following the sentencing hearing if the judge concludes that the crime was committed with the intent to intimidate or coerce the government.[12]

Another statute deals with "crimes of terrorism that transcend national boundaries" (18 USC §2332b) covering conduct that occurs outside the U.S. "in addition to the conduct occurring in the United States." Hence, this law could be used to prosecute the killing, maiming, assaulting, and kidnapping of any person within the U.S. when the execution of the crime has connections outside the U.S.

Before turning to the important provisions that criminalize material support for terrorism, here is a list of some of the many other ways terrorism figures into federal statutes.

- As noted in Chapter 6, when the FBI designates an investigation of an individual as involving domestic terrorism can be the predicate for expanding the investigation into an enterprise investigation.
- Under the Federal Rules of Criminal Procedure, Rule 41(b), in an investigation of domestic or international terrorism a judge may issue a warrant for persons or property within *or without* the district of the judge.
- Forfeiture of assets may happen to any individual or organization engaged in planning or perpetrating any federal crime of terrorism. 18 USC §981(g). Seizure is possible prior to conviction, based on a finding of probable cause that it is subject to forfeiture.
- The Internal Revenue Service may share taxpayer information with the FBI. 26 USC §6103(i)(3)(C).
- Disclosure of financial information. 12 USC §3414.
- The usual statute of limitations for a noncapital offense is extended from five to eight years. 18 USC §3286(a).

9 18 USC §4; 18 USC §1512(b)(3).
10 18 USC 2332b(g)(5)(A). See, also, *United States v Awan*, 607 F.3d 306 (2d Cir 2010).
11 Wadie E. Said, *Sentencing terrorist crimes*, 499 (cited in note 2).
12 Id at 500–501.

- There is no statute of limitation for a domestic terrorism crime if the offense resulted in, or created a foreseeable risk of death or serious bodily harm to another. 18 USC §3286(b).
- Pretrial detention is more likely. 18 USC §§3142(f)(1)(A) and (g)(1).
- The Attorney General may seek a court order requiring disclosure of education records relevant to an authorized investigation into one of the offenses listed in §2332b(g). 20 USC §1232g.
- Denying access to dangerous biological agents and toxins to people reasonably suspected of being involved in domestic or international terrorism. 42 USC §262a(e)(2)(D).[13]

In addition, see Chapter 4 regarding the granting of visas and the removal of alleged terrorists, and Chapter 5 regarding the placement of individuals on the No Fly and Selectee Lists.

II. Material support

The statutory provisions that have been frequently and successfully used in efforts to prosecute suspected terrorists are those that make it a crime to provide material support, 18 USC §2339A and in the case of terrorists or terrorist organizations, 18 USC §2339B. These statutes are anticipatory crimes such as conspiracy and attempt, but may be easier to prove. The material support statutes are at the heart of the FBI's forward leaning posture to prevent terrorism rather than waiting for it to occur.

Shown schematically, §2339A criminalizes providing support as follows:

Whoever
[knowingly]
  attempts to
  conspires to, or
  actually
provides material support or resources, or
conceals or disguises the
  nature of material support or resources,
  location of material support or resources,
  source of material support or resources, or
  ownership of material support or resources
knowing or intending that they be used
  in preparation for,
  in carrying out,
  in preparation for concealment or an escape from, or

13 See, also, Nicholas J. Perry, *The numerous federal legal definitions of terrorism: The problem of too many grails*, 30 J of Leg 249, 257 (2004).

in carrying out the concealment of an escape from an offense identified as a federal crime of terrorism.[14]

This provision could be likened to a form of a terrorism aiding and abetting statute.[15] Note the "mens rea" component of the statute – "knowing" or "intending" – an element of the crime that requires ingenuity to prove.

§2339B is different in that it does not address aiding and abetting a specific crime, but instead addresses providing material support to an organization designated as a "foreign terrorist organization (FTO)." The idea is that these organizations are themselves tainted by their criminal conduct, thus any contribution to the organization facilitates that conduct.[16] [Designation is governed by federal law that empowers the Secretary of State to make the designation according to a prescribed procedure, 8 USC §1189(a)(1). As of this writing there are approximately 60 designated foreign terrorist organizations listed on the Department of State's website.]

§2339B opens to criminal conviction:

Whoever
knowingly
  attempts to provide
  conspires to provide, or
  provides
material support or resources
to a foreign terrorist organization[17]
knowing that the organization
  has been designated a foreign terrorist organization, or
  engages or has engaged, in "terrorism" or "terrorist activity."

Each element listed can be and has been debated and often litigated in order to avoid "false positives" and to address unconstitutional vagueness.[18] Note the requirement of "knowing" the organization refers to a designated foreign terrorist organization.

14 Charles Doyle, *Terrorist material support: An overview of 18 USC §2339A and §2339B* 2 (Congressional Research Service, December 8, 2016) R41333) (a thorough analysis of the two sections).

15 Richard B. Zabel and James J. Benjamin, Jr., *In pursuit of justice: Prosecuting terrorism cases in the federal courts*, 26 (Human Rights First, May 2008), archived at https://www.humanrightsfirst.org/wp-content/uploads/pdf/080521-USLS-pursuit-justice.pdf.

16 Id at 34.

17 Section 1189 of Title 8 authorizes the Secretary of State to designate organizations as FTOs. To date there are approximately 60 entities on the list. Assets of an FTO in the US may be ordered frozen. An entity with presence in the US must be given notice of and an opportunity to be heard prior to the designation. An organization listed as an FTO may appeal the designation to the DC Circuit Court of Appeals. The FTO does not get to see the classified evidence used to designate it, and judicial review of the designation is deferential.

18 See, for example, *United States v Al-Arian*, 308 F Supp 2d 1322 (MD Fla 2004).

The elements of §§2339A and 2339B overlap with the definition of unprivileged enemy combatant discussed in Chapter 8.

The inherent sweep of what they criminalize, and the fact that the statutes have extraterritorial application, i.e., are not limited to application only within the U.S., adds to their potency.[19] The sweep of what §§2339A and 2339B criminalize can be explored by looking more closely at a few selected aspects of the provisions. What counts in both sections as "material resources" is defined in the statute as follows:

> [T]he term "material support or resources" means any property, tangible or intangible, or service, including currency or monetary instruments or financial securities, financial services, lodging, training, expert advice or assistance, safehouses, false documentation or identification, communications equipment, facilities, weapons, lethal substances, explosives, personnel (one or more individuals who may be or include oneself), and transportation, except medicine or religious materials.[20]

The term "training" as used in the provision means "instruction or teaching designed to impart a specific skill, as opposed to general knowledge." And "expert advice or assistance" must be advice or assistance derived from scientific, technical, or other specialized knowledge.

The statute requires "knowingly" providing material support to an FTO, but does not specify that the accused intended to further the FTO's terrorist activities. The Supreme Court has said all the statute requires is knowledge regarding the FTO's connection to terrorism, not a specific intent to further the FTO's terrorist activities.[21] (See the discussion of *Holder v Humanitarian Law Project* below.)

Note that the word "personnel" in the definition of "material resources" can include the accused themselves; thus a suspect who seeks terrorist training may be charged under the provisions. In fact, prosecution of individuals who have attempted to obtain or who have undergone terrorist training is a standard example of a basis for prosecution pursuant to these provisions.[22]

But the laws have reached further. Noor Salman, the wife of the Orlando killer, Omar Mateen, was herself indicated for violating §2339B by aiding and abetting her husband, based on the incorrect allegation that she accompanied her husband when he canvassed potential targets for his attack. (She was ultimately found not guilty.[23])

19 18 USC §2339B(d); Doyle, *Terrorist material support: An overview of 18 USC §2339A and §2339B*, at 11 (cited in note 14).

20 18 USC §2339A.

21 *Holder v Humanitarian Law Project*, 561 US 1 (2010). Compare *Scales v United States*, 367 US 203 (1961).

22 *United States v Mehanna*, 735 F3d 32 (1st Cir 2013); *United States v Faris*, 388 F3d 452 (4th Cir 2004); *United States v Goba*, 240 F Supp2d 242 (WD NY 2003) ("Lakawanna Six" Prosecution).

23 Patricia Mazzei, *Noor Salmon acquitted in Pulse nightclub shooting* (New York Times March 30, 2018), archived at https://www.nytimes.com/2018/03/30/us/noor-salman-pulse-trial-verdict.html.

In another case, Fahad Hashmi pled guilty after being prosecuted for letting another man who had "military gear" (a raincoat, poncho, waterproof socks) stay in his apartment, for letting him use his cell phone, for loaning him $300 to purchase a ticket to Pakistan, and for delivering his luggage to a member of al-Qaeda.[24] A doctor who provided medical services (as opposed to medicine, which is not covered) was convicted of providing material support and sentenced to 25 years in prison.[25] In another case, money that flowed to Palestinian charities, charities that the government claimed carried out the social programs of Hamas, was the basis for a conviction. The idea behind the prosecution was that the money was fungible, and hence money for the charity freed up funds that Hamas could use for terrorism.[26] Almost needless to say, most of these prosecutions and convictions are deeply controversial.

The statutes have also been used to pull in activities that are arguably protected by the First Amendment. The discussion of the controversies surrounding these applications of the provisions must begin with the Supreme Court's decision in *Holder v Humanitarian Law Project*.[27] The plaintiffs in this case trained members of a listed terrorist organization in how to use humanitarian and international law peacefully to resolve disputes; advocated politically on behalf of Kurds who lived in Turkey; taught members of the organization how to petition, for example, the United Nations for relief; and offered legal expertise in negotiating peace agreements. Fearing prosecution under §2339B, the plaintiffs sought a preliminary injunction against enforcement of the statute, claiming the law was unconstitutional as it applied to them. But the Supreme Court ruled against them saying that Congress constitutionally could outlaw the form of speech in which they engaged despite the First Amendment. The government had a compelling state interest to suppress terrorism, and the form of assistance here freed resources of the listed organizations to service illicit activities. A ruling for them would have lent legitimacy to the organization, and could strain diplomatic relations with the countries against whom the organization's terrorist activities might be directed.

Seeking an indictment and conviction when much of the evidence relied on consists merely of political statements by the accused, raises complex First Amendment problems. The Supreme Court in the *Holder* case said that §2339B only "reached material support *coordinated with or under the direction of* [italics added] a designated foreign terrorist organization. Independent advocacy that might be viewed as promoting the group's legitimacy is not covered." After finding §2339B constitutional after the "balancing" it did in this case, the Court also said it was not suggesting "that a regulation of independent speech would pass constitutional

24 Human Rights Watch, *Illusion of justice*, 67–69 (Human Rights Institute, Columbia Law School, July 2014), archived at https://www.hrw.org/report/2014/07/21ti/illusion-justice/human-rights-abuses-us-terrorism-prosecutions.

25 *United States v Farhane*, 634 F 3d 127 (2d Cir 2011).

26 Human Rights Watch, *Illusion of justice*, at 66 (cited in note 24).

27 561 US 1 (2010).

muster, even if the Government were to show that such speech benefits foreign terrorist organizations." Given these pronouncements, how might a court and jury use and weigh strong pro-terrorism statements by the accused submitted in evidence in a prosecution?

This question arose in *United States v Mehanna.*[28] Mehanna was convicted of violating both of the material support statutes, based partly on evidence that he had traveled to Yemen, presumably to obtain training in terrorism. An important part of the supporting evidence were statements Mehanna had made, testified to by conspirators, saying that he believed that engaging in jihad was a Muslim's duty, and that America was at war with Islam. In his failed attempts to get his conviction overturned, he argued that these comments were uncoordinated, pure political speech, and as such protected by the First Amendment. In the petition for a writ of certiorari, Mehanna said the question to be decided was whether his advocacy, "which the government conceded was *not* done at the direction of, or in any interchange with a [foreign terrorist organization], is material support." Phrased thusly, the question was misleading, since his statements were not by themselves the basis of his conviction, but were used as evidence to support the conclusion that his trip to Yemen was motivated by a desire to obtain terrorist training. The First Circuit, in upholding Mehanna's conviction, said the jury was entitled to see his comments as evidence of a scheme to obtain training and join al-Qaeda. Furthermore, there was other evidence buttressing that conclusion, e.g., emails of Mehanna that talked about the trip. Thus it seems that uncoordinated political speech could be used as part of evidence supporting his conviction under §2339B.

Another dimension of the case raises another First Amendment issue. The First Circuit noted Mehanna "began to translate Arab-language materials into English and post his translations on a website – at-Tibyan – that comprised an online community for those sympathetic to al-Qa'ida and Salafi-jihadi forums . . . [S]ome of the offerings that the defendant translated constituted al-Qa'ida-generated media and materials supportive of al-Qa'ida and/or jihad." The First Circuit was faced with a challenge regarding the district judge's jury instructions to the jury about the translation. But the First Circuit did not deal with the claim, made in the petition for certiorari, that the government theorized that anyone who posted a translation on at-Tibyan could be criminally liable under the material support statutes even if the posting were not coordinated with or under the direction of al-Qaeda. (The Supreme Court, as noted above, appears to have ruled that such theory was unconstitutional, but this was dictum on the part of the Court, not binding law.) We are thus still left with the question of whether a voluntary contribution of a translation of materials useful for the recruiting of English-speaking men and women who are on a track to be radicalized could be prosecuted under the material support statute §2339B without violating the First Amendment.

28 Cited in note 22.

A Congressional Research Service report in the wake of the Mehanna case has identified several free speech issues for which there is as yet no definitive judicial ruling: (a) Would it be constitutionally permissible simply to criminalize independent (uncoordinated) terrorist advocacy? (b) What if such a prohibition applied only to postings on the Internet? (c) Could the material support statutes be interpreted so as to apply to social media like Twitter and Facebook that provide accounts to foreign terrorist organizations?[29] As for the first question, such a law would most likely be deemed unconstitutional under *Brandenburg v Ohio*, 395 US 444 (1969). Even advocacy of violence is protected speech unless certain conditions are met, most notably the speech is imminently likely to produce violence. It also seems unlikely that focusing on the medium used, the Internet, would make a difference in the outcome. The third question is harder to answer as it turns on the interpretation of the statutes and the *Humanitarian Law Project* case. Would giving an account to such an organization meet the coordination requirement of the case? Also proving the social media company knew the account was held by a terrorist organization is likely to prove difficult, especially when the account holder goes to extreme efforts to hide the connection.

Brief note should be taken of 18 USC §2339C, which criminalizes the following:

> Whoever
> willfully
> by any means
>   directly or indirectly
>   provides or collects funds
> with the intention that such funds
>   be used, or
>   with the knowledge that such are to be used
>   fully or
>   in part
> to carry out an act that constitutes an offense within the scope of a treaty (specified in the statute) or any other act intended to cause death or serious bodily harm to a civilian when the purpose of the act is to intimidate a population or to compel a government or an international organization to do or abstain from doing any act.

III. Cyberterrorism

Cyberterrorism is defined by the Federal Emergency Management Agency (FEMA), as follows: "unlawful attacks, attempts to attack, and threats of attack against computers, networks, and the information stored therein when done to intimidate or

29 Kathleen Ann Ruane, *The advocacy of terrorism on the internet: Freedom of speech issues and the material support statutes*, 9, 11, 17 (Congressional Research Service, September 8, 2016, R44626).

coerce a government or its people in furtherance of political or social objectives."[30] The term "attack" can be defined as action taken to undermine the functions of computers, networks, or corrupt the information stored therein.[31] Specifically, this definition would cover harms to coaxial and optic cables, servers, routers, computers, regional and private networks, software that's part of the system, and satellite links. The mode of attack could, of course, be physical, e.g., cutting a cable, but also via the cyber system itself through the injection of malware, viruses, Trojan horses, altering of stored data, and denial of service attacks. Politically motivated actors are not ordinary criminals seeking financial gain (hence most likely are unprivileged enemy belligerents, lone wolves, foreign-connected terrorists, anarchists, or members of a domestic hate group). In addition, the definition used here would likely exclude lawful enemy belligerents and nation states engaged in a war as recognized by the laws of war.

Laws directed toward sabotage are a starting point for dealing with cyberterrorism directed against government computers.[32] A companion law is the federal statute that criminalizes the vandalism or destruction of government property.[33] Another provision is specifically directed toward the "willful, malicious destruction of radio, telegraph, telephone cable, line, station or system, or other means of communication, operated or controlled by the United States or used or intended to be used for military or civil defense functions of the United States" as well as toward willful or malicious interference with the working or use of these facilities, and the delay of the transmission of any communication over these facilities.[34] Finally, another provision extends protections to satellite operations.[35]

The principal statutory provision available for prosecuting cyberterrorism is the Computer Fraud and Abuse Act (CFAA). The act's coverage extends to "protected computers," a term so broadly defined that it effectively covers every computer used by the federal government and any computer connected to the Internet. A "protected computer" is a computer:

A exclusively for the use of a financial institution or the United States Government, or, in the case of a computer not exclusively for such use, used by or for a financial institution or the United States Government and the conduct constituting the offense affects that use by or for the financial institution or the Government; or

30 Quoted in Jeffery Thomas Biller, *Cyberterrorism: Finding a common starting point*, 4 J of L, Tech & the Internet 275, 304 (2013).

31 Onna A. Hathaway, Rebecca Crootof, Philip Levitz, Haley Nix, Aileen Nowlan, William Perdue, and Julia Spiegel, *The law of cyber attack*, 100 Cal L Rev 817, 826 (2012).

32 18 USC §§2153, 2155.

33 18 USC §1361.

34 18 USC §1362.

35 18 USC §1367.

B which is used in or affecting interstate or foreign commerce or communication, including a computer located outside the United States that is used in a manner that affects interstate or foreign commerce or communication of the United States.[36]

The breadth of the law is also reflected in the statutory definition of the term "computer":

> [T]he term "computer" means an electronic, magnetic, optical, electrochemical, or other high-speed data processing device performing logical, arithmetic, or storage functions, and includes any data storage facility or communications facility directly related to or operating in conjunction with such device, but such term does not include an automated typewriter or typesetter, a portable handheld calculator, or other similar device.[37]

Defined in this way the CFAA is applicable to the entire Internet and its related physical electronic hardware and software. The law specifies seven prohibited actions:

- Knowingly accessing a computer without authorization to obtain national security or other government-restricted data. **§1030(a)(1)**
- Intentionally accessing a protected computer without authorization to obtain certain information from:
  - a financial institution or consumer reporting agency;
  - the federal government; or
  - a protected computer. §1030(a)(2)
- Intentionally accessing and affecting the use of a government computer or a computer that is used by or for the government. §1030(a)(3)
- Knowingly accessing a protected computer to defraud and obtain anything of value. §1030(a)(4)
- Causing damage as specified in the statute to a protected computer by knowingly transmitting harmful items or intentionally accessing a protected computer. **§1030(a)(5)**
- Knowingly, with intent to defraud, trafficking in computer passwords. §1030(a)(6)
- Extortion involving threats to damage a protected computer. §1030(a)(7)

The term "cyberterrorism" is not a term used in the U.S. Code. But there are elements of the CFAA that do fall into what federal law calls a "Federal crime of terrorism."[38] As defined there, a federal crime of terrorism means an offense that "is calculated to influence or affect the conduct of government by intimidation

36 18 USC §1030(e)(2)(A) and (B).
37 18 USC §1030(e)(1).
38 18 USC §2332b(g)(5).

or coercion, or to retaliate against government conduct," and violates one or more specifically listed statutes within the CFAA. Among the statutes so listed are two prohibitions from the CFAA, §§1030(a)(1) and 1030(a)(5). A violation of §1030(a)(5) can be categorized a federal crime of terrorism only if the violation resulted in at least one of the following forms of damage:

- the modification or impairment, or potential modification or impairment, of the medical examination, diagnosis, treatment, or care of one or more individuals
- physical injury to any person
- a threat to public health or safety
- damage affecting a computer used by or for an entity of the United States Government in furtherance of the administration of justice, national defense, or national security
- damage affecting 10 or more protected computers during any one-year period.[39]

When a violation of CFAA is officially categorized as a federal crime of terrorism several legal consequences follow – the statute of limitations is extended, there is a presumption against release on bail, and there is an increase in the maximum term of supervised release.[40] The maximum sentence under the CFAA by itself is 10 years for a first offense, but when the violation is also classified as a federal crime of terrorism the maximum sentence increases to 25 years for damaging property.[41]

Importantly, CFAA violations that are deemed to be federal crimes of terrorism are in addition subject to the prohibition against providing material support under 18 USC §2339A when the support is given knowing or intending that it be used for carrying out a violation of any offense listed in §2332b(g)(5)(B) and, as just noticed, that includes the violation of either of two provisions of the CFAA. In short, providing support to a violation of the CFAA also violates §2339A. [Recall how broadly the term material support is defined in §2339A.] When the CFAA violation is also covered by §2339A, the possible sentence for committing the violation is 15 years for a non-capital offense instead of just 10 years for violating the CFAA alone.

> An aside: The interaction of CFAA and the other material support provision, §2339B, is not straightforward. A foreign terrorist organization that only engages in cyberterrorism as defined herein may not be subject to the prohibition of §2339B given that the definition of the type of organization covered by that provision focuses on organizations involved in actual

39 Id; 18 USC 1030(c)(4)(A).
40 18 USC §§3286, 3142(g)(1), and 3583(j).
41 18 USC §1030(c);18 USC §2332b(c).

physical violence: hijacking, kidnapping, assassination, the use of weapons of mass destruction.[42]

In 2001 Congress gave extraterritorial application to the CFAA.[43]

IV. The trial – challenges rooted in the Constitution

The Constitution lays out important rights for criminal defendants expressly in the Fourth, Fifth and Sixth Amendments, and also by implication in the First and Fourteenth Amendments. Some of the challenges that the defendant may raise in a prosecution based on these constitutional provisions have been dealt with both in previous chapters and earlier in this chapter. This section will continue the thread of those discussions by taking up additional topics of special relevance to the prosecution of suspected terrorists.

Prosecution following detainment often takes a while in these cases. This raises the possibility of the defendant complaining of a violation of his or her right to a speedy trial under the Sixth Amendment and 18 USC §3161.[44]

Despite the statute, it is not easy for a defendant to prevail on the speedy trial claim. Jose Padilla had to wait three years from the point of arrest until he was indicted.[45] In another case there was a five-year delay between initial custody of the accused (involved in bombing in Kenya) and his first appearance before a court.[46]

In developing surveillance and investigation policies the government has taken, and, indeed, should take into account the Fourth Amendment's prohibition against unreasonable searches and seizures (see Chapters 3 and 6). Failure to do so may mean prosecutors will be faced with motions to suppress evidence arguably obtained in violation of the Fourth Amendment whether obtained by a subpoena, other court order or a National Security Letter. This is precisely what occurred in the cell site location information case, *Carpenter v United States*, discussed in Chapter 6. The government collected seven days of cell site location information regarding the suspect; the Supreme Court ruled that despite the fact that there was a judicial order compelling the wireless carrier to disclose the information to the government, the order should have been premised on the issuance of a warrant based on probable cause. The reasons that evidence in an ordinary criminal proceeding may be suppressed are far too numerous for discussion in this book. We turn here to efforts to suppress evidence obtained by reliance on FISA.

42 18 USC §2339B; 8 USC §1182(a)(3)(B).

43 Paul N. Stockton and Michele Golabek-Goldman, *Prosecuting cyberterrorists: Applying traditional jurisdictional frameworks to a modern threat*, 25 Stan L & Pol R 211, 228 (2014).

44 Zabel and Benjamin, Jr., *In pursuit of justice: Prosecuting terrorism cases in the federal courts*, at 111 (cited in note 15).

45 Id at 113.

46 *United States v Ghailani*, 733 F3d 29 (2d Cir 2013). See, also, Wadie E. Said, *Crimes of terror*, 114–115 (Oxford 2015).

As the trial process gets underway federal law enforcement is required to provide the defendants with notice that it intends to use or disclose information obtained under FISA.[47] [FISA expressly permits the use of evidence obtained by electronic surveillance, physical searches, pen register or trap and trace devices in a criminal prosecution.[48]] This notice creates the opportunity for the defendant to challenge the introduction of this evidence at trial as having been acquired in violation of the Fourth Amendment or FISA itself. A motion to suppress then triggers a judicial *in camera, ex parte* review of the material to determine whether or not the statutory grounds for suppression have been met.[49] The constitutionality of this *ex parte* review has survived challenges that the procedure violates the defendant's right to due process despite the fact neither the defendant nor his attorney may see the relevant evidence.[50]

Recall that information collected pursuant to FISA is not collected under the rules that need to be followed in an ordinary criminal investigation. Hence the question may be asked: May FISA information, collected in conformity with FISA, be introduced in an ordinary criminal prosecution?

The short answer is "yes," given that the courts have rejected two lines of attack on this conclusion. In *United States v Duggan*, convicted members of the Provisional Irish Republican Army sought suppression of FISA-acquired evidence, claiming that FISA procedures violated the Fourth Amendment since authorization under the statute did not require a finding of probable cause that the defendants had committed a crime.[51] (Also see Chapter 3.) The Second Circuit Court of Appeals found FISA procedures constitutionally adequate in striking a balance between the individual's right and need to collect foreign intelligence.[52] FISA's procedures were "reasonable" under the Fourth Amendment in so far as the FISA court had to conclude there was probable cause that the target was a foreign agent. And if in targeting this foreign agent, the government discovered evidence of an ordinary domestic crime, it may use that evidence to prosecute for that offense.[53]

A second attack was directed at FISA's authorization permitting the executive to certify that the surveillance would serve "a significant" purpose to collect foreign intelligence, rather than having to certify that this was the "primary" purpose of the surveillance.[54] (See Chapter 3 and "the wall.") The concern here is that the

47 50 USC §1806(b), (c), (d).

48 50 USC §§1806(b), 1825(c), and 1845(b).

49 50 USC §§1806(f), 1825(h), 1845(g).

50 *United States v El-Mezain*, 664 F3d 467, 567 (5th Cir 2011); *United States v Belfield*, 692 F2d 141, 148-149 (DC Cir 1982); *United States v Elshinawy*, Criminal No. ELH-16-0009 (D. Md. March 20, 2017) (citing numerous cases).

51 *United States v Duggan*, 743 F2d 59 (2d Cir 1984).

52 See, also, *United States v Stewart*, 590 F3d 93, 126 (2d Cir 2009).

53 *United States v Ning Wen*, 477 F3d 896 (7th Cir 2010); *United States v Damrah*, 412 F3d 618 (6th 2005); *United States v Kashmiri*, Docket No. 09 CR 830-4. (N.D. Ill. November 10, 2010).

54 50 USC §1804(a)(6)(B).

government might be able to manipulate FISA to obtain authorization for surveillance for an ordinary criminal investigation without meeting the usual requirements for such an investigation. The Second Circuit rejected this attack, saying "For Fourth Amendment purposes, the critical question is not whether the executive can certify that obtaining foreign intelligence information is its 'primary' purpose, but whether it can certify that is a *bona fide* purpose of the surveillance."[55] The court said it did not have to decide at what point the asserted purpose was so trivial as to preclude it from being pursued in good faith. Significantly, the Second Circuit also said a FISA court reviewing the FISA application should not "second-guess the executive branch's certification; it is subject to minimum scrutiny by the courts."[56] (And when the government in good faith pursues both intelligence and law enforcement purposes it can choose whether to seek authority under FISA or Title III.)

Even incidentally collected communication of a U.S. person pursuant to §702 may be introduced as part of the case-in-chief against a criminal defendant despite the fact that incidental collection does not entail the use of a warrant, and does not involve any probable cause finding as discussed in Chapter 3.[57]

If the government were concerned that it could not effectively defend its FISA surveillance, the temptation would be to turn to "parallel construction." For example, the NSA may have collected evidence of a crime in the absence of a foreign intelligence purpose and turns that evidence over to the Drug Enforcement Agency (DEA). The DEA may use the information, but hide its origin, and with the advantage of having the NSA evidence, reconstruct a parallel (seemingly lawful) explanation of how the evidence was obtained. The evidence obtained in violation of the Fourth Amendment may then end up being used in a criminal case, its illegal origins having been laundered.[58]

The defendant still has the option under *Franks v Delaware* and FISA to seek to establish that the search authorization was based on intentionally false statements or statements said in reckless disregard of the truth.[59] FISA lets the district resolve these issues *in camera* and *ex parte* and only authorizes disclosure of the security-sensitive applications and other materials "where such disclosure is necessary to make an accurate determination of the legality of the surveillance." It is not easy to obtain such disclosure,[60] and one judge observed that given the secrecy surrounding the

55 *United States v Abu-Jihaad*, 630 F3d 102, 127 (2d Cir 2010).

56 *United States v Duggan*, at 77 (cited in note 51).

57 *United States v Mohamud*, 843 F3d 420 (9th Cir 2016); *United States v Muhtorov*, 187 F Supp3d 1240 (D Colo 2015).

58 Hanni Fakhoury, *DEA and NSA team up to share intelligence, leading to secret use of surveillance in ordinary investigations* (Electronic Frontier Foundation, August 6, 2013), archived at https://www.eff.org/deeplinks/2013/08/dea-and-nsa-team-intelligence-laundering.

59 438 US 154 (1978); 50 USC §§1806(f) and (g).

60 See, for example, *United States v Abu-Jihaad* (cited in note 55).

FISA proceeding, the chance of obtaining suppression would only occur in the most egregious of cases.[61]

The use of the confidential informant, discussed in Chapter 6, can easily morph into a "sting operation" where the target ends up committing a crime, and thus another constitutional issue is raised.[62] The "entrapment" defense:

> Entrapment is a complete defense to a criminal charge, on the theory that "Government agents may not originate a criminal design, implant in an innocent person's mind the disposition to commit a criminal act, and then induce commission of the crime so that the Government may prosecute." *Jacobson v. United States*, 503 US 540, 548 (1992). A valid entrapment defense has two related elements: (1) government inducement of the crime, and (2) the defendant's lack of predisposition to engage in the criminal conduct. *Mathews v. United States*, 485 US 58, 63 (1988). Of the two elements, predisposition is by far the more important.[63]

As the Court put it: "[W]hen the Government's quest for conviction leads to the apprehension of an otherwise law-abiding citizen who, if left to his own devices, likely would never run afoul of the law, the courts should intervene."[64] This defense has its origins in the common law, but is recognized as a requirement of the right to due process of law embodied in the Fifth and Fourteenth Amendments.[65]

Raising the entrapment defense initiates a dance between the defendant and the prosecution. The defendant starts off by providing evidence that a federal agent encouraged the defendant to commit the crime and that they lacked a predisposition to engage in that crime. After making this prima facie case the burden shifts to the government to establish beyond a reasonable doubt that entrapment did not occur.[66] The U.S. attorney handbook elaborates on the government's burden of proof regarding the matter of inducement.

> Inducement is the threshold issue in the entrapment defense. Mere solicitation to commit a crime is not inducement. *Sorrells v. United States*, 287 US 435, 451 (1932). Nor does the government's use of artifice, stratagem, pretense, or deceit establish inducement. *Id.* at 441. Rather, inducement requires a showing of at least persuasion or mild coercion, *United States v. Nations*, 764 F2d

61 *United States v Daoud*, 755 F3d 479, 486 (7th Cir 2014) (Rovner J., concurring).

62 Evan Osnos, *Do F.B.I. stings help fight Against ISIS?* (New Yorker, June 10, 2016), archived at http://www.newyorker.com/news/news-desk/do-f-b-i-stings-help-the-fight-against-isis.

63 https://www.justice.gov/usam/criminal-resource-manual-645-entrapment-elements. See. Wayne R. LaFave, Jerold H. Israel, Nancy J. King, and Orin S. Kerr, *Principles of criminal procedure: Investigation*, 2d ed., 249–263 (West 2009).

64 *Jacobson v United States*, 503 US 540, 553-54 (1992).

65 Compare http://law.justia.com/constitution/us/amendment-14/55-entrapment.html.

66 *United States v Montoya*, 844 F3d 63, 67 (1st Cir 2016).

> 1073, 1080 (5th Cir. 1985); pleas based on need, sympathy, or friendship, *ibid.*; or extraordinary promises of the sort "that would blind the ordinary person to his legal duties," *United States v. Evans*, 924 F2d 714, 717 (7th Cir. 1991). *See also United States v. Kelly*, 748 F2d 691, 698 (D.C. Cir. 1984) (inducement shown only if government's behavior was such that "a law-abiding citizen's will to obey the law could have been overborne"); *United States v. Johnson*, 872 F2d 612, 620 (5th Cir. 1989) (inducement shown if government created "a substantial risk that an offense would be committed by a person other than one ready to commit it").[67]

The lengths to which confidential informants may go to induce criminal behavior by the defendant are striking, including the informant suggesting a plan to, say, blow up a building.[68] Despite proof of inducement, proof of predisposition is fatal for the defendant. (This is the doctrine used in the federal courts.[69]) To this end, proof of a prior criminal conviction by the defendant is of course useful for the government. Other options include introducing evidence of the defendant's political and ideological statements and showing the jury extremist videos that were found on the defendant's computer. In the prosecution of James Cromitie, the government introduced both testimony from an undercover agent and multiple recordings of Cromitie speaking with the undercover agent and other co-conspirators.[70] This evidence was introduced to prove a predisposition that Cromitie was ready to commit the offense charged, once the opportunity had presented itself. The court also noted that the predisposition of potential terrorists available for recruitment was "to have a state of mind that inclines them to inflict harm on the United States, be willing to die like a martyr, be receptive to a recruiter's presentation . . . of the specifics of an operational plan, and welcome an invitation to participate."[71] The evidence in this case, the court concluded, established a predisposition in this sense. The evidence consisted of, among other things, the following statements volunteered by the defendant to the informant: "I want to do something to America." He "wanted to die like a shahid, a martyr." He indicated a willingness to join what he wrongly believed was a real terrorist organization. He wanted to buy "stuff" from the informant, i.e., guns and missiles. And he volunteered the idea of bombing a synagogue. [Cromitie and the other defendants were convicted on charges of conspiracy to use weapons of mass destruction against a Jewish temple, an airport, and conspiracy to kill officers and employees of the United States.]

67 https://www.justice.gov/usam/criminal-resource-manual-645-entrapment-elements.

68 Said, *Crimes of terror*, at 36–39, 42 (cited in note 46).

69 LaFave, Israel, King, and Kerr, *Principles of criminal procedure: Investigation*, 2d ed., at 252 (cited in note 63).

70 *United States v Cromitie*, 727 F3d 194 (2d Cir 2013).

71 Id at 208.

On appeal the defendants raised several constitutional arguments. They argued that the government's conduct in the case was so outrageous as to have violated the Fifth Amendment's due process clause. While theoretically possible, courts have never actually overturned a conviction on this basis. The Second Circuit, which disallowed the defendant's argument, said "the existence of a due process violation must turn on whether the government conduct, standing alone, is so offensive that it 'shocks the conscience' regardless of the extent to which it led the defendant to commit his crime."[72] The sting operation in this case did not cross that line even when it involved monetary inducements, created the opportunity to commit the crime, and made use of an emotional attachment the defendant had for the informant.[73]

Relief from convictions is also possible if the defendant proves coercion. While there is no doubt that the defendant has standing to claim he/she had been coerced, it remains unsettled whether the defendant has standing to claim a witness was coerced.[74] The starting point for understanding coerced testimony is not the due process clause of the Fifth Amendment, but rather the Fifth Amendment's stipulation that no person "shall be compelled in any criminal case to be a witness against himself."

Challenges to the use of statements by the accused based on the Fifth Amendment only succeed if the defendant can establish that the pressure imposed by the government amounted to compulsion. This plunges the courts into sifting through all the facts regarding the interrogation in order to apply the voluntariness test. That approach "examines 'whether a defendant's will was overborne' by the circumstances surrounding the giving of a confession . . . The due process test takes into consideration 'the totality of all the surrounding circumstances – both the characteristics of the accused and the details of the interrogation'."[75] From the defense's perspective, proof to establish lack of voluntariness has proven difficult to sustain since these interrogations have taken place outside the U.S., and the courts have given credence to the testimony of officials denying coercion where the defendant was held, and have had their doubts about the credibility of the defendant.[76] Case in point, might threatening to shift a terrorist suspect to solitary confinement amount to compulsion sufficient to negate a confession based on the Fifth Amendment privilege?[77]

72 Id at 218.

73 See, also, *Hampton v United States*, 425 US 484 (1976); *United States v Russel* 411 US 423 (1973) (touching on the issue whether there may be some circumstances in which entrapment would be available even to a defendant found to be predisposed).

74 Katherine Sheridan, *Excluding coerced witness testimony to protect a criminal defendant's right to due process and adequately deter police misconduct*, 38 Fordham Urban L J 1221, 1224 (2010). See *United States v Gonzales*, 164 F3d 1285 (10th Cir 1999); But see *Samuel v Frank*, 525 F3d 566 (7th Cir 2008) (coerced witness testimony not a constitutional issue; only an evidentiary issue for the jury).

75 *Dickerson v United States*, 530 US 428, 434 (2000) (reviewing the history and viability of the voluntariness test).

76 Human Rights Watch, *Illusion of justice*, at 78–81 (cited in note 24).

77 Compare *McKune v Lile*, 536 US 24 (2002).

Another way in which the privilege against self-incrimination can come into play is when evidence to be submitted in the trial was obtained by subpoena or warrant from the defendant, and the defendant claims this violates their right against self-incrimination.[78] In the end, at least, this much seems settled: A suspect may be required by a court order or subpoena to give the government specific documents even if they contain incriminating evidence because the original creation of the document was not itself compelled or coerced.[79]

Government demands for passwords and decryption raise Fifth Amendment issues. In an Eleventh Circuit Court of Appeals case the defendant claimed that by decrypting the contents of his computer, "he would be testifying that he, as opposed to some other person, placed the contents on the hard drive, encrypted the contents, and could retrieve and examine them whenever he wished." He thus invoked the protection of the self-incrimination clause of the Fifth Amendment in refusing to decrypt the contents of his computer. The court agreed that the accused did properly invoke the Fifth Amendment privilege.[80] Professor Orin Kerr has taken exception to this ruling by offering a very narrow interpretation of what the accused is "testifying" to if he were to comply with the order to decrypt. Kerr says the only testimony implied by the act of decryption is "I know the password." He then claims that knowing the password does not mean that you know what files are stored on the computer, and it is not equivalent to identifying the computer's contents. In his view, the Fifth Amendment is focused on the "testimony" implicit in the suspect's act, the act of decryption, per se.[81] It of course remains to be seen how the Supreme Court rules on this issue if and when it reviews these cases.

Intertwined with the Fifth Amendment issues noted above is a body of law regarding the Miranda warning informing the accused of the right to remain silent, that anything he says can be used against him in a court of law, that he has the right to the presence of an attorney, and if he cannot afford an attorney one will be appointed for him prior to any questioning if he so desires.[82] This is not the place to examine the large body of law that has arisen around the warning, but this much can be said. Suspects whose statements and confessions were elicited by foreign officials outside the U.S. are out of luck if they seek to suppress evidence for having failed to be provided with the Miranda warning.[83] If, however, the questioning

78 Compare *United States v Doe*, 465 US 605 (1984).

79 *United States v Hubbell*, 530 US 27, 35-36 (2000).

80 *United States v Doe (In re Grand Jury Subpoena Duces Tecum Dated Mar. 25, 2011)*, 670 F3d 1335 (11th Cir 2012).

81 Orin Kerr, *The Fifth Amendment limits on forced decryption and applying the "foregone conclusion doctrine"* (Washington Post, June 7, 2016), archived at https://www.washingtonpost.com/news/volokh-conspiracy/wp/2016/06/07/the-fifth-amendment-limits-on-forced-decryption-and-applying-the-foregone-conclusion-doctrine/?utm_term=.4f0dbd6a240d.

82 *Miranda v Arizona*, 384 US 436 (1966); *Dickerson v United States*, 530 US 428 (2000).

83 *United States v Yousef*, 327 F3d 56, 145 (2d Cir 2003).

was a joint undertaking between U.S. and non-U.S. officials and was so brutal as to "shock the conscience," suppression would be a possibility.[84]

Questioning by U.S. agents of suspects, whether occurring outside or inside the U.S., triggers the Miranda warning requirement.[85] Failure to issue the warning or to cease questioning when the suspect requests an attorney and refuses to speak, will lead to the suppression of any statements elicited from that point forward. Voluntary waiver is possible, but whether or not the rights were voluntarily waived may, of course, become an issue in a suppression hearing. When an attorney is requested the questioning must stop until one is made available.[86] One analysis states that agents may not get around the Miranda warning by obtaining a confession without giving the warning and then eliciting the same confession "this time for the record."[87] However, Charlie Savage has reported another way President Obama's legal team worked around the Miranda warning.[88] The suspect might make self-incriminating statements prior to the Miranda warning while incarcerated for months in the inherently coercive environment of the brig of a naval ship at sea. Fearing these statements could not be admissible in a court the suspect was given a break from questioning and given access to the Red Cross. Then a different set of interrogators, a "clean team" of FBI agents, who did not know of the earlier self-incriminating statements, would arrive, provide the Miranda warning, and begin the questioning again. If the suspect willingly continues to talk, his statements might now be admissible. No court has specifically ruled on this gambit.[89]

The idea of providing a suspected terrorist with the Miranda warning leading to the suspect's silence and the possibility of other co-conspirators going about their business, has not set well with members of Congress who have proposed various pieces of legislation regulating the use of the Miranda warning, such as prohibiting its use with high-value enemy belligerents.[90] [The definition of enemy belligerent is taken up in Chapter 8.] When one of the two Boston marathon bombers was captured on Friday April 19, 2013 he was first questioned without being given the Miranda warning until a judge delivered it in his hospital room on the following Monday.[91] Shortly after the arrest of Dzhokhar Tasrnaev, Senators Lindsey Graham and John McCain issued a statement urging President Obama to place him in military custody as an enemy combatant without the right to a Miranda warning.[92]

84 *United States v Abu Ali*, 395 F Supp2d 338, 373-74 (ED Va 2005).

85 *United States v Bin Laden*, 132 F Supp2d 168, 173-79 (SD NY 2001).

86 Charles Doyle, *Terrorism, Miranda, and related matters*, 2 (Congressional Research Service, April 24, 2013).

87 Id.

88 Charlie Savage, *Power wars*, 344–347 (Little Brown & Company 2015).

89 FeiFei Jiang, *Dancing the two-step abroad: Finding a place for clean time evidence in Article III Courts*, 47 Colum J L & Soc Probs 453, 455 (2014).

90 Doyle, *Terrorism, Miranda, and related matters*, at 9 (cited in note 86).

91 Savage, *Power wars*, at 505 (cited in note 88).

92 Id at 506.

Wholly denying the Miranda warning to such suspects, there is an option made possible by the Supreme Court in *New York v Quarles*, 467 US 649 (1984) that created a public safety exception to the requirement in a case in which the police were concerned about finding a missing gun, given the empty holster of the arrested suspect. So, the police asked for the location of the gun before reading him his rights, a step the Court upheld, noting that the "case represented a situation where concern for public safety must be paramount." The Court said the police were confronted with the immediate necessity to find the gun, which the police suspected the defendant had sequestered somewhere inside the store in which he was arrested. The Court saw this as a narrow exception to the basic Miranda requirement, as have the lower courts.[93] The Quarles exception was used to uphold the use of statements made by a bomb maker who was questioned without the warning in his hospital room following his arrest.[94]

The FBI, in a memo reported in the *New York Times*, has outlined an expansive conception of the public safety exception, a conception which has not yet been judicially ruled on. Norman Abrams provided this useful summary of the memo:[95]

> First, "without advising the arrestee of his Miranda rights," FBI agents could ask "any and all questions" prompted by public safety concerns. The guidelines then indicate that "although all relevant public safety questions have been asked," agents are authorized to continue with "unwarned interrogation . . . [where it is] necessary to collect valuable and timely intelligence not related to any immediate threat, and . . . [where] the government's interest in obtaining this intelligence outweighs the disadvantages of proceeding with unwarned interrogation."

Abrams continues with this quote from the memo:

> [S]uch [public safety] interrogation might include, for example, questions about possible impending or coordinated terrorist attacks; the location, nature, and threat posed by weapons that might post [sic] an imminent danger to the public; and the identities, locations, and activities or intentions of accomplices who may be plotting additional imminent attacks.

Given the Court's emphasis that the public safety question is "narrow," it seems unlikely it would go along with the FBI's interpretation of its opinion if and when information from the interrogation were introduced in a trial. In any event, Abrams

93 Doyle, *Terrorism, Miranda, and related matters*, at 4, n.31 (cited in note 86).

94 *United States v Khalil*, 214 F3d 111 (2d Cir 2000).

95 Norman Abrams, *Terrorism prosecution in US federal court: Exceptions to constitutional evidence rules and the development of a cabined exception for coerced confessions*, 4 Harv Nat Secur J 58, 84 (2012). The memo itself is archived at http://www.nytimes.com/2011/03/25/us/25miranda-text.html?mcubz=0.

offers these additional observations. (i) Information obtained without the Miranda warning may still be useful intelligence. (ii) Even if the public safety exception applies the reliability of the information remains to be tested in the trial. (iii) Using the statement in a trial of another suspect would likely be blocked by the evidentiary rule against the use of hearsay, not to speak of a possible violation of this suspect's Sixth Amendment right to confront witnesses against him. [This right plays a role regarding the use of secret information taken up in another section below.]

The Sixth Amendment specifies that the accused shall enjoy the right "to have compulsory process for obtaining witnesses in his favor." Defendants such as Zacarias Mousaoui, of 9/11 infamy, may seek to exercise the right by demanding that the government produce witnesses to testify that the government, for reasons of national security, may not want to. Faced with such a demand, the government has two options, either to suffer dismissal of the case, or to produce a substitute for the testimony that will provide the defendant with substantially the same ability to make his defense.[96] How a court is to determine whether the substitute meets the required standard is not fully settled law. Abrams suggests that the Fourth Circuit opinion regarding Moussaoui stands for this proposition – "a special reliability rationale can be used to address the Sixth Amendment compulsory process challenge posed when the government declines to produce witnesses on grounds of national security and offers as a substitute hearsay records of the statements that the witnesses made to interrogators who had been seeking *intelligence* rather than gathering evidence for *prosecution*."[97] [italics added] The idea is that reliability is more assured if the statements were collected for intelligence purposes rather than for prosecution purposes.

The Sixth Amendment also states the accused shall enjoy the right "to be confronted with the witnesses against him." While the right to compulsory process includes the right to call favorable witnesses, the confrontation clause provides the right to question opposing witnesses. Again, the government for national security reasons may not want the defendant to be able to question these witnesses directly. This problem is handled by the Classified Information Procedures Act (CIPA), taken up below.[98] Also taken up below is the "state secrets privilege," originally a common law doctrine that the Supreme Court has recognized as giving the President authority to invoke to prevent the disclosure of information.

Although there may be evidence and witnesses that the government may keep successfully at one remove from the trial, there is other evidence that the government

96 *United States v Moussaoui*, 382 F3d 453, 476–477 (4th Cir 2004). The criteria to be used to determine an adequate substitute the Fourth Circuit adapted from the Classified Information Procedures Act (CIPA) – discussed below – for use in this Sixth Amendment compulsory process case.

97 Abrams, *Terrorism prosecution in US federal court: Exceptions to constitutional evidence rules and the development of a cabined exception for coerced confessions*, at 68–69 (cited in note 95).

98 See these Supreme Court opinions interpreting the Sixth Amendment clause and creating an exception to it that may be of relevance in a terrorism prosecution in the future. *Crawford v Washington*, 541 US 36 (2004); *Davis v Washington*, 547 US 813 (2006); *Michigan v Bryant*, 562 US 344 (2011).

must submit even when not asked for by the defendant, namely, exculpatory and impeachment evidence. The manual for United States Attorneys summarizes this obligation as follows:

> Government disclosure of material exculpatory and impeachment evidence is part of the constitutional guarantee to a fair trial. *Brady v. Maryland*, 373 U.S. 83, 87 (1963); *Giglio v. United States*, 405 U.S. 150, 154 (1972). The law requires the disclosure of exculpatory and impeachment evidence when such evidence is material to guilt or punishment. *Brady*, 373 US at 87; *Giglio*, 405 U.S. at 154. Because they are Constitutional obligations, *Brady* and *Giglio* evidence must be disclosed regardless of whether the defendant makes a request for exculpatory or impeachment evidence. *Kyles v. Whitley*, 514 US 419, 432-33 (1995). Neither the Constitution nor this policy, however, creates a general discovery right for trial preparation or plea negotiations.[99]

The obligations rest on the due process clauses of the Fifth and Fourteenth Amendments. Among the important pieces of information that must be disclosed – information that could be an issue in many trials – is an agreement not to prosecute a witness in exchange for the witness's testimony ("Giglio Policy"). The *Brady* case involved wrongful withholding from the defense of a written confession to the killing by Brady's companion. An example of an FBI terrorism prosecution "going south" is the so-called "Detroit Sleeper Cell" case in which the FBI seemed to win a celebrated conviction based on evidence that the defendants had "cased" various sites for an attack.[100] But subsequently the FBI acknowledged "that its trial team had violated *Brady* by failing to tell the defendants that, among other things, a sketch alleged to show terrorist plotting against a U.S. airbase in Turkey instead was just a map of the Middle East and that a video alleged to reveal terrorist surveillance of U.S. attractions such as Disneyland and Las Vegas was merely a tourist videotape depicting young Tunisians visiting the United States." The terrorism convictions were dismissed, the prosecutors were charged with obstruction of justice, and the jury acquitted.[101]

Similarly, defendants have a right to compel the government to disclose evidence it has that bears on the credibility of the government's witnesses.[102] The statute cited in the footnote provides the procedures for dealing with materials the government does not want to disclose, which in the extreme could lead to the dismissal of the case.

99 https://www.justice.gov/usam/usam-9-5000-issues-related-trials-and-other-court-proceedings.

100 Zabel and Benjamin, Jr., *In pursuit of justice: Prosecuting terrorism cases in the federal courts*, at 92 (cited in note 15).

101 Id.

102 *Jencks v United States*, 353 US 657 (1957); 18 USC §3500 (Jencks Act).

V. The trial – challenges rooted in statutes

Since statutory challenges that could be raised in the course of a prosecution are far too numerous to be canvassed here, this section will focus on three statutory challenges arguably at the heart of many terrorist prosecutions; namely, challenges based on two electronic surveillance statutes (Title III and FISA), and a third challenge involving the Classified Information Procedures Act (CIPA). Keep in mind the challenges pursuant to these three statutes are so numerous that only a few central issues will be highlighted.

In a trial, a defendant might try to exclude evidence based on the claim that it was collected in violation of a statute. This is not always possible. The pen register and trap and trace statute, 18 USC §3121 et. seq., does not have a statutory exclusion rule, while the FISA pen register and trap and trace statute, 50 USC §1845, does. 50 USC §1861, regarding the collection of "tangible things," and the Stored Communications Act, 18 USC §§2701-2712 both do not.[103] What happens when statutes do not have a suppression provision is discussed below.

Title III of the Omnibus Crime Control and Safe Streets Act of 1988 (18 USC §§2510 to 2522) is the basic wiretap law used in ordinary criminal investigations. Section 2517(3) permits the introduction into a trial of information concerning wire, oral, or electronic communication that was obtained by authorized interception. Statutory challenges raised in the course of a criminal prosecution must seek to suppress that evidence by attacking (putting aside a constitutional attack) the original authorization for the wiretap and/or the execution of the authorization as not being in conformity with the authorization.[104]

Situation 1: Courts do not suppress Title III evidence lightly. In *United States v Chavez* the Supreme Court said that not "every failure to comply fully with any requirement in Title III would render the interception of wire and oral communications 'unlawful'." A violation of Title III is "unlawful" and warranting suppression only if it entails a failure to meet the statute's requirements that "directly and substantially implement" Congress's intent to limit wiretapping "to those situations clearly calling for" its use.[105] The Congressional Research Office puts the point this way: "Mere technical noncompliance is not enough; the defect must be of a nature that substantially undermines the regime of court-supervised interception for law enforcement purposes."[106]

103 §2708 limits remedies to those described in the chapter (i.e., civil damages and criminal punishment), thus ruling out exclusion of data from a trial as a remedy. *United States v Smith*, 155 F3d 1051 (9th Cir 1998).

104 See 18 USC §2515 prohibiting the use in any trial of intercepted wire or oral communication if disclosure of the information would be in violation of this chapter. 18 USC §2518 (10). See, also, James G. Carr and Patricia L. Bellia, Evan A. Creutz, *The law of electronic surveillance* (Clark Boardman Callaghan 2017).

105 416 US 562, 574–75 (1974).

106 Gina Stevens and Charles Doyle, *Privacy: An overview of federal statutes governing wiretapping and electronic eavesdropping*, 34 (Congressional Research Office, October 9, 2012, 98-326).

Just as Title III specifies the grounds for seeking suppression, so does the Foreign Intelligence Surveillance Act (FISA). An aggrieved person is permitted to seek suppression on two grounds: (1) the information was unlawfully acquired; or (2) the surveillance was not made in conformity with the order of authorization or approval.[107]

Situation 2: FISA-acquired information may be used when the government, as required by the statute, provides notice of use of FISA data.[108] The defendant may then move to suppress the evidence on the grounds just noted and, to this end, seek disclosure of the original application. The government may oppose disclosure of the application on grounds of national security, 50 USC §§1806(f) and 1825(g). The court may then disclose, under appropriate security procedures portions of the application, order, and other materials "only where such disclosure is necessary to make an accurate determination of the legality of the surveillance or search."[109] 50 USC §§1806(f), 1825(g). This may then lead to an *in camera* and *ex parte* determination by a court regarding the legality of the search.[110] (Discussed above.) Note there has been a history of the government violating FISA by not providing a defendant notice of its intent to use FISA-acquired information.[111]

If the FISA court determines that the surveillance was not lawfully authorized or conducted, it "shall" suppress both the evidence that was unlawfully obtained as well as evidence that was derived from that evidence.[112] Hence what is sometimes called "the fruit of the poisonous tree" also would be suppressed. But getting a court to suppress the evidence is not easy, and the entire process is tilted toward the government.

First, the court that is initially requested to authorize tends to err on the side of national security and defers to the administration's request for the application with an occasional required modification.[113] The law, 50 USC §1805(a)(4), only requires that the certification not be clearly erroneous. Second, when the original certification is challenged at trial, the review by the court of the motion to suppress will not be intense. The application need only be reviewed to determine if the government's certification was clearly erroneous.[114] That is, once the certification is made it is subject to minimal scrutiny based on the presumption the certification was valid.[115] Accordingly, the FISA court will usually follow the pattern of those courts

107 50 USC §§1806(e) (electronic surveillance), §1825(h) (physical search), §1845(e) (pen register and trap and trace).

108 50 USC §§1806(c), 1825(d).

109 Compare *United States v Abu-Jihaad*, 630 F3d 102 (2d Cir 2010).

110 *United States v Osmakac*, 868 F3d 937 (11th Cir 2017).

111 Patrick C. Toomey, *Why aren't criminal defendants getting notice of Section 702 Surveillance – Again* (December 11, 2015), archived at https://www.justsecurity.org/28256/arent-criminal-defendants-notice-section-702-surveillance-again/.

112 50 USC §1806(g); 50 USC 1845(g).

113 Elizabeth Goitein and Faiza Patel, *What went wrong with the FISA Court*, 37 (Brennan Center for Justice 2015), archived at https://www.brennancenter.org/publication/what-went-wrong-fisa-court.

114 50 USC §1805(a)(4) and §1824(a)(4).

115 *United States v Abu-Jihaad*, at 130 (cited in note 55); *United States v Hassan*, 742 F3d 104, 138-139 (4th Cir 2014); *United States v Badia*, 827 F2d 1458, 1463 (11th Cir 1987).

reviewing Title III suppression motions and not order suppression for "minor" violations of FISA, i.e., only those violations that transgress Congress's concerns in adopting the legislation.[116]

Note: Both Title III and FISA have provisions for the appeal of a court's granting or denying a motion to suppress.[117]

Among the most constitutionally sensitive problems that can arise in the trial of a terrorist is the matter of handling classified or secret information. First, the government asks (itself) if the information is subject to discovery – must it be revealed to the defendant? If it is exculpatory it must be shared with the defendant pursuant to *Brady v Maryland* or *Jencks v United States* discussed above. Second, the government may want to use evidence, which if fully revealed, might arguably endanger national security. In that case, the defendant's Fifth Amendment due process right and Sixth Amendment right to confront the evidence, to be personally present at the trial, and to cross-examine witnesses, indicate the evidence must be revealed if it is used. Third, a defendant may want to use classified information or to subpoena a witness to testify either because the information is genuinely relevant or is part of an effort to engage in what is called "graymail" (described below). Fourth, the Sixth Amendment affords the defendant a compulsory process to obtain witnesses and to have a public trial with a jury, all of which create difficulties when it comes to the use of sensitive national security information and witnesses whose identify the government does not want to reveal. Fifth, the Sixth Amendment's right to counsel may create an "awkwardness" if the counsel is not cleared to see classified information.

Attorneys at the Brennan Center for Justice have listed five options the government has for dealing with classified information relevant to the prosecution of a terrorism suspect.[118] The first two options, "filtering" and "restricted disclosure," are addressed by the Classified Information Procedures Act (CIPA).[119] The other options are workarounds the government might use, namely: declassify the information; bring different charges that do not require the use of classified information; delay the prosecution until other evidence is gathered. Of course, dropping the effort to prosecute remains yet another option.

The CIPA is Congress's way of balancing the criminal defendant's constitutional rights and the government's right to protect sensitive classified and unclassified information in the interest of national security.[120] This sets up a combination of

116 David S. Kris and J. Douglas Wilson, *National security investigations & prosecutions*, 30-6 (Thomson-West 2007).

117 18 USC §2518; 50 USC §1806(f) and (h); 50 USC §1845(h).

118 Serrin Turner & Stephen J. Schulhofer, *The secrecy problem in terrorism trials*, 17 (Brennan Center for Justice 2005), archived at https://www.brennancenter.org/publication/secrecy-problem-terrorism-trials.

119 18 USC app. 3.

120 Despite its name, the CIPA has been interpreted to also apply to *unclassified* materials the government believes the disclosure of which would harm national security. *United States v Drake*, 818 F Supp 2d 909 (D Md 2011).

procedures and tools available to the trial judge who executes the law in the course of the trial. The procedures include *in camera* (away from the jury) and even *ex parte* (without the defendant present) hearings in which the sensitive evidence is revealed to the judge. In dealing with this evidence, the judge has several options. Evidence can be excluded from the trial, or its use required as in the case of *Brady* and *Jencks* materials.[121] In addition, the judge may authorize the use of summaries provided by the government; the use of redacted versions of the evidence; or permit the government to admit to the facts the information tends to prove.[122] In executing these options that judge is bound by the statutory rule that any substitution of the defendant's or prosecution's evidence provides the defendant with the same ability to make his defense as would disclosure of the classified information. (§6 of CIPA).

As these issues are being worked out the government is authorized to seek an "interlocutory appeal" to an appeals court regarding disclosure of sensitive information.[123] This kind of appeal can happen before or during the trial. (Absent the right to seek an interlocutory appeal the defendant has to wait until after conviction to appeal.) If the appellate judge orders disclosure of the evidence, and no summary or redaction is acceptable to the trial judge, and the government still refuses to disclose, the trial judge may dismiss all or part of the indictment.

Judicial decisions reveal a mixed picture. In one case, the Second Circuit upheld against a constitutional challenge the exclusion of the defendant from evidentiary hearings considering classified information issues.[124] In another case, the Fourth Circuit ruled it was "harmless error" when the jury got to see an unredacted version of a document, but the defendant and his counsel (who did not have security clearance) could not.[125] Zacaroas Mousaoui, a co-conspirator with those who executed the 9/11 attack, tried to compel access to witnesses that government held captive as enemy belligerents. It was agreed that Moussaoui had a powerful interest in obtaining the witnesses the government refused to produce. Rather than dismissing the case, the Fourth Circuit sought a way to find an acceptable substitute and pointed to relying as a starting pointing government reports regarding these witnesses' statements prepared prior to trial as presumptively reliable.[126] In another case, the defendant succeeded in claiming that the government's proffered substitute summaries were too general and unspecific to be of use of the defendant.[127]

121 18 USC app. 3; *Brady v Maryland*, 373 US 83 (1963); *Jencks v United States*, 353 US 657 (1957); Jencks Act, 18 USC 3500. Brady materials are exculpatory materials. Jencks materials are materials that tend to undermine the credibility of a government witness.

122 18 USC app. 3, §4.

123 18 USC app. 3, §7. See, also, *United States v Moussaoui*, 333 F3d 509 (4th Cir 2003).

124 *In re Terrorist Bombings of United States Embassies in East Africa*, 552 F3d 93, 157, 177 (2d Cir 2008).

125 *United States v Abu Ali*, 528 F3d 210 (4th Cir 2008).

126 *United States v Moussaoui*, 382 F3d 453, 476, 478 (4th Cir 2004).

127 *United States v Fernandez*, 913 F2d 148 (4th Cir 1990). See, also, *United States v Rosen*, 487 F Supp 2d 703 (ED Vir 2007) (prohibiting the use of a "silent witness" method of presenting evidence).

VI. The trial – challenges rooted in federal rules

Criminal trials not only have to comply with the Constitution and many relevant statutes, but also with the Federal Rules of Evidence.[128] A piece of classified evidence may be used in a trial by the defendant, but if that evidence does not satisfy the standard rules of evidence it would not be admitted. For example, the evidence must be relevant; but even if relevant and probative it may be excluded if its value is substantially outweighed by the danger of unfair prejudice. Character evidence may not, generally speaking, be introduced to prove a person's character in order to prove that on a particular occasion the person acted in accordance with that character. Impeaching a witness's credibility based on his/her religious beliefs is not permissible. Hearsay evidence is generally excluded but there are many exceptions to this rule, e.g., statements made in the course of the conspiracy by one co-conspirator. A "privilege" may exempt a witness from testifying, e.g., a client may prevent his attorney from disclosing a confidential communication. (Recall the Fifth Amendment protects the privilege against self-incrimination.) In addition, real and documentary evidence needs to be authenticated, that is, there must be proof the item is what its proponent claims it is (was this email written by the defendant?) Of course, today the issue of authentication and reliability has gotten very technical, requiring computer forensics (how were the data copied from the computer, what are the qualifications, expertise, and reliability of the expert witness?).

A few rules of evidence are of particular relevance to terrorism prosecutions. As noted, character evidence cannot be introduced simply to prove that the defendant committed the crime he or she has been charged with. But the Federal Rules of Evidence do permit character evidence to be introduced in several situations: (a) when the defendant has offered character evidence, the prosecution may seek to rebut it; and (b) if evidence of previous crimes, wrongs, and *other acts* have been introduced to prove motive, opportunity, intent, preparation, plan, or knowledge.[129] Matters also get complicated when the defendant claims entrapment. Rule 405 lays out various methods of proving character, including testimony about the person's reputation, presumably useful in connection with (a) above. Thus the Rules regarding character evidence do open the door to the presentation of evidence of radical behavior and perhaps even radical speech such as emails celebrating a terrorist action.

Rule 403 authorizes the judge to exclude even relevant evidence "if its probative value is substantially outweighed by a danger of . . . unfair prejudice." This is precisely the problem that arose in *United States v Al-Moayad*,[130] in which the court said the evidence was both unrelated to the guilt of the defendant on a charge of material support based on 18 USC §2339B, and was prejudicial. The evidence in question was evidence of a terrorist bombing that took place in Tel Aviv on the day

128 FRE 101-1103.

129 FRE 404.

130 545 F3d 139 (2d Cir 2008).

that the defendant was attending a wedding in Yemen. That evidence consisted of photos of the destroyed bus, and a video of a news story about the bombing. Other prejudicial evidence was about a terrorist training program, and multiple images of Bin Laden and Al-Zawahiri. On appeal, the Circuit Court vacated the conviction and remanded the case to the federal district court for the case to be tried before a different judge.

The rule against hearsay provides another basis for a challenge. [Hearsay is defined in Federal Rule 801 as a statement the declarant did not make while testifying at the trial (i.e., it was made out of court) and a party offers it in evidence to prove the truth of the matter asserted in the statement. An example: an email by Joe in which Joe says that Dan blew up the building. This email is inadmissible hearsay if introduced to prove Dan blew up the building.] The Federal Rules of Evidence regarding hearsay contain many exceptions that the prosecutor can use to work around the basic prohibition of hearsay. First, hearsay defined in Rule 801 allows prior statements to be admitted into evidence by a witness if the statements were given under penalty of perjury and are consistent with the testimony currently being provided by the witness. The same rule says a statement made by one co-conspirator "during or in furtherance of the conspiracy" may be admitted against the defendant con-conspirator. Thus the email example noted above would be admissible if it had been sent during the conspiracy.

Importantly, hearsay also may be introduced under Rule 803 to prove motive, intent, or plan. Thus a statement such as "I'm joining the team tomorrow for the planned action" may be introduced to prove both that the declarant joined the action, and *perhaps* also that the "team" was also part of the action.[131]

Hearsay has also been admitted into evidence in hearings addressing a petition for habeas corpus as discussed in Chapter 10.

VII. Pulling a few threads together

A look at one terrorist prosecution will help pull a number of the threads of this chapter together. Tarek Mehanna, a U.S. citizen, was convicted on multiple charges, including a charge of providing two types of material support, conspiracy and making false statements to federal officers.[132] The investigation into Mehanna's activities involved a confidential informant. Investigators checked out Mehanna's work on a website, searched his computers on the authority of a FISA court; recorded him; got testimony from co-conspirators; kept track of his traveling; and interviewed Mehanna himself prior to his arrest. On appeal to the First Circuit Mehanna raised (a) two constitutional issues (the sufficiency of the evidence against him and his conviction based on his work for a website); (b) numerous evidentiary issues;

131 Compare *Mutual Life Ins Co v Hillman*, 145 US 285 (1892); *United States v Persico*, 645 F3d 85 (2d Cir 2011).

132 *United States v Mehanna* (cited in note 22).

and (c) a challenge based on federal sentencing guidelines. After the First Circuit affirmed the convictions, Mehanna unsuccessfully sought a writ of certiorari from the Supreme Court that focused on his conviction based on the work he did for an Islamic website.

- *Investigative techniques*: The use of confidential informants and the recording of the defendant with the consent of the informant is permissible. Not discussed earlier were physical searches pursuant to FISA. For a FISA authorization to have been properly issued the FISA would have had to find, based on probable cause, that Mehanna was a foreign agent (i.e., involved in international terrorism) and that the property to be searched had been used by a foreign agent.[133] In addition, the FISA court would have had to find that the certification submitted to the court was complete in that it had "checked off all the boxes" stating that a significant purpose of the search was to obtain foreign intelligence; and that the information could not be obtained by normal investigative techniques. To pass muster, if the target were a U.S. person, the certification had to be not clearly erroneous. The FISA court also would have had to find that the proposed minimization procedures met statutory requirements.[134]
- *First Amendment issue*: Mehanna was charged and convicted of providing material support in two ways. One was his effort to obtain terrorist training (discussed more fully below) and the other was his translating Arab-language materials into English, which the government described as jihadist propaganda, for publication on a password-protected jihadist website. Section 2339B served as the basis for the charge that he provided material support to a listed federal terrorist organization, al-Qaeda.

This much was clear, but there was a sharp dispute between the defendant and the government over what the defendant knew when he carried out these activities and what his intent was. He certainly had the intent to further his radical ideology, but his attorneys claimed he did not have knowledge of coordination between al-Qaeda and the website to which he had submitted his translation. The defense said he did not know the website posted translated material at al-Qaeda's request. And the defendant disputed the government's claim that he intended to aid the website's goal of aiding al-Qaeda. The defense argued Mehanna had no direct links with al-Qaeda, did not coordinate with al-Qaeda, and did not operate under the direction of al-Qaeda. At best, he provided moral support and was perhaps arguably "associated" with al-Qaeda.

The next leg of the defendant's argument was that §2339B had not been interpreted by *Holder* to extend criminality to this kind of linkage, that *Holder* left the application of §2339B to these facts undecided – it had left the issue to another

133 50 USC §1824(a).
134 Id.

day – and, now that that day had arrived, it could not, consistent with the First Amendment, be interpreted to criminalize his behavior. Section 2339B could only be interpreted to criminalize speech activities when the following was true:

> [T]he person [providing the alleged support] must have a direct connection to the group [foreign terrorist organization (FTO)] and be working directly with the group [FTO] for it to be a violation of the statute.[135]

Thus to the extent that the trial court and the First Circuit rejected the defendant's interpretation of the facts and rejected the *Holder* decision, Mehanna's conviction was unconstitutional; hence he petitioned for the writ of certiorari. Any interpretation of §2339B that allowed criminalization on the facts of this case opened the door to punishing people simply for expressing their political viewpoints, infringing upon their First Amendment rights.

This line of argument was not successful and ultimately unpersuasive in obtaining the writ of certiorari. The First Circuit Court of Appeals said the trial court's interpretation of *Holder* in its instructions to the jury was correct, which said that the defendant could be found guilty of making the translation if this was done in:

> coordination with or at the direction of a foreign terrorist organization. Advocacy that is done independently of the terrorist organization and not at its direction or in coordination with it does not violate the statute.
>
> Put another way, activity that is proven to be the furnishing of material support or resources to a designated foreign terrorist organization under the statute is not activity that is protected by the First Amendment; on the other hand, as I've said, independent advocacy on behalf of the organization, not done at its direction or in coordination with it, is not a violation of the statute.

But the First Circuit sidestepped the issue by saying it would not review the sufficiency of the government's factual evidence regarding the "link" between Mehanna and al-Qaeda since it was not necessary to do so. Why not? Because the conviction for providing material support could stand solely on the fact that Mehanna had tried to go to a training camp and provide his fighting services to al-Qaeda.

Mehanna then petitioned the Supreme Court for a writ of certiorari. The core of Mehanna's argument to the Supreme Court was that the trial court and First Circuit (i) reached the wrong conclusions on the facts regarding his relationship with al-Qaeda; (ii) improperly interpreted *Holder*, and used jury instructions that did not properly reflect the meaning of *Holder*, and the instructions were vague and ambiguous. (iii) Consequently, both courts applied the wrong law to an erroneous factual conclusion, making it possible to find Mehanna guilty of an activity that was

135 *United States v Mehanna* at 50 (cited in note 22).

protected by the First Amendment. The result was precedent that created a dangerous slippery slope. This dangerous and harmful precedent says that the government now has the legal authority to characterize protected behavior – advocacy of an ideological viewpoint, and the voluntary translation of controversial material (the moral support of al-Qaeda) – as the criminal activity of material support of a terrorist organization.

Was the evidence sufficient to prove the constitutional minimum necessary link between Mehanna and al-Qaeda? Maybe or maybe not, depending on what that constitutional minimally necessary link must be according to the First Amendment and *Holder*. This is where the law gets somewhat ambiguous. *Holder* said that minimum necessary link had to entail a speech activity done in "coordination" with al-Qaeda or at the "direction" of al-Qaeda in order for it not to be protected. The jury instructions said this along with saying that if the speech activity was "independent" of al-Qaeda it could not be the basis of criminal conviction. But neither *Holder* nor the courts involved in the Mehanna prosecution defined these terms, leaving the law on this point ambiguous.

In its reply brief to the Mehanna petition for certiorari, the government finally came up with a definition of coordination. Quoting *Webster's Third New International Dictionary* 501 (2002) the government said the word "coordinate" meant bringing into common action, movement or condition" or to "regulate and combine in harmonious action."

What is not clear is whether the jury relied on this definition of coordination. It is possible the jury's conception of coordination might have included the mere occurrence of two actions in a close temporal sequence, e.g., al-Qaeda made it known it was open to support from volunteers, and Mehanna without any message directly conveyed to him personally stepped forward as a volunteer.[136] Take this example. Al-Qaeda lets it be known it would be useful for the cause if Muslims wrote letters to the editor on behalf of the cause, and learning of this, a Muslim writes such a letter. Was this letter written in coordination with or at the direction of al-Qaeda or was it an exercise in free speech by the letter writer? If this is an example of unlawful coordination, a whole new batch of speech activity has been newly criminalized.

- *Due process and evidentiary issues*: The First Circuit Court of Appeals says that to be guilty under §2339A, the defendant must have "provide[d] support or resources with the knowledge or intent that such resources be used to commit specific violent crimes."[137] In this case, the jury convicted Mehanna of violating §2339A

136 When "jurors have been left the option of relying upon a legally inadequate theory" as a result of the trial court's charge to the jury this could be grounds for reversal. *Griffin v United States*, 502 US 46, 59 (1991). But the First Circuit said that if this did occur in this case, it was nevertheless a harmless error since conviction was still possible exclusively on the charge of violating §2339B.

137 *United States v Mehanna*, at 43 (cited in note 22).

> based on the finding that he sought to obtain terrorist training in Yemen with the intent of providing his services to al-Qaeda and to kill persons abroad, especially Americans. (See 18 USC §§956 and 2332.) Mehanna argued on appeal that there was insufficient evidence to support his convictions. A claim of insufficient evidence ultimately rests upon the due process clause of the Fifth and Fourteenth amendments. ("[T]he Due Process Clause protects the accused against conviction except upon proof beyond a reasonable doubt of every fact necessary to constitute the crime with which he is charged."[138])

To make the case of insufficient evidence, the defendant argued that in the First Circuit various pieces of evidence that the government introduced should not have been admitted. A quick look at these arguments provides a good illustration of how the government goes about prosecuting terrorists. The categories of evidence involved included: (a) Mehanna's own statements; (b) statements from co-conspirators; (c) terrorist-related media – videos and propaganda; (d) evidence of Mehanna's efforts at covering up; and (e) evidence that he traveled to Yemen. Items (a) through (d) were introduced to prove that his intent in going to Yemen was to become trained as a terrorist, to provide his support to al-Qaeda to carry out killings.

The First Circuit upheld the trial court's rulings, admitting into evidence all these pieces of evidence; hence the First Circuit concluded there was sufficient evidence to convict. Looking at item (c), the Court of Appeals admitted that dozens of media items were introduced and that in a number of cases there were graphically violent images such as beheading. The legal question was whether this mass of evidence was relevant to proving the defendant's intent, or might its probative value be substantially outweighed by creating unfair prejudice.[139] Taking a very deferential posture toward the trial court, the First Circuit upheld the introduction of all this evidence. The evidence was "relevant," said the court, in proving the defendant's intent and motive. Further, the government "posited," and the court agreed, that the defendant was inspired by the terrorist rants, and developed an anti-American animus which culminated in his decision to travel to Yemen to join al-Qaeda. And the court said this evidence was "very probative" in rebutting the defendant's claim that his moderate beliefs prevented him from attacking Americans.

The statements from co-conspirators (b) were hearsay, but under the rule noted above, could be introduced to prove what the hearsay asserted, namely, that the defendant intended to obtain terrorist training in Yemen. A tricky point here was whether the conspiracy started before the trip to Yemen and continued past the trip to Yemen. That was a crucial point because the statements of conspirators could only be admitted if they were uttered in the course of the conspiracy. The First Circuit took a broad view of the duration of the conspiracy and even admitted statements

138 *In re Winship*, 397 US 358, 364 (1970).
139 FRE 403.

made prior to Mehanna's having joined the conspiracy. The Circuit court noted precedent which allowed the admission of such statements prior to the defendant joining the conspiracy: "[A] conspiracy is like a train. When a party knowingly steps aboard, he is part of the crew, and assumes the conspirator's responsibility for the existing freight." (*United States v Baines*, 812 F2d 41, 42 (1st Cir. 1987).)

(d) Evidence tending to prove that Mehanna was attempting to cover up the real purpose of the trip was admitted based on the precedent that said evidence of a cover-up can be probative regarding the elements of the underlying crime, in this case, intent to aid al-Qaeda. And, of course, Mehanna's own statements would be relevant to and probative of this state of mind, which the court said was relevant to the issue of his intent.

8

MILITARY DETENTION AND INTERROGATION

On November 13, 2001 President Bush, acting as commander-in-chief, issued a military order announcing a new policy of the United States, namely, that it was possible for the Secretary of Defense to detain members of al-Qaeda (and others) without trial, and if the detainees were tried, they would be tried by military commissions.[1] This chapter deals with detention and interrogation, and Chapter 9 covers trials by military commissions.

This chapter assumes that the President as commander-in-chief has the authority to command the military to detain without trial unprivileged enemy belligerents, even U.S. citizens, seized on foreign battlefields.[2] The chapter does not address what authority, if any, Congress may use to regulate this assumed authority of the President.

> Terminology: The term "belligerent" is used instead of "combatant," a commonly used term, for two reasons. (1) In non-legal English "combatant" connotes that the individual must have personally acted violently, but the people discussed here may not have. (2) In legal-English the term "combatant" arises in the context of international law dealing with conflicts between

1 Detention, Treatment, and Trial of Certain Non-Citizens in the War Against Terrorism §1(a), 66 Fed. Reg. 57,831 (November 13, 2001), (hereinafter Military order), archived at https://fas.org/irp/offdocs/eo/mo-111301.htm.

2 Philip B. Heymann, Essay: *Detention*, 2 Harv Nat Sec J, archived at http://harvardnsj.org/volume-2/. Consider. *Ex Parte Quirin*, 317 US 1, 28 (1942). See, also, Oona Hathaway, Samuel Adelsberg, Spencer Amdur, Philip Levitz and Freya Pitts, *The power to detain: Detention of terrorism suspects after 9/11*, 38 Yale J Inter L 123, 146 (2013). John Walker Lindh and Yasir Hamdi, both U.S. citizens, were seized on foreign battlefields. Lindh pled guilty and was given a 20-year sentence. Hamdi sought release leading to a Supreme Court case discussed below.

recognized states (i.e., international armed conflicts); note the terrorism discussed here legally is a non-international conflict in so far as it does not involve recognized states.[3]

The chapter explores the use of the military to detain people seized in the U.S without trial, perhaps indefinitely. The following issues are addressed:

1 Does the President enjoy preclusive authority as commander in chief to determine who may be detained, or *must* Congress play a role in establishing the applicable law? A related question: Under what circumstances, if at all, may the President and Congress use the military domestically to detain? (Is the U.S. a battlefield under the law of war in the so-called "war on terror?")
2 Constitutionally, may U.S. citizens or legal residents be subjected to military detainment, or must citizens/residents be dealt with by civilian authorities?
3 Assuming the military may detain U.S. citizens, what are the sufficient and/or necessary conditions to detain? What are the boundaries of the authority to detain?
4 What procedural due process rights do people seized by the military enjoy to challenge their status as persons who may be detained?
5 Once detained, what rights regarding treatment during detainment do detainees have? When must detention cease?

Section I of this chapter takes on the first question. Section II addresses the second; Sections III–V cover question 3; Section VI turns to question 4; and Section VII question 5.

A brief chronology: Three days after 9/11 Congress passed the "Authorization to Use Military Force" (AUMF), which became an important basis for the President to claim authority to detain unprivileged enemy belligerents. On November 13, 2001 Bush issued a military order specifically addressing detention. With the passage of the Military Commissions Act (MCA) in 2006 and 2009 two other statutes relevant to detention were passed. In 2012 the National Defense Authorization Act (NDAA) specifically authorized detention by the President. The Department of Defense issued a manual on the law of war. And on January 30, 2018 President Trump issued E.O. 132824, ordering Guantanamo to remain open, reversing President Obama's E.O. 13492 that sought its closure.

I. Presidential domestic exercise of the Constitution's Article II military-detention authority

This section focuses on the President's Article II authority to use the military to detain unprivileged enemy belligerents, without congressional authorization, in the U.S. The section does not describe precisely the kind of person who may be detained; for this see Sections II through V.

3 Knut Dörmann, *The legal situation of "unlawful/privileged combatants,"* 85 IRRC 45 (March 2003).

John Yoo and Robert Delahunty have argued that "Article II of the Constitution, which vests the President with the power to respond to emergency threats to the national security, directly authorizes use of the Armed Forces in domestic operations against terrorists."[4] Note the double claim here: first, *that it is legally permissible to use military authority* (which would include the authority to detain enemy belligerents), and, second, *that the President alone can invoke that authority*. Another 2002 memo out of the Office of Legal Counsel also claimed there was legal precedent for the President's authority; Article II and federal statutes allowed the President to detain as an enemy belligerent a U.S. citizen (Jose Padilla) captured in the U.S.[5] This same argument was made to the Supreme Court.[6] In 2008 another memo from the Office of Legal Counsel warned that caution should be exercised before relying on the Yoo-Delahunty argument.[7]

Turning to the first Yoo-Delahunty claim, there are two Supreme Court cases arising out of the Civil War that are relevant, but do not settle the issue. One is the so-called *Prize Cases* in which the Court ruled that even in the absence of a declaration of war and despite the fact the enemy was not an acknowledged independent nation, there was an ongoing "de-facto war."[8] The case seems at first glance to support Yoo and Delahunty. But the facts of the situation in the *Prize Cases* (insurrection) are markedly different from the current situation, thus making it inapplicable to the conflict with al-Qaeda.[9]

Another case cuts against the domestic use of the military today. The Supreme Court asked itself whether a military commission had jurisdiction when it tried and sentenced Lampdin P. Milligan. The Court said "no," making the point that "the laws and usages of war . . . can never be applied to citizens in states that have upheld the authority of the government, and where the courts are open and their process unobstructed."[10] As for relying on "martial law," the Court cut that option off, writing that "Martial rule can never exist where the courts are open and in the proper and unobstructed exercise of their jurisdiction."

4 Memorandum for Alberto Gonzales, Counsel to the President and William J. Haynes, General Counsel, Department of Defense from John C. Yoo, Deputy Assistant Attorney General and Robert J. Delahunty, Special Counsel, Re: Authority for Use of Military Force to Combat Terrorist Activities Within the United States 4 (October 23, 2001), archived at https://nsarchive2.gwu.edu/torturingdemocracy/documents/20011023.pdf.

5 Memorandum for the Attorney General from Jay S. Bybee, Assistant Attorney General, Re: Determination of Enemy Belligerency and Military Detention (June 8, 2002), archived at https://www.hsdl.org/?abstract&did=741720.

6 Brief for Respondents on Writ of Certiorari, 13–18, *Hamdi v Rumsfeld*, Supreme Court (March 2004), archived at https://supreme.findlaw.com/supreme_court/briefs/03-6696/03-6696-mer-resp.html.

7 William C. Banks and Stephen Dycus, *Soldiers on the homefront*, 222–223 (Harvard 2016).

8 *The Brig Amy Warwick; The Schooner Crenshaw; The Barque Hiawatha; The Schooner Brilliante*, 67 US 635 (1862).

9 See, also, *Miller v United States*, 78 US (11 Wall) 268 (1870).

10 *Ex Parte Milligan*, 71 US 2, 104 (1866).

In a World War II decision, *Ex Parte Quirin*, the Court allowed the use of military authority to detain and try a U.S. citizen caught on U.S. soil who was fighting for Germany.[11] Regarding the President's authority, the Court said it was not necessary in this case "to determine to what extent the President as commander in chief has constitutional power to create military commissions [and detain enemy belligerents] without the support of Congressional legislation."[12] The Court got around *Milligan* when it claimed that Milligan won his writ of habeas corpus because Milligan himself was simply not an enemy combatant. (Incidentally, Justice Scalia, dissenting in *Hamdi v Rumsfeld*, 2004, concluded that the *Quirin* Court reversed *Milligan* rather than described it.[13]) (More about *Milligan* and *Quirin* below.)

The authority of the President to act as commander-in-chief domestically came up again before the Supreme Court in *Hamdi v Rumsfeld*. The President argued that he did not need explicit Congressional authorization to detain in a military brig Yasir Hamdi, a U.S. citizen seized in Afghanistan and transferred to the United States as an enemy combatant. President Bush claimed he had plenary authority as commander-in-chief under Article II to detain Hamdi, a power that was "fully engaged," given the "armed conflict that the United States is now fighting against the Al-Qaeda terrorist network." Bush argued, "Especially in the case of foreign attack, the President's authority to wage war [and detain combatants] is not dependent on 'any special legislative authority'."[14] While the Court acknowledged the President's claim, it did not rule on it since the President had the necessary authority under the AUMF.[15]

The Second Circuit Court of Appeals took on the issue avoided by the Supreme Court.[16] Jose Padilla, a U.S. citizen, was arrested on May 8, 2002 in Chicago when he flew into the U.S. from Pakistan. Shortly after his arrest President Bush designated him an enemy belligerent and ordered that the military detain him. It was believed he had come back to the U.S. on behalf of al-Qaeda to execute a plan to build and detonate a "dirty bomb." Proceedings and various rulings in the federal district court led to an appeal to the Second Circuit, which ruled that the detention of Padilla was a proper exercise of the President's power as commander-in-chief, and that the AUMF also gave the President the authority despite 18 USC §4001(a)

The Second Circuit concluded that the President lacked inherent constitutional authority to detain a U.S. citizen on American soil. The court looked at various provisions of the Constitution (e.g., the habeas corpus suspension clause, Article 1, §9, cl 2) and concluded that *Congress* had the power to deal domestically with

11 317 US 1 (1947).
12 Id at 29.
13 *Hamdi v Rumsfeld*, 542 US 507 (2004), J. Scalia, Dissenting.
14 Brief for the Respondents, *Hamdi v Rumsfeld* at 13 (cited in note 6).
15 *Hamdi v Rumsfeld*, at 516–517 (cited in note 13). Justice Thomas dissented relying on *Moyer v Peabody*, 212 US 78 (1909).
16 *Padilla ex. rel. Newman v Bush*, 352 F3d 695 (2d Cir. 2003), rev'd sub. nom., *Rumsfeld v Padilla*, 542 US 426 (2004).

such crises. In addition, the President did not have statutory authorization. As for precedent, the court pointed out that the *Quirin* decision rested on the existence of congressional authorization for the use of military tribunals to try unlawful belligerents, and that the *Quirin* combatants were admitted soldiers in the German army, thus *Quirin* did not support the detention of Padilla.

The legal proceedings regarding Padilla continued for many more years. In 2004 the Supreme Court ruled he should have appealed his detention to the Fourth Circuit, not the Second Circuit, since he was being held in South Carolina, not New York. The case thus ended up in the Fourth Circuit Court of Appeals, which held that the President was authorized by the AUMF to detain Padilla, and that the *Quirin* decision supported that conclusion, and the decision in *Milligan* was distinguishable.[17]

Like Quirin, Padilla was "associated with the military arm of the enemy," like the defendants in *Quirin*, he was seized on U.S. soil, and the decision upholding detention in *Hamdi* did not hinge on the fact he was captured outside of the U.S. The Court also concluded that the fact that Padilla could have been prosecuted in a civilian criminal court "was not determinative of the power to detain."

> Equally important, in many instances criminal prosecution would impede the Executive in its efforts to gather intelligence from the detainee and to restrict the detainee's communication with confederates so as to ensure that the detainee does not pose a continuing threat to national security even as he is confined – impediments that would render military detention not only an appropriate, but also the necessary, course of action to be taken in the interest of national security.[18]

[In 2005 the administration changed course, obtained a criminal indictment in a civilian court, and in 2008 a conviction and a sentence of 17 years.[19]]

In sum, precedent in this area is unsettled in two respects. First, it is not firmly settled that the President, on his own, may choose to exercise military authority domestically. (However, as discussed below, Congress arguably has granted the President this authority. At least five Justices agree *Congress* may authorize the President to use military detainment authority domestically.[20] See Sections IV and V discussing such Congressional authorization.)

17 *Padilla v Hanft*, 423 F3d 386 (4th Cir 2005).

18 Id at 395.

19 http://www.cnn.com/2005/LAW/11/22/padilla.case/index.html; Peter Whoriskey and Dan Eggen, *Judge sentences Padilla to 17 years, cites his detention* (Washington Post, January 23, 2008), archived at http://www.washingtonpost.com/wp-dyn/content/article/2008/01/22/AR2008012200565.html.

20 See, also, *Al-Marri v Wright*, 487 F3d 160 (4th Cir. 2007), vacated, *Al-Marri v Pucciarelli*, 534 F3d 213 (4th Cir. 2008) (per curiam, en banc) (Traxler, J concurring), vacated sub nom. *Al-Marri v Spagone*, 555 US 1220 (2009).

Two concluding observations. First, the Yoo and Delahunty argument is not conclusively supported by precedent, and Professors Neil K. Katyal and Laurence H. Tribe argue that the Constitution's text, structure, and logic demand approval by Congress if life, liberty, or property are to be significantly curtailed or abridged.[21]

Second, the Posse Comitatus Act, passed in the wake of the Civil War and Reconstruction, prohibits the use of the military to execute the civilian laws unless expressly authorized by the Constitution or by an act of Congress.[22] And in the Non-Detention Act of 1971 (18 USC §4001) Congress provided that "No citizen shall be imprisoned or otherwise detained by the United States except pursuant to an Act of Congress." These two laws taken together point to the necessity of Congressional legislation to authorize the military to detain a citizen suspected of violating either the law of war or civilian criminal law.

II. The detention of U.S. citizens seized on U.S. soil

Even assuming an act of Congress, may the government constitutionally detain as an unprivileged enemy belligerent a U.S. citizen or legal resident alien seized on U.S. soil? There is a long history touching on the detainment of U.S. citizens by the military. As noted above, Milligan was arrested and tried by Lincoln's military, only to be released. A state governor in Colorado, was exonerated in his detention of a labor union leader.[23] In what is now a discredited opinion, the Supreme Court rejected a claim that the equal protection clause had been violated by a military exclusion order directed to people of Japanese ancestry in California, thereby constitutionally approving the internment during World War II of Japanese-Americans without any proof they were in fact disloyal or a security risk.[24] On the same day, in *Ex parte Endo* the Court ruled that the authority to exclude persons of Japanese ancestry from declared military areas did not include the authority to detain concededly loyal Americans.[25] While the Japanese internment cases have been disavowed by the Supreme Court, "the constitutionality of detention of citizens during war who are deemed dangerous has never expressly been ruled *per se* unconstitutional."[26] Yet the use of the phrase "conceded loyal" in *Ex Parte Endo* seems to imply there is a Fifth

21 Neal K. Katyal and Laurence H. Tribe, *Waging war, deciding guilt: Trying the military tribunals*, 111 Yale L J 1259, 1266 (2002).

22 18 USC §1385. See Charles Doyle and Jennifer K. Elsea, *The Posse Comitatus Act and related matters: The use of the military to execute civilian law* (Congressional Research Service, August 16, 2012 R42659).

23 *Moyer v Peabody* (cited in note 15).

24 *Korematsu v United States*, 323 US 214 (1944). In *Trump v Hawaii*, No. 17.965 *38 (U.S. June 26, 2017) the Court wrote, *Korematsu* was gravely wrong the day it was decided, has been overruled in the court of history, and—to be clear—"has no place in law under the Constitution."

25 *Ex Parte Endo*, 323 US 283 (1944).

26 Jennifer K. Elsea, *Detention of U.S. persons as enemy combatants*, 31 (Congressional Research Service, January 23, 2014, R42337).

Amendment guarantee of procedural due process applicable to the determination of loyalty or dangerousness.[27]

In the *Quirin* decision,[28] denying an application for a writ of habeas corpus filed by the defendants, and upholding their trial by military commission, the Supreme Court said that the U.S. citizenship of Herbert Hans Haupt did not relieve him from the consequences of violating the law of war as an enemy combatant. Approximately 60 years later the Supreme Court again affirmed, citing the *Quirin* decision, that "There is no bar to this Nation's holding one of its own citizens as an enemy combatant."[29] And as discussed below the detainment of U.S. citizens seized on U.S. soil has been upheld by the courts.

III. Limits on the substantive grounds for detention

May the U.S. government declare that mere political opponents of the President are unprivileged enemy belligerents? Most certainly "no." Binding treaty obligations (Article VI, clause 2) and possibly also customary international law, comprised of those principles not agreed to in treaty but generally recognized by states are likely to stand in the way. And declaring the President's opponents to be detainable unprivileged enemy belligerents, would violate many Constitutional provisions including the First Amendment's free speech clause, the Fifth Amendment's due process clause, and the Fourteenth Amendment's equal protection clause.

But what about declaring mass murderers such as Timothy McVeigh and Dylan Root as militarily detainable unprivileged enemy belligerents? (Whether McVeigh and Root are terrorists under civilian criminal law is a separate issue, see Chapter 7.) What about a lone wolf who, espousing the extremist views of a radical organization such as the Real Irish Republican Army, commits a violent act? May a radical Muslim cleric who personally committed no violent acts but who preached extremist beliefs and contributed money to Hezbollah charities be militarily detained? (See Chapter 7 regarding possible criminal prosecution.) Could the government legally adopt a policy/law that treated Mehanna (Chapter 7) as an unprivileged enemy belligerent? Treaty and international customary law gets increasingly complex when applied to each of the above examples.

Sections IV, V, and VI address the policy and law the President and Congress have actually adopted. Section VII turns to judicial efforts to define the scope of a President's detention authority in light of the Constitution, the statutes, and international law. (Material in the footnote provides a starting point for exploring discussions on these issues.[30])

27 Id at 30.

28 *Ex Parte Quirin*, 317 US 631 (1947).

29 *Hamdi v Rumsfeld* (cited in note 13).

30 Onna Hathaway, Samuel Adelsberg, Spencer Amdur, Philip Levitz, and Freya Pitts, and Sirine Shebaya, *The power to detain: Detention of terrorism suspects after 9/11*, 38 Yale J Int L 123(2013); Laurie R. Blank,

IV. The President and the Department of Defense

Bush's military order of November 13, 2001 specified who would be detained, *but excluded from its coverage U.S. citizens.* Roughly, the order covered members of al-Qaeda and broadly swept up anybody (other than citizens) who engaged, aided, abetted, conspired in international terrorism (all undefined terms), or who harbored a terrorist.[31] Bush not only used his own undefined terms in the order, he also detained people if he felt the facts indicated there was a "reason to believe" someone fit the undefined terms. The military order did not exclude its application domestically. [Remember Jose Padilla was seized and detained as an enemy belligerent on May 8, 2002, as was Ali Saleh Kahlah Al-Marri on June 23, 2003. Several years later, The Fourth Circuit Court of Appeals in two decisions concluded that the AUMF provided authorization for both detentions; both were U.S. citizens arrested in the U.S.[32] When authorizing their detentions President Bush apparently ignored or effectively amended his own Military Order that excluded the detention of U.S. citizens.]

The Department of Defense's (DOD) view of the military's authority to detain is different and broader. It says that "an individual who is not entitled to the distinct privileges of combatant status (e.g., combatant immunity [as would apply to a uniformed enemy soldier]), but who by *engaging in hostilities* [against the U.S.] has incurred the corresponding liabilities of combatant status [e.g., is subject to detention]."[33] (Drawing the distinction between lawful and unlawful belligerents can get into complex issues of international law.[34])

Several points regarding this claimed authority need to be made. First, it appears to rest wholly on the President's Article II authority. Second, the term "engaging in hostilities" seems to have two prongs to it. One prong involves the individual personally doing things intended to cause harm to the enemy, namely, the U.S. This means either engaging in combat and carrying out acts "that are an integral part of combat operations or that effectively and substantially contribute . . . to the conduct of sustained combat operations." It would not include doing something equivalent to buying "war bonds."[35] The other prong, according to the DOD manual, is when the individual is "part of a non-state armed group that is engaged in hostilities."[36] Thus DOD also claims the authority to detain individuals who

A square peg in a round hole: Stretching law of war detention too far, 63 Rutgers L R 1169 (2011); David Mortlock, *Definite detention: The scope of the President's authority to detain enemy combatants*, 4 Harv L Pol R 375 (2010).

31 Military order (cited in note 1).

32 *Padilla v Hanft* (cited in note 17); *Al-Marri v Pucciarelli* (cited in note 20).

33 Department of Defense Directive, No. 2310.01E, Aug 19, 2014, Incorporating Change 1, May 24, 2017, archived at https://www.hsdl.org/?abstract&did=757296.

34 See, for example, *United States v Hamidullin*, No. 15-4788 (4th Cir. 2018).

35 Id; Office of General Counsel, *Department of defense law of war manual*, 224–228 (June 2015), archived at https://www.defense.gov/Portals/1/Documents/pubs/Law-of-War-Manual-June-2015.pdf.

36 Id at 160; Department of Defense Directive, No. 2310.01E (cited in note 36).

"substantially support" (undefined) an enemy non-state armed group.[37] (Recall the crime of providing material support discussed in Chapter 7.)

In sum, a U.S. citizen who engaged him- or herself in a violent act against the U.S., substantially contributed to such an operation, who became "part of" a *group* involved in these activities, or who substantially supported an enemy non-state armed group, could be detained. It is important to note that there is disagreement regarding whether the detention authority that the government has (however defined) "extends to entities other than al-Qaeda and the Taliban, and there is disagreement regarding which entities are sufficiently affiliated with al-Qaeda or the Taliban so as to be indistinguishable from them."[38] The chapter does not address this "group" issue, but only the individual factors that make a person detainable.

How the DOD policy squares with what the *judiciary* has said about the authority of the government to detain unprivileged enemy belligerents is taken up in Section VII. Meanwhile, it is instructive to consider how the DOD policies apply to the case of Tarek Mehanna (discussed in Chapter 7). Recall that Mehanna, a U.S. citizen, was tried under civilian criminal law. He had espoused militant beliefs, attempted to obtain terrorist training in Yemen, and provided a translation of radical Islamist materials for release via a webpage associated with al-Qaeda. He was successfully prosecuted for violating several criminal laws including the prohibition against providing material support. But under the DOD policy, it seems as if he could have just as easily been detained as an unprivileged enemy belligerent. Whether this application of the policy is constitutional is a separate question.

V. Congressional authorization of detention

The Constitution does not per se block the military detainment of U.S. citizens seized on U.S. soil simply because they are citizens, and the Posse Comitatus (18 USC §1385) and Non-Detention Act (18 USC §4001) permit the detention of U.S. citizens if authorized by Congress.

Congress has passed several laws authorizing detention. First came the AUMF of September 14, 2001, which said:

> The President is authorized to use all necessary and appropriate force against those nations, organizations, or persons he determines planned, authorized, committed, or aided the terrorist attacks that occurred on September 11, 2001, or harbored such organizations or persons, in order to prevent any future acts of international terrorism against the United States by such nations, organizations or persons.[39]

37 Id.

38 Robert B. Chesney, *Who may be held? Military detention through the habeas lens*, 52 Boston College L Rev 769, 770 (2011).

39 50 USC §1541, Note.

The AUMF made no specific mention of an authority to detain, but Bush said the phrase "necessary and appropriate force" included the power to detain. As discussed below, the judiciary agreed.

Between the AUMF (2001) and 2012 Presidents Bush and Obama and Congress further elaborated on the authority to detain.[40] The National Defense Authorization Act (NDAA) of 2012 explicitly authorized the President to detain and also defined who may be detained.[41]

A IN GENERAL. – Congress affirms that the authority of the President to use all necessary and appropriate force pursuant to the Authorization for Use of Military Force (Public Law 107–40; 50 USC 1541 note) includes the authority for the Armed Forces of the United States to detain covered persons (as defined in subsection (b)) pending disposition under the law of war.

B COVERED PERSONS. – A covered person under this section is any person as follows:

  1 A person who planned, authorized, committed, or aided the terrorist attacks that occurred on September 11, 2001, or harbored those responsible for those attacks.
  2 A person who was a part of or substantially supported Al-Qaeda, the Taliban, or associated forces that are engaged in hostilities against the United States or its coalition partners, including any person who has committed a combatant act or has directly supported such hostilities in aid of such enemy forces.

The NDAA kept detention authority focused on those directly involved in 9/11 and people who were part of al-Qaeda, the Taliban, or associated forces (the associational criterion), or who substantially supported certain groups, or who "engaged in hostilities" against the U.S. and coalition partners.[42]

The NDAA does not prevent its application domestically. Additionally, existing law regarding the detention of U.S. citizens was expressly left untouched by the NDAA. The NDAA (18 USC §4001) says that no citizen may be detained except pursuant to an act of Congress. The AUMF arguably satisfies this requirement, at least when it comes to U.S. citizens captured outside the U.S.[43] (Also significant is

40 Military Commissions Act of 2006, Pub L No 109-366, 120 Stat. 2600, codified at chapter 47A of Title 10, US Code (2006), archived at https://www.loc.gov/rr/frd/Military_Law/pdf/PL-109-366.pdf. The statute authorized military commissions to try "unlawful enemy combatants" as defined in the statute and by logical implication authorized the detainment of these people.

41 National Defense Authorization Act for Fiscal Year 2012, H.R. 1540, 112th Cong (2011); 10 USC §801 note.

42 See, also, *Hedges v Obama*, 724 F3d 170 (2d Cir 2013), cert. denied, 134 S Ct 1936 2014 (offering an interpretation of the provision and dismissing based on lack of standing).

43 *Hamdi v Rumsfeld* (cited in note 13).

the fact that the NDAA expressly stated it was not intended to expand or limit the President's authority (presumably under Article II), or limit the scope of the AUMF (10 USC 801 note).)

There is also the Military Commissions Act of 2009 that authorized military commissions, and in doing so specified the jurisdiction of those commissions regarding persons.[44] The DC Circuit Court relied on this provision to say that any person subject to a military commission trial was also subject to detention.[45] Summarizing, the MCA 2009 allows the detention of *aliens* who have engaged in hostilities against the U.S. or coalition partners; who have purposefully and materially supported such hostilities; or, who were a member of al-Qaeda at the time the offense occurred.

VI. Taking stock: statutes and DOD policy

The President has multiple sources of authority to detain: (i) Article II authority as commander-in-chief – arguably the provisions of the DOD manual rest on this authority; (ii) the AUMF; (iii) the NDAA, which is narrower than the AUMF. Note that Congress did not intend for the NDAA to supersede the AUMF (thereby limiting the AUMF's broader authority).[46] Likewise the NDAA does not limit the more sweeping policy of the DOD, neither does it expand or limit the President's authority.

The DOD manual, AUMF, and NDAA all authorize the detainment of U.S. citizens, even those seized on U.S. soil, as long as they also satisfy the definitions of a "covered person." (The MCA 2009 addresses aliens.) Besides those who actually acted violently toward the U.S., covered persons included those who were "part of" designated groups, or who "substantially supported" the groups.

These last two categories of covered persons lack clear-cut boundaries, and defining those boundaries has been left to the judiciary. Judge Wilkinson of the Fourth Circuit stated in wrestling with these boundaries that "there must be appropriate criteria for determining when the government may constitutionally detain a suspected terrorist as an enemy combatant."[47]

VII. The judicial determination of the authority to detain[48]

In this still somewhat unsettled area of the law at least one point is established. Yaser Esam Hamdi, a U.S. citizen, was seized in Afghanistan where he was a weapon-carrying member of a Taliban fighting unit engaged in armed conflict with the

44 10 USC §948a (6–7).

45 *Al-Bahini v Obama*, 590 F3d 866 (DC Cir 2010), rehearing en banc denied, 619 F3d 1 (DC C 2010).

46 National Defense Authorization Act for Fiscal Year 2012, §1021(d) (cited in note 44).

47 *Al-Marri v Pucciarelli*, at 313 (Wilkerson, J concurring in part and dissenting in part) (cited in note 23).

48 A question of importance not addressed here is which bodies of law are relevant to determining the scope of attention authority. Chesney, *Who may be held? Military detention through the habeas lens*, at

U.S. The Supreme Court ruled that the AUMF authorized the President to detain Hamdi, saying that the detainment of Hamdi as an unlawful combatant/belligerent was by universal agreement an important incident of war.[49]

Few would argue that *Hamdi* was not detainable, but the case of Ghaleb Nassar Al-Bihani posed a more difficult fact scenario for the D.C. Circuit Court.[50] Al-Bihani was a Yemini citizen captured on a foreign battlefield who worked as a cook for the brigade; he carried a brigade-issued weapon but did not engage in combat. The unit he worked for had been occasionally commanded by a member of al-Qaeda and he followed the commands of his brigade. Relying on MCA 2006 and 2009 as well as the AUMF, the Circuit Court concluded he was "part of" a belligerent group, and purposefully and materially supported hostilities; hence he was detainable. The court rejected his argument that he was only a civilian contractor rendering services.

The following case posed a yet more complex problem for the Fourth Circuit; the case resulted in a sharply divided en banc panel.[51] Here are the facts: Ali Saleh Kahlah al-Marri was a legal resident of the United States and a citizen of Qatar. He was arrested in Peoria, Illinois, spent some time in ordinary jails, was declared on June 23, 2003 by President Bush to be an enemy belligerent, then taken to the Naval Consolidated Brig in South Carolina where he was held without charge. In 2004 he sought a writ of habeas corpus, which the government resisted in part by providing the court with a declaration that asserted al-Marri was associated with al-Qaeda, trained in an al-Qaeda training camp, had volunteered for a "martyr mission," was ordered to enter the U.S. prior to 9/11 as a "sleeper agent," and was given money to buy a computer. While in the U.S. he gathered information about poisonous chemicals, undertook to obtain various false documents, communicated with known terrorists, saved information about jihad and 9/11, and had a picture of Bin Laden on his computer. Al-Marri denied these factual allegations, but did

---

782 (cited in noted 41); the D.C. Circuit Court has wrestled with the relevance of law of war for interpreting domestic statutes. In one case, Judge Brown, writing in *Al-Bihani v Obama*, rejected the view that Congress intended international laws of war to serve as extra-textual limits on the AUMF, MCA 2006, and the MCA 2009. (*Al-Bahini v Obama* at 871 (cited in note 48).) That approach to the interpretation of the statutes was thrown into doubt in the D.C. Circuit when a majority of the circuit judges, while denying a petition for en banc review, also said the rejection of international law by the decision under review was dicta. (*Al-Bahini v Obama*, 619 F3d 1 (DC Cir 2010).) Judges on the Fourth Circuit Court of Appeals have turned to the laws of war to interpret the meaning of the AUMF and the definition of enemy combatant. Thus the relevance of international law for interpreting the meaning of the statutes is not settled but Martin Lederman and Steve Vladeck have argued that Congress did intend for the AUMF and the NDAA to be interpreted in light of the law of war. (Marty Lederman and Steve Vladeck, *The NDAA: The good, the bad, and the laws of war – Part II* (Lawfare, December 31, 2011), archived at https://www.lawfareblog.com/ndaa-good-bad-and-laws-war-part-ii.) This raises issues not only regarding the legal status of a detainee but also regarding other issues such as the treatment of detainees and the length of their detention. (See Section VIII.)

49 *Hamdi v Rumsfeld* (cited in note 13).

50 *Al-Bahini v Obama* (cited in note 48).

51 *Al-Marri v Wright* (cited in note 23).

not file rebuttal evidence, contending that the government had the initial burden to prove he was an enemy belligerent and that the declaration was not sufficient. When a federal district court denied the writ of habeas corpus, he appealed to the Fourth Circuit Court of Appeals, which in a 2-1 vote concluded that the President did not have the authority to seize and indefinitely detain al-Marri even assuming that the government's declaration was correct. He did commit grave crimes, but the court found no authority that al-Marri could be treated as an enemy belligerent or as anything other than a (criminal) civilian.

The government sought and got an en banc review of the decision by the Fourth Circuit, which it won with a fractured nine-member panel voting 5-4 that al-Marri could be detained as an enemy combatant.[52] A slightly different 5-4 majority also concluded that the case needed to be remanded to the district court because al-Marri had not been provided with sufficient process to challenge his designation as an enemy combatant. [Procedural issues are taken up separately below and in Chapter 10.]

One member of the 5-4 majority upholding detention, Judge Traxler, said the allegations regarding al-Marri were sufficient to detain him – allied with al-Qaeda, volunteering for a martyr mission, getting training and money, getting sent to the U.S. as a sleeper agent.[53] His opinion did not spell out what he would say were "necessary" conditions in order to detain, that is, he did not demark the outer boundaries of AUMF's grant of detention authority. Judge Wilkinson wrote a more sophisticated opinion supporting detention that did strongly hint at the outer boundaries of the government's detention authority.[54] A first necessary condition was that the individual be an "enemy." An enemy, he said, is a person who is a "member" of an organization (or nation) against whom Congress has authorized the use of military force. A second necessary condition was that they had to be a "combatant." "In light of today's realities, a combatant is a person who knowingly plans or engages in conduct that harms or aims to harm persons or property for the purpose of furthering the military goals of an enemy nation or organization. . . . Under this criterion . . . members of an enemy sleeper terrorist cell that have taken steps, even if preliminary in nature, toward an act of destruction are also considered combatants."[55] Based on these criteria, Judge Wilkinson said that Timothy McVeigh could not be designated an enemy combatant because he was not a member of an enemy organization. However, he concluded that al-Marri easily fit all the requirements of being classified as an enemy combatant. In reaching this conclusion, Judge Wilkinson seemed to say that detention based on membership alone was insufficient; there had to be some showing of knowing involvement in violent activities.[56]

52 *Al-Marri v Pucciarelli* (cited in note 23).
53 Id at 253.
54 Id at 293.
55 Id at 324.
56 Chesney, *Who may be held? Military detention through the habeas lens*, at 822 (cited in note 41).

Judge Motz in dissent laid out a different necessary condition in order to detain. She said detainment required that the detainee had to be affiliated during wartime with the military arm of the enemy and to have fought alongside them.[57] In effect, she claimed the *Hamdi* decision laid out the outer boundaries of the government's detention authority and al-Marri did not fit within those boundaries. Hence al-Marri was but a civilian who was planning on committing a crime on behalf of an enemy organization and could only be prosecuted in the civilian courts for a crime.

The Supreme Court ultimately vacated the Fourth Circuit en banc opinion after the administration charged al-Marri with a federal crime and placed him in the ordinary criminal justice system.[58]

The District of Columbia federal circuit courts have wrestled with related but different sufficient conditions to detain. As Judge Wilkinson said some form of direct participation in hostilities would be sufficient. But what the D.C. courts have focused on is whether membership and support are sufficient conditions. Several scholars who have carefully reviewed the relevant opinions have concluded that the D.C. courts have answered "yes" to both questions with several qualifications.[59] Thus a person may be found detainable because they were a member of al-Qaeda (or an associated organization); and attending a training camp or staying at a guest house seems to be sufficient evidence of membership. Other evidence that is relevant, but not by itself sufficient, includes association with, say, al-Qaeda members, carrying a large amount of cash when captured, attending a religious school where other recruits attended, etc. Proof of being part of the chain of command of the organization is sufficient but not necessary. There seems to be no geographic constraint in determining membership.

Opinions regarding support as a sufficient condition yield an even murkier picture. Whether support – independent of proof of membership – is sufficient is not clearly settled, but most likely the answer is "yes." Recall that the DOD and the NDAA both authorize detainment of those who provided "substantial support" to certain groups. However, it remains to be seen whether the independent support criterion must be limited to people captured or to those who carried out hostile actions in certain geographic locations such as Afghanistan. Also not settled is the kind and extent of support that has to be proved, and whether proof of a specific intent to contribute to violence is required. Two other commentators say the meaning of the phrase is going to have to be worked out on a case-by-case basis in light of each specific fact situation.[60]

57 Id at 217.

58 *Al-Marri v Spagone* (cited in note 23).

59 Benjamin Wittes, et al., *The emerging law of detention 2.0: Project on law and security*, 24 (Harvard Law/Brookings April 2012), archived at https://www.brookings.edu/research/the-emerging-law-of-detention-2-0-the-guantanamo-habeas-cases-as-lawmaking/; Chesney, *Who may be held? Military detention through the habeas lens*, at 829, 845 (cited in note 41).

60 Marty Lederman and Steve Vladeck, *The NDAA: The good, the bad, and the laws of war – Part II* (Lawfare December 31, 2011), archived at https://www.lawfareblog.com/ndaa-good-bad-and-laws-war-part-ii.

Looking back at DOD policy and at the NDAA on detainment it seems that those provisions as written, *on their face* satisfy what the judiciary has said, except with regard to the unqualified claim of the DOD that the military may detain individuals who "substantially support" an enemy non-state armed group. Given the evolving definition of unprivileged enemy belligerent it is unlikely such a belligerent legally would also be a "lone wolf." But if support independent of membership is a sufficient condition to be an unprivileged enemy belligerent, it is possible that such a person could be both an unprivileged enemy belligerent and a lone wolf.

VIII. Procedural due process and proving detainability

Given that the body of law reviewed above tilts toward detainability, due process issues (Fifth Amendment) such as the standard of proof and the use of hearsay evidence become especially important. The procedures available to detainees occur in three settings: one set of procedures is carried out by the military "jailors" (discussed later in this section). Chapter 9 takes up the procedures of military commissions; Chapter 10 addresses judicial hearings when dealing with a petition for a writ of habeas corpus filed by a detainee.

In the early years of Guantanamo, detainees had no legally required neutral forum in which they could challenge their statuses as unprivileged enemy combatants. Yaser Esam Hamdi's situation is illustrative. He was interrogated by military officials and otherwise received no process; on the basis of that interrogation he was classified as an enemy combatant. Subsequently, a Supreme Court case led the Bush administration to institute what was called the Combatant Status Review Tribunal (CSRT). *Hamdi v Rumsfeld*, 542 US 507 (2004) ruled that due process demands some system for a detainee to refute his classification, and to have a fair opportunity to rebut the government's factual assertions before a neutral decisionmaker. In 2004 the CSRT was established, ostensibly to satisfy the due process rights of the detainee as spelled out in the 2004 decision.[61] In saying that the citizen detainee had certain procedural rights, the Court said that those rights might be "met by an appropriately authorized and properly constituted military tribunal." The specific requirements of the *Hamdi* decision will be returned to in Chapter 10.

Combatant Status Review Tribunals afforded the detainee only a very limited set of procedural rights.[62] The CSRT is a non-adversarial proceeding run by three military officers. The detainee is represented by an officer who may see and comment on classified information, but does not act as an advocate for the detainee. The

61 Another decision at the time also motivated the administration to create the CRST, *Rasul v Bush*, 542 US 466 (2004), extended the writ of habeas corpus to the detainees held in Guantanamo.

62 This account of the Combat Status Review Tribunals draws heavily on Jennifer K. Elsea, and Michael John Garcia, *Enemy combatant detainees: Habeas corpus challenges in federal courts* (Congressional Research Service, February 3, 2010, RL33180). See Office of General Counsel, *Department of Defense law of war manual*, at 181–182 (cited in note 38).

rules of evidence do not apply; the CSRT looks to see if statements introduced were obtained by coercion, hence their probative value. The detainee can only present evidence that is "reasonably available."[63] One commentator said the CSRT was a "kangaroo court": "Detainees are presumed guilty unless they can prove their innocence. They have neither lawyers nor the means to gather evidence of innocence from their home countries, nor do they have access to the details and sources of the evidence against them. This evidence consists mostly of hearsay from unreliable people without firsthand knowledge and statements given during brutally coercive interrogations by other detainees seeking lenience."[64] (The CSRT is taken up again in Chapter 10.)

It is interesting to note here that the reports that identified Jose Padilla as a suspect were based in part on information obtained by the "enhanced interrogation" of other detainees.[65] If Padilla had appeared before a CSRT, the tribunal would only have had to look at the "probative value" of the hearsay reports of statements of other detainees made as a result of "enhanced interrogation."

In this time frame Congress passed laws that blocked detainees from seeking the writ of habeas corpus, and provided for a review of CSRT determination in the D.C. Circuit Court of Appeals only. In addition, the Circuit Court's authority to review was sharply limited by not being allowed to re-examine the underlying facts of the detainment. This arrangement was struck down by the Supreme Court.[66] (The CSRT itself was not struck down.) In any event, today the habeas hearing is the primary judicial venue that affords detainees a modicum of procedural due process protection when it comes to determining their status as unprivileged enemy combatants. (See Chapter 10.)

IX. Indefinite detention, forced feeding and torture

The length of time a detainee may be detained has proved to be a contentious issue. The basic principle derived from the law of war requires unprivileged enemy belligerents, if not charged with a crime or tried, to be released at the end of hostilities.[67] (If tried and convicted they may be held past the end of hostilities.) The plurality opinion in *Hamdi* stated that "indefinite detention for the purpose of interrogation is not authorized."[68] That is, the capture and detention of unprivileged enemy

63 Id at 7–8. See, also, Thomas R. Johnson, *Combatant status review tribunals: An ordeal through the eyes of one "enemy combatant,"* 11 Lewis and Clark L Rev 943 (2007).

64 Stuart Taylor, Jr., *This time, let's get it right* (The Atlantic, December 2006), archived at https://www.theatlantic.com/magazine/archive/2006/12/this-time-lets-get-it-right/305527/.

65 Brian Bennett, *Did CIA torture yield key information? Report says no; defenders disagree* (LA Times, December 10, 2014), archived at http://www.latimes.com/world/middleeast/la-fg-torture-effectiveness-20141211-story.html.

66 *Boumediene v Bush*, 553 US 573 (2008).

67 *Hamdi v Rumsfeld*, at 518-519 (cited in note 13). See Office of General Counsel, *Department of Defense law of war manual*, at 164 (cited in note 38).

68 *Hamdi v Rumsfeld*, at 521 (cited in note 13).

belligerents must have as its purpose the disabling of the enemy and the prevention of their return to hostilities.[69] But, of course, the "war on terror" seems to have no end, thus opening the door to the possible indefinite detention of unprivileged belligerents pursuant to both the laws of war and the AUMF. The *Hamdi* court acknowledged as much, and, at this point, there appears to be no accepted legal doctrine to work around this conclusion.[70] Furthermore, the District of Columbia Circuit Court of Appeals has said that the determination of when hostilities have ceased is a decision for the President, so it defers to the President on this matter, at least in the absence of a Congressional declaration terminating the war.[71]

On March 7, 2011 President Obama issued E.O. 13567 requiring the periodic review (every four years) of detainees held at Guantanamo to determine if their detention is "necessary to protect against significant threat to the United States."[72] If this standard is not met, efforts have to be made to find an appropriate location to which to transfer the detainee. However, even if the standard were met, the military still had the option of considering whether the individual ought to be charged and tried. Obama's order was enacted into law by the NDAA, §1023.[73] The NDAA also authorized detention without trial until the end of hostilities covered by the AUMF, but when President Obama signed the law on December 31, 2011, he said his administration would not authorize indefinite military detention without trial of American citizens. And he said he would not adhere to an across-the-board requirement of military detention for non-U.S. persons. Finally, he expressed his opposition to §§1026–1028, which blocked the transfer of detainees from Guantanamo Bay to the United States or its territories.[74]

Whether periodic reviews will actually result in detainees being released since President Trump took office is in doubt since his January 3, 2017 tweet that said "There should be no further releases from Gitmo."[75] In the wake of this and other comments from Trump, 11 detainees who have been held at Guantanamo for between 10 and 16 years without charge or trial filed in February 2018 for a writ of

69 Id at 148.

70 Hathaway, et al., *The power to detain: Detention of terrorism suspects after 9/11*, at 158–159 (cited in note 2). See, also, Blank, *A square peg in a round hole: Stretching law of war detention too far*, at 1179ff (cited in note 33); Stephen Dycus, Arthur L. Berney, William C. Banks, Peter Raven-Hansen, and Stephen I. Vladeck, *National security law*, 6th ed., 951 (Wolters Kluwer 2016).

71 *Al-Bihani v Obama*, at 874 (cited in note 48). See, also, *Al-Alwi v Trump*, 236 FSupp3d 417 (D DC 2017).

72 https://obamawhitehouse.archives.gov/the-press-office/2011/03/07/executive-order-13567-periodic-review-individuals-detained-guant-namo-ba.

73 National Defense Authorization Act for Fiscal Year 2012, §1023 (cited in note 44). See Office of General Counsel, *Department of Defense law of war manual*, at 504 (cited in note 38).

74 Statement of the President on H.R. 1540, December 31, 2011, archived at https://obamawhitehouse.archives.gov/the-press-office/2011/12/31/statement-president-hr-1540; Jennifer K. Elsea and Michael John Garcia, *Wartime detention provisions in recent defense authorization legislation* (Congressional Research Service, March 14, 2016, R42143).

75 https://twitter.com/realdonaldtrump/status/816333480409833472?lang=en.

habeas corpus.[76] An interesting question yet to be addressed is whether a detainee who was originally and properly classified as an unprivileged enemy belligerent may constitutionally continue to be held if the conflict is ongoing, but the detainee himself is no longer a threat.

Long-term detention is one thing, and how the detainees are treated while in detention is another. On February 7, 2002 Bush issued a memorandum entitled the "Humane Treatment of Taliban and Al-Qaeda Detainees."[77] In it, he said that Geneva Conventions regarding the treatment of prisoners of war and Common Article 3 of the Geneva Conventions – which prohibit "mutilation, cruel treatment, and torture" – did not apply to al-Qaeda or Taliban captives. This was because neither al-Qaeda nor the Taliban was a signatory to the conventions and because the relevant conflicts were international (but not in the sense that involved recognized states) in scope, and Common Article 3 applied only to "armed conflict not of an international character." The crime of torture consists of the infliction of "severe physical or mental pain or suffering" for purposes such as "obtaining information or a confession, punishment, intimidation or coercion or for any reason based on discrimination of any kind."[78]

Before looking at the matter of torture it should be noted the Supreme Court relied in part on Common Article 3 in *Hamdan v Rumsfeld*, 587 US 557 (2006) in finding the military commission procedures were not legal. Thus at least part of the Geneva Conventions did apply to the detainees, suggesting the detainees had more legal rights to humane treatment than acknowledged by the Bush administration.[79]

In 2002 lawyers in the Office of Legal Counsel (OCL) in the Department of Justice issued documents – the infamous torture memos – that offered a legal justification for various enhanced interrogation techniques including "temperature extremes, shackling, stress positions, sleep and sensory deprivation, loud noises, bright lights, nudity, isolation, shaking, head and stomach slaps, and waterboarding – a technique designed to simulate the sensation of drowning."[80] In time Bush's OCL backed off from the position laid out in the torture memos, and it appears that the CIA stopped waterboarding sometime in 2003.[81] (In 2009 the Office of Professional Responsibility in the Department of Justice concluded that John Yoo, who wrote the "torture memos," had committed "intentional professional misconduct when he violated his duty to exercise independent legal judgment and render thorough, objective and candid legal advice."[82])

76 Archived at https://ccrjustice.org/sites/default/files/attach/2018/01/AlBihani_et_al_v_Trump_MotionforOrderGranting Writ.pdf.

77 Archived at https://www.aclu.org/sites/default/files/field_document/20100615_dos_release_1_doc_-_already_released.pdf.

78 18 USC §2340.

79 Jack Goldsmith, *The terror presidency*, 136 (W.W. Norton 2007).

80 William Ranney Levi, *Interrogation's law*, 118 Yale L J 1434, 1436 (2009).

81 Jack Goldsmith provides an account of the issuance and withdrawal of the torture memos (cited in note 81).

82 Office of Professional Responsibility, Department of Justice, *Investigation into the Office of Legal Counsel's memoranda concerning issues relating to the Central Intelligence Agency's use of "enhanced interrogation techniques" on suspected terrorists*, 11 (July 29, 2009), archived at https://web.archive.org/web/20110728023830/judiciary.house.gov/ hearings/pdf/OPRFinalReport090729.pdf.

Congress stepped into the torture controversy in December 2005 with the Detainee Treatment Act (DTA) that said no one in custody of the Department of Defense could be subjected to any technique of interrogation not authorized by the *U.S. Army Field Manual on Intelligence Interrogation.*[83] The manual at this point prohibited inhumane treatment, electric shock, pain through bondage, beating, deprivations, chemicals, mental torture, but it did not mention waterboarding. The DTA, however, did not apply to the CIA.

Yet Bush was uncomfortable with having to abide by the Army field manual. Thus, when he signed the law he also issued a signing statement on December 30, 2005 in which he clung to his power as President. He said "The executive branch shall construe [the law] in a manner consistent with the constitutional authority of the President . . . as commander in chief."[84] A senior administration official, who spoke on condition of anonymity to Charlie Savage, then on the *Boston Globe* staff, said Bush was reserving his right to use harsh interrogation methods.[85]

Despite Bush's obvious desire to hold onto harsh methods of interrogation, on September 6, 2006, the Army released an updated version of the Army field manual. The revised manual prohibited cruel, inhuman, and degrading treatment. Notably, eight techniques are expressly prohibited from being used in conjunction with intelligence interrogations:

- Forcing the detainee to be naked, perform sexual acts, or pose in a sexual manner.
- Placing hoods or sacks over the head of a detainee; using duct tape over the eyes.
- Applying beatings, electric shock, burns, or other forms of physical pain.
- Waterboarding.
- Using military working dogs.
- Inducing hypothermia or heat injury.
- Conducting mock executions.
- Depriving the detainee of necessary food, water, or medical care.

On July 20, 2007, the Justice Department provided further protection specifically for the CIA in a memorandum discussing six interrogation techniques, one of which was waterboarding, and concluded they were lawful.[86] On March 8, 2008 Bush vetoed the Intelligence Authorization Act, which would have limited CIA interrogations to the techniques authorized by the Army field manual. Bush said it "would take away one of the most valuable tools on the war on terror . . . This is no time for Congress to abandon practices that have a proven track record of keeping America safe."[87]

83 42 USC §2000dd-2.
84 http://www.presidency.ucsb.edu/ws/index.php?pid=65259.
85 Archived at http://archive.boston.com/news/nation/articles/2006/01/04/bush_could_bypass_new_torture_ban/.
86 Archived at https://www.justice.gov/olc/olc-foia-electronic-reading-room.
87 http://www.washingtonpost.com/wp-dyn/content/article/2008/03/08/AR2008030800304.html.

Then on January 22, 2009 President Obama issued Executive Order 13491 that was applicable across all government agencies – the Department of Defense, the CIA – that prohibited the use of any interrogation technique not listed in the Army field manual. The order also made clear that Common Article 3 was going to be followed regarding all individuals detained in any armed conflict.[88] The Obama administration also ordered an investigation of the torture program by the Department of Justice with a view to possibly bringing criminal charges against those involved, but the investigation concluded without charges being brought.[89] A lengthy report by a Senate Committee, among other findings, concluded that the interrogation methods were not effective; that coercive interrogation methods were used that were not approved by the Department of Justice or authorized by CIA headquarters; that the CIA impeded oversight of the program by Congress, the White House, and the CIA's own inspector general; and that no one in the CIA was disciplined for significant violations. The report also identified the contract psychologists who devised the interrogation program.[90] These psychologists were in turn sued in October 2015 by the American Civil Liberties Union on behalf of three men who were "tortured and experimented on using methods developed by the CIA-contracted psychologists James Mitchell and John 'Bruce' Jessen."[91] The Justice Department did not seek to block the suit by arguing that the suit would reveal state secrets, and in August, 2017 the suit was settled out of court. The settlement agreement has not been made public.

President Trump has said, however, that he would be open to bringing back waterboarding.[92] He might accomplish this by (i) requiring a change in the Army field manual, (ii) by working to repeal the law noted above requiring enforcement of the Army field manual, or (iii) simply claiming authority to waterboard as commander-in-chief.

Harsh treatment of detainees was not limited to "enhanced" interrogation techniques. Detainees who refused to eat unless and until they were released were subjected to "enteral feeding" – forced feeding using "nasogastric tubes" inserted through the nose into the stomach, a painful procedure that took 30 to 40 minutes. A group of detainees sought to end this procedure by seeking the assistance of the courts, but they were turned down. The court said that even if forced feeding "burdens fundamental rights," it served "legitimate penological interests." This was true even though a detainee had already been cleared for release.[93]

88 http://www.presidency.ucsb.edu/ws/?pid=85669.

89 https://www.justice.gov/opa/pr/statement-attorney-general-eric-holder-closure-investigation-interrogation-certain-detainees.

90 Senate Select Committee on Intelligence, *Committee study of the Central Intelligence Agency's detention and interrogation program*, December 13, 2012, declassified revisions December 3, 2014, archived at https://www.feinstein.senate.gov/public/index.cfm/senate-intelligence-committee-study-on-cia-detention-and-interrogation-program.

91 https://www.aclu.org/news/cia-torture-psychologists-settle-lawsuit.

92 Dan Merica, *Trump on waterboarding: "We have to fight fire with fire"* (CNN, January 26, 2017), archived at https://www.cnn.com/2017/01/25/politics/donald-trump-waterboarding-torture/index.html.

93 *Aamar v Obama*, 742 F3d 1023 (DC Cir 2014).

9

MILITARY COMMISSIONS: TRIALS

Having looked at the detainment of unprivileged enemy belligerents in Chapter 8, this chapter turns to their trial by military commission. The terrorists who are the subjects of these chapters are terrorists with a foreign connection, not domestic (even jihadist-motivated domestic terrorists).

On September 14, 2001, right after the attacks of 9/11, Congress adopted the Authorization to Use Military Force (AUMF), which empowered the President to "use all necessary and appropriate force against those nations, organizations, or persons he determines planned, authorized, committed, or aided the terrorist attacks . . . in order to prevent any future acts of international terrorism against the United States by such nations, organizations or persons."[1] Approximately one month later President Bush issued his military order of November 13, 2001, discussed in Chapter 8, and without explicit authorization from Congress, President Bush ordered the creation and use of a system of military commissions to try and convict unlawful enemy combatants (offender jurisdiction) who allegedly violated "all offenses triable by military commission" (offense jurisdiction).[2] President Bush could have used civilian Article III courts to try accused terrorists, but instead chose to create military commissions. Jane Mayer quoted Vice President Cheney as saying: "We think it [the military commission] guarantees that we'll have the kind of treatment of these individuals that we believe they deserve."[3]

1 115 Stat. 224; 50 USC §1541 note.

2 President Bush relied on a memo from the Office of Legal Counsel. *Legality of the use of military commissions to try terrorists*, US Dept of Justice, Office of Legal Counsel 25 Op ICL 238 (2001), archived at https://www.justice.gov/sites/ default/files/olc/opinions/2001/11/31/op-olc-v025-p0238_0.pdf.

3 Meyer's quote of the Vice President appears in Stephen Dycus, Arthur L. Berney, William C. Banks, Peter Raven-Hansen, and Stephen I. Vladeck, *National security law*, 6th ed., 1161 (Wolters Kluwer 2016).

I. Article III courts and courts-martial

To understand the military commission, it is useful to begin with a discussion of ordinary civilian Article III courts and military courts-martial. Article III courts include the Supreme Court and those "inferior courts" that Congress may establish. The judges of Article III courts hold their offices during "good behavior" and enjoy compensation that may not be reduced during their time in office. The offender and offense jurisdiction of these courts is spelled out both by the Constitution and by federal statute. It is in these courts that civilian federal crimes, such as murder, theft, and the crime of providing material support to terrorists[4] are tried. Significantly, crimes tried in these courts must be by jury.[5] People tried in Article III courts also enjoy the protections of the Fourth, Fifth, and Sixth Amendments, e.g., public trial, jury trial, compulsory process, and right to counsel. The standard federal rules of criminal procedure and evidence are also applicable. Article III courts serve as the gold standard regarding criminal prosecutions.

The courts-martial are established by Congress for the trial and conviction of people closely associated with the military,[6] and accused of violating 50 crimes listed in the Uniform Code of Military Justice or violations of the "General Article" (Article 134).[7] Military judges, however, do not have the same constitutional independence as do Article III judges, namely, life tenure and independence from Presidential control.[8]

Over the years the procedures and rights in courts-martial have evolved to come to resemble Article III courts at least in criminal cases.[9] Yet there are significant rights available in Article III courts that are not available in courts-martial: indictment by a grand jury, trial by jury as covered by Article III and the Sixth Amendment.[10]

Non-military people may not be tried by courts-martial, and thus prevents the government from avoiding the fully panoply of rights available in Article III courts.[11] As Justice Black put it: "Every extension of military jurisdiction is an encroachment on the jurisdiction of the civil courts, and, more important, acts as a deprivation of the right to jury trial and of other treasured constitutional protections."[12]

4 18 USC §§2339A and 2339B.

5 US Const Art III, §§1 and 2.

6 10 USC §802(a) (2012). See, also, R. Chuck Mason, *Military justice: Courts-martial, an overview* (Congressional Research Service, August 12, 2013, R41739).

7 10 USC §934 – Article 134. See Stephen I. Vladeck, *Military courts and Article III*, 103 Georgetown L J 933, 941 (2015).

8 *United States ex rel. Toth v Quarles*, 350 US 11, 17 (1955). See, also,. 10 USC §942 – Art. 142.

9 Stephen I. Vladeck, *Military courts and Article III*, 103 Georgetown L J 933, 941 (2015).

10 *O'Callahan v Parker*, 395 US 258, 263–265 (1969); Vladeck, *Military courts and Article III*, at 961 (cited in 9).

11 Stephen I. Vladeck, *The laws of war as a constitutional limit on military jurisdiction*, 4 J of Natl Security L & Pol 295, 308 (2010).

12 *Reid v Covert*, 354 US 1, 20 (1956).

II. Military commissions

Military commissions are yet a different animal.

> "The military commission, a tribunal neither mentioned in the Constitution nor created by statute, was born of military necessity." Unlike courts-martial, military commissions have historically been irregular courts with carefully circumscribed jurisdiction. One species of commissions has served as martial law or occupation courts exercising general criminal jurisdiction in exceptional situations. The other has entertained prosecutions of enemy belligerents for violations of the international laws of war—such as the body that convicted the Nazi saboteurs in *Ex Parte Quirin* and the numerous war crimes tribunals convened by the United States after World War II. Whether these courts operated with express congressional authorization, their procedures, rules, and judges were entirely controlled by the Executive Branch (and basically unregulated by statute).[13]

After President Bush's military order of November 13, 2001 (noted earlier), the Department of Defense issued Military Order No. 1 on March 21, 2002, which spelled out in more detail the commissions that Bush had ordered established. (President Bush's creation of military commissions was not a wholly novel development in U.S. history. Military commissions have been used from time to time over the centuries, most notably during the Civil War and World War II.)

The March 2002 order addressed the offender and offense jurisdictions of the military commissions, their procedures, rules of evidence, and the rights of the accused. (There was a subsequent amendment issued in 2005 that is not of importance here.) It did not provide for judicial review of the final orders of the military commissions. In 2005, when the Detainee Treatment Act was passed, exclusive reviewing jurisdiction was given to the D.C. Circuit Court of Appeals, which was authorized to undertake a sharply restricted review of the final orders of the military commissions. Also in 2005, the Supreme Court in the *Hamdan v Rumsfeld* decision concluded that (1) the offense jurisdiction of the military commissions exceeded the authority Congress had provided for in 10 USC §861 (aka Article 21 of the Uniform Code of Military Justice); and that (2) the procedures used by these commissions did not comply with requirements of the Uniform Code of Military Justice and were not consistent with Common Article 3 of the Geneva Conventions.[14]

A few more words about *Hamdan v Rumsfeld.* Salim Ahmed Hamdan was captured by militia forces in Afghanistan, turned over to the U.S., and transported to Guantanamo Bay. He was charged with conspiracy and was slated for trial by military commission. He filed a petition for a writ of habeas corpus challenging the use of

13 Vladeck, *Military courts and Article III* (cited in note 9), Georgetown L. J. 933, 944 (2015).

14 *Hamdan v Rumsfeld*, 548 US 557, 567 (2006) (plurality).

the military commission to try him. The Court decided not to answer the question of whether a President may constitutionally convene military commissions "without the sanction of Congress" since various statutes "acknowledge a general Presidential authority to convene military commissions."[15] But that left unanswered the question of the scope of that Congressional authorization, and whether Bush's military commission was in compliance with that authorization. The Supreme Court ended up deciding that the President lacked the statutory authority to create a commission that could try detainee Hamdan for conspiracy, because the military commission Congress authorized was one "incident to the conduct of war." The offense jurisdiction of such a commission had to be limited to offenses cognizable during time of war. As such this kind of commission had jurisdiction to try only two kinds of offense: (a) violations of the law and usages of war cognizable by military tribunals only, and (b) breaches of military order or regulations not legally triable by courts-martial under the Articles of War.[16] In *Hamdan v Rumsfeld*, the commission was authorized to address a charge of conspiracy, which was not historically triable by military commission.

This decision triggered the passage of the Military Commission Act of 2006 (MCA 2006) in which Congress for the first time provided a general statutory foundation for military commissions. Offender jurisdiction was extended to any "alien" who was an "unlawful combatant." (See Chapter 8.)

MCA 2006 sported a long list of crimes subject to the law's offense jurisdiction, including the following:

> [M]urder of protected persons; attacking civilians, civilian objects, or protected property; pillaging; denying quarter; taking hostages; employing poison or similar weapons; using protected persons or property as shields; torture, cruel or inhuman treatment; intentionally causing serious bodily injury; mutilating or maiming; murder in violation of the law of war; destruction of property in violation of the law of war; using treachery or perfidy; improperly using a flag of truce or distinctive emblem; intentionally mistreating a dead body; rape; sexual assault or abuse; hijacking or hazarding a vessel or aircraft; terrorism; **providing material support for terrorism**; wrongfully aiding the enemy; spying; contempt; perjury and obstruction of justice. 10 USC §950v. **Conspiracy** (§950v(b)(28)), attempts (§ 950t), and solicitation (§950u) to commit the defined acts are also punishable.[17]

Thus the law included "providing material support for terrorism" and "conspiracy," both of which were not traditional violations of international law. Hence it was now not the President, but Congress, flirting with violating Article III of the Constitution,

15 Id at 594–595.

16 Id at 598.

17 Jennifer K. Elsea, *The Military Commissions Act of 2006 (MCA 2006): Analysis of procedural rules and comparison with previous DOD rules and the Uniform Code of Military Justice*, 10–11 (Congressional Research Service, January 26, 2007, RL33688).

and the Fifth and Sixth Amendments. The MCA 2006 did not change the limited review available in the District of Columbia Court of Appeals as specified in the Detainee Treatment Act. MCA 2006, however, amended the Detainee Treatment Act by stripping the judiciary of habeas jurisdiction in all detainee cases, including pending cases, a provision the Supreme Court struck down.[18] [The legal conflict over the suspension of habeas corpus is taken up in Chapter 10.] However, no challenge to military commissions created by MCA 2006 reached the Supreme Court.[19]

When President Obama took office he halted proceedings under MCA 2006, and started efforts to close Guantanamo, which, in the face of Congressional opposition, he did not succeed in doing before leaving office. As for military commissions, in May 2009 the administration said it was considering restarting the use of military commissions with some procedural changes. The Department of Defense issued modifications to the Manual for Military Commissions effective July 14, 2009, and on October 28 Congress enacted the Military Commissions Act of 2009, which included reforms of MCA 2006 that the administration supported.[20]

The MCA 2009 amendments affected both offender and offense jurisdictions. Regarding offender jurisdiction, the terminology changed from "alien unlawful combatant" to "alien unprivileged enemy belligerent." (The term "lawful combatant" was dropped in favor of "privileged belligerent.") Being "part of the Taliban" no longer automatically excluded someone from being a "*privileged* belligerent."[21] Offense jurisdiction remained the same as under MCA 2006 but with the express requirement that the offenses occurred "in the context of and associated with hostilities."[22]

Also amended were the rules of evidence and other provisions enhancing the protections of the accused. MCA 2009 made possible judicial review of the decisions of the military commissions based on insufficiency of evidence to support the verdict, and ultimate review by the Supreme Court.

III. The authority of a President to establish and use military commissions

May Presidents, *on their own say-so*, set up a military commission without Congressional approval? Neal K. Katyal and Laurence H. Tribe stated their opposition to such a claim of authority as follows:

> In our view, a president who sets out to put on trial and then to punish offenders against the laws of war in the course of a constitutionally directed

18 *Boumediene v Bush*, 533 US 723 (2008).

19 Elsea, *The Military Commissions Act of 2006: Analysis of procedural rules and comparison with previous DOD rules and the Uniform Code of Military Justice*, at 2 (cited in note 17).

20 Jennifer K. Elsea, *The Military Commissions Act of 2009 (MCA 2009): Overview and legal issues*, 2–3 (Congressional Research Service, Augzut 4, 2014, R41163).

21 Id at 10, 38.

22 10 USC §950p(c).

> military campaign must generally be regarded as no different from a president who sets out to try and punish those whom he regards as offenders against any other body of law, domestic or international, whom the officials, properly directed by the president in any of his other core functions, happen to encounter and detain in the course of carrying out presidential instructions. So, for instance, if a president is traveling down Pennsylvania Avenue to give his State of the Union address (or is engaged in an exercise of his power to veto, pardon, make recess appointments, receive ambassadors, call out the militia to protect a state from invasion, or negotiate treaties), and a gang of thugs attempts to obstruct an exercise of any of these powers, whatever inherent power the President might possess to intercept and detain members of the gang so as to immobilize them from further interference or obstruction does not extend to the very different power to create and administer tribunals to adjudicate their guilt and to mete out punishment. This is so even if the tribunals provide the full panoply of Article III safeguards and Bill of Rights protections, for the Constitution explicitly gives to Congress, not the President, the power to make law, to define and punish offenses against the law of nations, and to create tribunals inferior to the Supreme Court.[23]

In short, Katyal and Tribe believe that Congress must specifically authorize the use of military tribunals before their use is allowed.[24] The structure of the Constitution, they say, means that the concurrence of all three branches is normally required when, for example, basic constitutional guarantees are put at risk.

The commander-in-chief clause does not alter this basic constitutional arrangement. (1) "Nothing less is meant by the Constitution's simple but majestic command that no person 'be deprived of life, liberty, or property, without due process of law'." (2) Other passages in the Constitution "create a framework that requires legislative approval for all significant deprivations of liberty." Here they specifically point to a list of Congressional powers in Article I – to define and punish offences against the law of nations, to make rules for the regulation of the military, and to constitute tribunals inferior to the Supreme Court. They agree that the President could set up military commissions in a theater of war and arguably even during a domestic emergency. However, they point to the danger to the Republic if any inherent emergency powers the President had were stretched to include the authority to issue the November 13, 2001 military order. That emergency power, they argue, "must be most sparingly used, for without the sturdiest limits that power could eclipse all our constitutional guarantees."[25] "[N]othing said by the President or by anyone speaking on his behalf remotely supports the proposition that circumstances are too exigent

23 Neal K. Katyal and Laurence H. Tribe, *Waging war, deciding guilt: Trying the military tribunals*, 111 Yale L J 1259, 1270–1271(2002).

24 Id at 1284.

25 Id at 1273.

to make timely congressional action a realistic option . . . [T]he most that might be established is the magnitude of the peril the nation faces – not the necessity for unilateral executive action responding to that peril with institutional measures that are ordinarily impermissible without authorization from Congress."[26]

In dramatic contrast to the analysis of Katyal and Tribe, Patrick F. Philbin – an attorney in the Office of Legal Counsel – in a memorandum dated November 6, 2001 for the President, argued that as commander-in-chief the President had inherent authority to establish military commissions. His argument was multipronged.[27] (1) Punishing enemy belligerents for violations of the laws of war was a necessary incident of authority over the conduct of military operations in war. (2) There is a history of Presidents creating military commissions based on their inherent authority. (3) Justice Douglas in a concurring opinion in *Hirota v MacArthur*, 338 U.S. 197 (1948) agreed with the plurality opinion dismissing petitions for the writ of habeas corpus filed by citizens of Japan held for trial by a military commission after World War II. In his opinion, Justice Douglas recognized the authority of the president to work with other nations to establish the multinational tribunal without first getting Congressional authorization. The memo also cited the use of a military commission, without Congressional authorization, to try those accused of being part of the plot to assassinate President Lincoln.

As noted, the Supreme Court in *Hamdan v Rumsfeld*, a case challenging Bush's military commission, raised the question of whether the President may constitutionally convene military commissions "without the sanction of Congress" in situations of "controlling necessity."[28] Having raised the issue, the Court said it did not need to answer that question because various statutes acknowledged a general presidential authority to convene military commissions under circumstances where they were justified under the Constitution and laws. This, of course, leaves the issue of the President's authority wide open.[29]

IV. Are there limits on the authority of Congress and the President to establish military commissions?

The military commission was designed to deal with a different category of terrorist than those addressed in previous chapters; specifically, it was established to deal with the unprivileged enemy belligerent.[30] Again, it is Article I, Section 8 that provides the authority of Congress to establish military commissions.

26 Id at 1276.

27 *Legality of the use of military commissions to try terrorists*, US Dept of Justice, Office of Legal Counsel 25 Op ICL 238 (2001), archived at https://www.hsdl.org/?abstract&did=38273.

28 *Hamdan v Rumsfeld*, at 592 (cited in note 14).

29 Id at 594–595.

30 For a discussion of international law regarding the terms unlawful/unprivileged enemy combatants, prisoner of war, civilian, and the privileges and immunities of these categories under international law, see Knut Dörmann, *The legal situation of "unlawful/unprivileged combatants,"* 85 Int'l L R Red Cross 45 (2003), archived at https://www.icrc.org/ eng/assets/files/other/irrc_849_dorman.pdf.

But are there *constitutional* limits regarding Congress's authority? Did Congress act constitutionally when it enacted MCA 2006 and 2009 authorizing a military commission that could try alien unlawful enemy belligerents on charges of conspiracy, and/or material support? MCA 2006 and 2009 only extend to offenders who are aliens; could Congress extend offender jurisdiction to *citizens* who were "unprivileged enemy belligerents?" And might that category be extended beyond those, to people who are "part of" al-Qaeda, to lone wolves, to Tarek Mehanna, a U.S. citizen discussed in Chapter 7, to Timothy McVeigh who blew up a government building and killed government employees, to Alex Fields who ran people down with a truck in Charlottesville, Virginia, or to the racist Dylan Roof who killed nine African-Americans in a Charleston church? Might the offense jurisdiction of military commissions be extended to hate crimes like those in 18 USC §249? It is conceivable that offender and offense jurisdictions of military commissions could become so broad as to usurp the place of the Article III courts, thus avoiding having to comply with various constitutional protections, like the right to a jury trial, that are part and parcel of Article III tribunals. This possibility of course raises the specter of a serious curtailing of the protections in Article III and the Fifth and Sixth Amendments.

With this background, recall from Chapter 8 the evolving specification of those who could be detained by the military. Note the authority to detain may not be the same as the authority to try by military commission. There are two dimensions to the jurisdiction of military commissions. First is offender jurisdiction. Offender jurisdiction of the MCA 2009 matched the authority to detain under the National Defense Authorization Act of 2012.[31] Offender jurisdiction applied only to aliens. While Congress chose not to extend offender jurisdiction to citizens, it probably could have, given the decision in *Ex Parte Quirin*, 317 US 1 (1947) upholding the use of the military commission to try a U.S. citizen. (See also Chapter 8.) Second is offense jurisdiction. Offense jurisdiction as defined in MCA's 2009 provisions (10 USC §950t) include a long list of offenses. To summarize, the list includes a variety of violent activities against persons and property, as well as: (1) terrorism; (2) conspiracy; and (3) material support for terrorism. (The statute makes clear that material support means the same thing as in 18 USC §2339A.) Thus Congress in both MCA 2006 and 2009 indeed extended military commission jurisdiction beyond well-established offenses under the law of war. Stated differently, Congress, having authorized the detainment and trial of unlawful enemy belligerents under the law of war, now said those belligerents could be charged and convicted by military commissions of crimes not well established under the law of war.

> Procedural note: A detainee has several procedural options to seek review, and to "collaterally" challenge the offender and offense jurisdiction of military commissions. These options are briefly addressed below at the end of Section V.

31 National Defense Authorization Act for Fiscal Year 2012, H.R. 1540, 112th Cong (2011). See, also, Elsea, *The Military Commissions Act of 2009 (MCA 2009): Overview and legal issues*, at 9 (cited in note 20).

(1) May Congress define a violation of the law of nations not recognized in the law of nations itself? (2) Even if the answer is yes, may Congress subject such crimes to trial by military commission in light of Article III and the Fifth and Sixth Amendments?[32] Stephen Vladeck concludes that the answer to the first question has generated conflicting views among scholars regarding how much deference is owed to Congress when it "defines" as offenses actions that have not in the traditional law of nations been deemed to be offenses. Regardless, the discussion above about Article III and the Fifth and Sixth Amendments suggests that even if Congress could expand the list of violations of the law of nations, the answer to question (2) should be "no." Thus the current law regarding military commissions is, or could be, subject to constitutional attack in so far as it has provided for trial by military commissions offenses that are also ordinary crimes and have not been traditionally recognized as violations of the law of war.

The legality of Congress expanding the list of offenses subject to military commissions was addressed by the D.C. Circuit Court of Appeals in *Hamdan v United States* (2012) (*Hamdan II*)[33] and *al Bahlul v United States* (2016).[34] The *Hamdan II* case arose following the decision by the Supreme Court in the original *Hamdan* case that struck down the Bush military commission's authority to try individuals for conspiracy. After Congress passed MCA 2006, which established military commissions and authorized prosecutions for conspiracy and for providing material support for terrorism, Hamdan was recharged with both conspiracy and material support. He was convicted only for providing material support. His appeal to the Court of Appeals involved several issues, but the one of importance here was whether providing material support to terrorism was a war crime, and hence properly tried by a military commission. The Circuit Court concluded "no" and the conviction was reversed. But reversal was based on the grounds that applying MCA 2006 to Hamdan was not possible since Congress did not authorize retroactive enforcement of MCA 2006 unless the conduct (material support) was already prohibited under existing U.S. law as a war crime triable by military commission. Since material support was not a war crime triable by commission prior to 2006, the MCA 2006 could not be used to prosecute Hamdan. Thus the majority on the court avoided deciding the question of whether Congress could expand the list of war crimes triable by military commission. However, Judge Kavanaugh, who as of this writing is a recent appointee to the Supreme Court, claimed in a footnote to the main opinion that under Article I Congress did have this authority.

The scope of Congress's Article I authority to identify new war crimes subject to military commission returned to the D.C. Circuit Court in *al Bahlul v United States*. A six-judge majority, relying on different rationales, upheld al Bahlul's conviction

32 Vladeck, *The laws of war as a constitutional limit on military jurisdiction*, at 327–328 (cited in note 11).

33 696 F3d 1238 (DC Cir 2012).

34 *Al Bahlul v United States*, 840 F3d 757 (DC Cir 2016) (en banc) (per curiam), cert denied, October 10, 2017.

by military commission of the crime of conspiracy. Four of the six judges' opinions (Brown, Griffith, Henderson, and Kavanaugh) rested on the proposition that Articles I and III of the Constitution permitted Congress to make conspiracy punishable by military commission. This rationale will be addressed below. [The three dissenters took issue with these four judges, in particular expressing their concern that their approach took an expansive view of the authority of the political branches of the government.] Judges Millet and Wilkins, whose votes were needed to make up the majority, affirmed on narrower grounds. What follows is a summary of two of the opinions of the judges, one in the majority and the other a dissent. These summaries focus on Article I and Article III issues.

The three out of the four judges in the majority (Judges Kavanaugh, Brown and Griffith) summarized their position in one paragraph:

> This case therefore raises one central legal question: Under the U.S. Constitution, may Congress establish military commissions to try unlawful enemy combatants for the offense of conspiracy to commit war crimes, even if conspiracy is not an offense under the international law of war? The answer is yes. We know that from the text and original understanding of the Constitution; the structure of the Constitution; landmark Supreme Court precedent; longstanding congressional practice, as reflected in venerable and contemporary federal statutes; and deeply rooted Executive Branch practice, from the 1800s to the present.[35]

In their view, Congress's authority to establish military convictions and make offenses triable by military commission was found in Congress's authority under Article I to declare war and other war-power clauses in Article I that make no reference to international law, neither do they impose international law as a constraint. They argued that these clauses, along with the necessary and proper clause, provided ample authority to do what Congress did, whatever international law may say. Thus they also brushed aside the argument that the controlling Article I authority for Congress was the Article I clause that deals with defining and punishing offenses against the laws of nation. Further, they said, the idea that international law defines the scope of Congressional authority does not make sense – the framers did not give foreign or international bodies power to constrain U.S. war making authority acting through the international law of war. Precedent, they said, also supported their view in that the Court in *Quirin* upheld a commission conviction for espionage even though espionage was not an offense under the international law of war. And they noted the military commission trials of the Lincoln conspirators and the Nazi saboteurs in *Quirin* were trials based on charges of conspiracy. In sum, the historical practice of Congress has been one of regularly going beyond international law in specifying offenses that may be tried by military conviction.

35 Id at 760.

After recounting the history that supported these claims, the three judges turned to the important last claim, namely, that Article III confines the offense jurisdiction of military commissions. They began with al Bahlul's argument that Article III vests judicial power in Article III courts and requires the use of a jury. Their response was to note that there was a long recognized "exception" to Article III for military commissions, and if historical practice demonstrated that an offense is triable by military commission, that resolved the Article III issue. They referred back to their history of military commissions trying non-international-law-of-war offenses. [They did not address why, as a matter of constitutional interpretation and theory, this practice, assuming there was such a practice, means Article III ought not to serve as the kind of constraint argued for by al Bahlul.] Next, they turned to a dispute over the interpretation of *Quirin*. Did or did not that opinion limit the Article III exception to the international law of war offenses? They concluded not, arguing that it made little sense to read *Quirin* this way when the opinion itself rejected the Article III argument directed against a statute that made spying – a non-international-law-of-war offense – triable by military commission. An offense's status as an international law offense was sufficient, but not *necessary*, to make the offense triable by military commission. The three judges did concede that the Constitution did not grant Congress unlimited authority to designate crimes as triable by military commission. What that limit was on Congress's power, however, was not their job to decide. It was enough if an offense was an international law of war offense, *or* had historically been tried by U.S. military commission. The latter was sufficient to uphold Congress's authority in this case.[36]

As noted previously, the opinion of Judges Kavanaugh, Brown, and Griffith was joined by Judge Henderson.[37] Judge Henderson's own opinion went further in two respects. She would ground Congress's authority on the same Article I clauses relied on by Kavanaugh, Brown, and Griffith, as well as Congress's authority to "define" offenses "against the law of nations." Regardless of what the international community did, Congress could, under the "define and punish" clause, push beyond the international community. After several other arguments, and taking note that her colleagues wanted to police Congress's Article I powers stringently, Judge Henderson doubled down, saying "when it comes to issues of national security and foreign affairs, abstention – not aggressive policing – has always been our watchword."[38]

As for Article III serving as a limitation on Congress, Judge Henderson noted that historically there had been exceptions to the Article III judicial power clause that placed judicial power in Article III courts. One of these exceptions was the military commission. Judge Henderson expressly equated the scope of the exception

36 Id at 769.

37 Judge Henderson concurred in the Court's judgment, doing so for the reasons she stated in her dissent in *Al Bahlul v United States*, 792 F3d 1, 27–72 (D.C. Cir. 2015) which incorporated as her opinion 840 F3d 757 (DC Cir 2016).

38 Id at 62.

with the scope of Congress's Article I powers, i.e., whatever Congress does regarding the military commissions falls within the Article III exception. She offered an alternative argument that applied a balancing test to determine if Congress had violated Article III and concluded that national security was an "overriding reason" for choosing to go the military commission route. She then ticked off concerns she had regarding Article III courts trying alleged terrorists.

> [T]he potential disclosure of highly classified information; the efficiency of military-commission proceedings; the military's expertise in matters of national security; the inability to prosecute enemy combatants due to speedy-trial violations; the inadmissibility of certain forms of evidence; and, later, the risk of terrorist attacks on domestic courts.[39]

Her final nail in the Article III argument was that "Even if the Criminal Jury Clause did limit military-commission jurisdiction, it has no application here because Bahlul is neither a U.S. citizen nor present on U.S. soil."[40]

The three dissenters, Judges Rogers, Tatel, and Pillard were alarmed by the road down which the majority's views could take the country. "[I]t would seem that Congress and the President could vest military commissions with authority to try enemy belligerents for almost any crime so long as it related in some way to 'hostilities'." They suggested this hypothetical situation to illustrate the concern.

> What if the FBI . . . discovered that three U.S. citizens sent $200 to the humanitarian wing of an organization that the United States designated a foreign terrorist organization, earmarked for training in human-rights advocacy that the donors hope will turn the organization away from terrorist activities? Could the three be shipped off to a military base and tried for material support for terrorism – an offense unrecognized under international law but made punishable under the Military Commissions Act? The government seems to think so.[41]

They backed up their concern with a legal argument. They agreed that it had been established that Congress may place judicial power in non-Article III tribunals such as military commissions, but that this was a narrow authority. Congress's authority in this area had two different authorities: one was the authority to define offenses against law or nation; the other was the authority to actually authorize and pay for military commissions. The authority to define offenses springs from the define and punish clause, and this clause was bound by the laws of nations. That is, Congress had the authority to define the law, but not to invent it wholesale. And inventing a

39 Id at 67.
40 Id at 71.
41 *Al Bahlul v United States*, at 837 (cited in note 34).

new unrecognized war crime is what has happened here. Inchoate conspiracy has never been a war crime, or a crime under the laws of nations. The necessary and proper clause, in their view, did not come to the rescue because that clause did not allow Congress to do what it otherwise was expressly barred from doing. Neither did it help to claim that historical practice supported Congress's authority to define conspiracy as a crime under the law of nations, since there simply was no robust history supporting this claim.

V. Military commission procedures

At the heart of the debate regarding the offense jurisdiction of military commissions was the concern that shifting a wide range of criminal cases into military commissions meant the government could work around a significant number of constitutional protections. This concern was most marked regarding the original military commission established by President Bush as it existed prior to the passage of MCA 2006 and 2009. As noted earlier, the presiding officer and the three other members of the commission did not have the protection of independence afforded Article III judges. The accused did have to be provided with a copy of the charges, both in English and his or her own language; was entitled to a presumption of innocence; and was entitled to an appointed military counsel, but could only hire civilian counsel of his own choosing at his own expense as long as this person was a U.S. citizen with a security clearance. Although the accused's access to evidence was protected, there were important limitations.[42]

1 The accused could obtain witnesses and documents but only if reasonably available.
2 Although the prosecution had to provide the defense with the evidence it intended to introduce at trial, the accused and his civilian counsel could be excluded from, and precluded from ever learning about evidence presented during the part of the proceeding that was "closed" because the evidence was classified.
3 Appointed military counsel could attend these closed sessions but could also be forbidden to reveal anything about the session to the accused.
4 Moreover, the accused and his civilian counsel could be denied access to evidence in the form of "protected information" (which included classified information as well as "information protected by law or rule from unauthorized disclosure" and "information concerning other national security interests," as long as the presiding officer concludes that the evidence is "probative" and that its admission without the accused's knowledge would not "result in the denial of a full and fair trial."

42 *Hamdan v Rumsfeld* (cited in note 14).

The rules of evidence also opened the door to potentially unreliable evidence in a way not allowed in Article III courts. Any evidence that "would have probative value to a reasonable person" was admissible, including hearsay evidence and evidence obtained as a result of coercion. Prior statements of the accused could be admitted, even if obtained by coercion. Neither in-court witnesses nor written statements had to be sworn. And only a two-third's vote was necessary for a verdict of guilt. All appeals were confined to the level of the Department of Defense and ultimately the President, not to the Article III courts.

The plurality in *Hamdan* concluded that these procedures were not lawful. A federal statute required military commissions to conform to the procedures of courts-martial unless the President determined this was not practicable. Here the Court concluded that here the President's "practicability" determination was insufficient to justify variances from the courts-martial. Of special concern was the failure to assure a fundamental protection, available in courts-martial, of the right to be present. The Court then added this observation:

> The military commission was not born of a desire to dispense a more summary form of justice than is afforded by courts-martial; it developed, rather, as a tribunal of necessity to be employed when courts-martial lacked jurisdiction over either the accused or the subject matter.[43]

Next, the Court concluded the procedures violated Common Article 3 of the Geneva Conventions which required "judicial guarantees which are recognized as indispensable by civilized peoples." One such guarantee was the right to be tried in one's presence. And the military commissions did not meet the Common Article 3 requirement that these courts be "regularly constituted," since without a satisfactory explanation they departed from the rules applicable in courts-martial.

As previously noted, this decision led to Congress's adoption of MCA 2006.[44] Although MCA 2006 changed the procedures by taking them a step closer to the procedures afforded the accused in Article III courts, the procedures remained sufficiently different so as to cause alarm. Here are several examples: MCA 2006 established that the accused could be required to testify against himself (10 USC §948r(a)), but the statute did not expressly prohibit drawing adverse inferences from the failure to testify. The accused could be questioned prior to the trial by military commission, but the courts-martial rule that required a kind of Miranda warning before questioning was expressly made not applicable (10 USC §948b(d)). The rules governing the admissibility of hearsay evidence strongly favored its admissibility.

43 Id at 624.

44 The summary of MCA 2006 is not intended to address all the provisions of the act, e.g., eligibility requirements for judges, openness of the proceedings, roles of prosecuting and defense counsel, court reporters, service of charges, deliberation and voting procedures, sentencing, and a number of other provisions.

These and other concerns with MCA 2006 ultimately led to the adoption of MCA 2009.[45] Has MCA 2009 alleviated the concern regarding the expansion of the offense jurisdiction of military commissions? The answer is yes, somewhat, but the full panoply of protections an accused person enjoys in an Article III court are still not available in a military commission trial, thereby seeming to increase the likelihood a prosecution in a military commission will be successful.[46]

Along with the limitations noted earlier, note should be made of the rules of evidence and burden of proof. The accused is presumed innocent, and guilt must be established beyond a reasonable doubt.[47] Unlike in civilian criminal proceedings, statements of the defendant in the absence of a Miranda warning are admissible.[48] The defendant, however, cannot be compelled to be a witness against himself.[49] And the statements must have been made "voluntarily."[50] In determining voluntariness several factors have to be looked at including "the lapse of time, change of place, or change in identity of questioners between the statement sought to be admitted and any prior questioning of the accused." This opens the door to first conducting a coercive questioning, then moving the defendant to another location where he is questioned again by a new group of people (a "clean team") in order to solicit the same information "voluntarily," which is now admissible. (See Chapter 7.) This approach seems to provide a way around the prohibition against admitting into evidence testimony that was obtained through the use of torture, or by cruel, inhuman, or degrading treatment.[51] Derivative evidence obtained using a coerced statement is not barred.[52] And hearsay evidence is admissible.[53] Neither does the MCA itself prohibit the admission of evidence obtained in violation of the Fourth Amendment. Classified information may be used according to rules like those found in the Classified Information Procedure Act.[54] (See Chapter 7.) And the law opens the door to allowing the government to make exceptions in the applicability of the procedures and rules of evidence that would apply in general courts-martial as required by "the unique circumstances of the conduct of military and intelligence operations during hostilities or by other practical need consistent with this chapter."[55]

Despite provisions like these designed to make conviction by military commission more probable, the track record of commissions does not compare favorably

45 10 USC §§948a–950t.

46 For a more detailed examination of MCA 2009, see Elsea, *The Military Commissions Act of 2009 (MCA 2009): Overview and legal issues* (cited in note 20).

47 10 USC §949l; 10 USC §949i.

48 10 USC §948b(d).

49 10 USC §948r(b).

50 10 USC §948r(c).

51 10 USC §948r(a).

52 Elsea, *The Military Commissions Act of 2009 (MCA 2009): Overview and legal issues*, at 41 (cited in note 20).

53 10 USC §949a(b)(3)(D).

54 10 USC §§949p-1–949p-7.

55 10 USC 949a(b)(1).

with prosecutions undertaken in civilian criminal courts. Between 2001 and 2011 the ordinary courts handled 578 jihadist cases; 431 were resolved and of these 87% resulted in conviction.[56] During the same period military commissions at Guantanamo completed seven cases.[57]

Final note. Obtaining what is called an interlocutory appeal (an appeal of a commission ruling prior to the conclusion of the trial) is a possibility.[58] The MCA 2009 (10 USC §950b) also provides for direct appeals of final decisions of a commission to the United States Court of Military Commission Review, and following that to the D.C. Circuit Court, and ultimately the Supreme Court.[59] As discussed in Chapter 10, the detainee can seek a "collateral" review (a review that is not part of a direct review) by seeking the writ of habeas corpus.

56 Terrorist Trial Report Card, September 11, 2001–September 11, 2011, 7 (Center on Law and Security, NYU Sch of Law, 2011), archived at https://www.lawandsecurity.org/wp-content/uploads/2011/09/TTRC-Ten-Year-Issue.pdf.

57 https://www.hrw.org/video-photos/interactive/2017/03/30/guantanamo-facts-and-figures.

58 *In re Al-Nashiri*, 791 F3d 71 (DC Cir 2015).

59 Challenges have been raised regarding the makeup of the court military commission review. *In re Khadr*, 823 F3d 92 (DC Cir 2016); Steve Vladeck, *The misbegotten court of military commission review* (LawFare, May 24, 2016, archived at https://www.lawfareblog.com/misbegotten-court-military-commission-review.

10

PROTECTION AGAINST BEING "DISAPPEARED"

The "Great Writ" of habeas corpus is the legal process in which an independent judge has the authority to decide whether the executive branch of the government may continue to detain a particular individual. "Colloquially, the writ of habeas corpus could be styled as protection against being 'disappeared'."[1]

During the Bush administration the question arose as to whether or not Guantanamo could operate as a place from which people could be "disappeared," free from judicial oversight, free from the scrutiny of Article III courts, which could consider a detainee's petition for a writ that would command the President to release him. The Bush administration sought three times to block the availability of the writ to Guantanamo detainees, and three times, in 2004, 2006, and 2008, the Supreme Court stepped in to make the writ available to them.[2] Thus aliens held at Guantanamo were entitled to seek the writ, and the first habeas corpus trials began in November 2008. [Incidentally, undocumented immigrants who were "apprehended within hours of surreptitiously entering the United States" were not.[3]]

Bagram Air Force Base in Afghanistan continues to be a black hole. Lower courts have refused to extend the writ and the Suspension Clause (discussed below) to aliens held there.[4] [The Supreme Court has assumed that U.S. persons outside the U.S. are protected by the Suspension Clause, thus the writ would be available to them unless it was properly suspended.[5]]

1 Stephen Dycus, Arthur L. Berney, William C. Banks, Peter Raven-Hansen, Stephen I. Vladeck, *National security law*, 6th ed., 831 (Wolters Kluwer 2016).

2 *Rasul v Bush*, 542 US 466 (2004); *Hamdan v Rumsfeld*, 548 US 557 (2006); *Boumediene v Bush*, 553 US 723 (2008).

3 *Castro v US Dep't of Homeland Security*, 835 F3d 422 (3d Cir 2016).

4 Const Art I, §9, cl 2; *Al Maqaleh v Gates*, 605 F3d 84 (DC Cir 2010). See, also, *Al Maqaleh v Hagel*, 738 F3d 312 (DC Cir 2014).

5 Dycus, Berney, Banks, Reven Hansen, Vladeck, *National security law*, 6th ed., at 857, n.1 (cited in note 1).

I. The writ of habeas corpus: background

The writ of habeas corpus predated the Constitution. The Suspension Clause of the Constitution presumes the existence of habeas corpus by prohibiting its suspension "unless when in Cases of Rebellion or Invasion the public safety may require it."[6] Since 1789 habeas corpus practice has been a result of federal legislation.[7] Statutes specify who may seek the writ, what burden of proof the government must satisfy to the justify the detention, the hearing procedures, and the relief that may be granted. Section 2241 specifies that the writ will not be issued unless the detainee "is in custody in violation of the Constitution or laws or treaties of the United States."[8] The Supreme Court has said that the writ was vital for securing freedom from unlawful restraint, and as such was specifically provided for in the Constitution.[9]

An application for a writ must satisfy various statutory requirements that vary depending whether the petitioner is held in custody by federal or state officials.[10] One requirement that has loomed up in cases involving the detainment of alleged enemy belligerents is that the writ must be directed to the person who has custody of the petitioner. This requirement blocked the use of a writ filed by Jose Padilla in a New York district court when it was directed to the Secretary of Defense, instead of to the commander of the brig in South Carolina where Padilla was being held. Because the brig commander was in South Carolina, the New York district court did not have jurisdiction to entertain the petition.[11]

Filing a petition for a writ of habeas corpus triggers a procedure that starts with the court considering the application. The court may "forthwith award the writ" or "issue an order directing the respondent to show cause why the writ should not be granted."[12] The person to whom the writ is directed "shall make return certifying the true cause of the detention." And the person detained "may, under oath, deny any of the facts set forth in the return or allege any other material facts." Once an order to show cause is issued and a return has been filed by the government, a hearing is held by the court. Section 2246 notes that "evidence may be taken orally or by deposition, or, in the discretion of the judge, by affidavit. If affidavits are admitted, any party shall have the right to propound written interrogatories to the affiants, or to file answering affidavits."[13] Section 2243 also includes a requirement that unless the application for the writ and the return present only issues of

6 Const Art I, §9, cl 2.

7 28 USC §§2241–2255.

8 28 USC §2241(c)(3).

9 *Boumediene v Bush* (cited in note 2).

10 Convicted state criminals face an exhaustion of remedies requirement, 28 USC §2254. If the state prisoner did not raise his federal claim in state court as required by state law it cannot now be raised in the petition for the writ. *Wainwright v Sykes*, 433 US 72 (1977). State prisoners also face a one-year statute of limitations to file the petition, 28 USC §2244(d).

11 *Rumsfeld v Padilla*, 542 US 426 (2004).

12 28 USC §2243.

13 28 USC §2246. See, also, 28 USC §2247 regarding other documentary evidence.

law, the person who has custody of the detainee must produce the detainee at the hearing. The statute requires the courts to "summarily hear and determine the facts, and dispose of the matter as law and justice require." [There are other requirements specifically applicable to the conduct of hearings triggered by petitions filed by state prisoners following conviction in a state court, or by federal prisoners challenging their sentence.[14]]

The federal statutory hearing requirements leave many questions open, especially regarding detainees held by the command of the President in the name of national security.[15] Section 2243 outlines only a skeleton set of procedures.

The Suspension Clause specifies the circumstances under which the writ may be suspended but does not expressly provide which branch of government – Congress or the President – has the authority to suspend. (Justice Taney, sitting as a judge in a habeas hearing in 1861, said a writ could only be suspended by Congress.[16]) Bush's efforts to suspend the writ operated by denying the judiciary jurisdiction to hear petitions for the writ. But even if such a suspension were upheld, there would still be the question of what the legal consequence of the suspension would be. The practical effect would be that those in custody remain in custody as long as the President chooses to detain them. (There are other possible effects not addressed here.)[17]

II. Attempts to deny the availability of the writ

Subsequent to the attacks on 9/11 the United States created an internment facility along the southeastern border of Cuba on a piece of land, Guantanamo, over which the U.S. had control because of a long-term lease agreement originally reached in 1903 with the then newly independent Republic of Cuba. Detainees in Guantanamo claiming that they had never been a combatant against the United States or engaged in any terrorist acts filed petitions for writs of habeas corpus relying on 28 USC §2241, which, as noted above, authorized the federal courts to issue the writ of habeas corpus.[18] The federal district court where the petition was filed and the D.C. Circuit Court of Appeals dismissed the petitions for want of jurisdiction. The D.C. Circuit Court said the Supreme Court ruling in *Johnson v Eisentrager*, 339 US 763 (1950) held that the writ did not extend to aliens in military custody who were not in territory over which the United States was sovereign. That decision was appealed to the Supreme Court. Justice Stevens, writing for the Court, stated that the question before the Court was whether the habeas statute conferred a right to a judicial review of the legality of the President's detention of aliens "in a territory

14 28 USC 2254.

15 Marc D. Falkoff, *Back to basics: Habeas corpus procedures and long-term executive detention*, 86 Denver U L Rev 961, 962 (2009).

16 *Ex Parte Merryman*, 17 F Cas 144 (CC D Md 1861).

17 See. Dycus, Berney, Banks, Reven Hansen, Vladeck, *National security law*, 6th ed., at 846 (cited in note 1).

18 *Rasul v Bush* (cited in note 2).

over which the United States exercises plenary and exclusive jurisdiction, but not 'ultimate sovereignty'."[19]

The Court answered yes. Justice Stevens distinguished the case from *Johnson v Eisentrager* in two ways. First, the Guantanamo detainees were unlike those in *Johnson*, in that they were imprisoned in territory over which the United States exercised exclusive jurisdiction and control. Second, this case was about the meaning of federal statute §2241, whereas *Johnson* addressed whether the detainees had a constitutional right to seek the writ. The *Rasul* court concluded that the reach of §2241 did not depend on where the detainee was located, but only on where the custodian was located. A district court acts within its jurisdiction as long as the custodian can be reached by service process. No party questioned the District Court's jurisdiction over the detainees' custodians.

On the same day that the Court issued the *Rasul* decision, it also issued its decision in *Hamdi v Rumsfeld*.[20] In that case a U.S. citizen held in a South Carolina brig was allowed by the Court to proceed with the petition for the writ under §2241 since all the parties agreed that suspension of the writ had not occurred. The Court in *Hamdi* also ruled that a citizen held in the United States as an enemy belligerent had to be provided with notice of the factual basis for his classification, and a fair opportunity to rebut the government's factual assertions before a neutral decisionmaker.

The decisions in *Rasul* and *Hamdi* led the Bush administration in 2004 to establish Combatant Status Review Tribunals (CSRTs), an administrative process designed to determine if a detainee at Guantanamo were an enemy combatant. (See Chapter 8.) Detainees took advantage of the availability of the writ to file numerous petitions in the U.S. District Court for the District of Columbia. Then in 2005 Congress passed the Detainee Treatment Act of 2005 (DTA).

The DTA amended §2241 of Title 28 by adding a provision that denied the federal courts jurisdiction to hear or consider an application for the writ filed by or on behalf of any alien held in Guantanamo.

Regarding the military-run CSRTs that were now in effect being substituted for a habeas corpus hearing in an Article III court, the DTA provided that the D.C. Circuit Court of Appeals would have exclusive jurisdiction to determine the validity of the final decisions of the CSRTs. The scope of the review that the Court of Appeals was allowed to undertake was limited to looking at purely legal questions: (i) did the CSRT comply with standards and procedures laid out by the Secretary of Defense; and (ii) was the application of federal statutes and the Constitution – to the extent applicable – consistent with those provisions. The Circuit Court, thus, was not authorized to look at the underlying facts used to determine if the detainee were an unprivileged enemy belligerent. As noted in Chapter 8, one commentator said the CSRT was a "kangaroo court."

19 Id at 475.
20 542 US 507 (2004).

The DTA's provision that eliminated federal court jurisdiction was partially blocked by the Supreme Court in 2006 when it ruled that the provision was inapplicable to cases that were pending at the time the DTA was enacted, thus the courts were given a green light to continue to entertain the petitions filed prior to the enactment of the DTA.[21] This decision of course left the courts closed to those detainees who wanted to file for the writ of habeas corpus following the enactment of the DTA.

The next act of the drama over the writ of habeas corpus featured the enactment of the Military Commissions Act of 2006 (MCA 2006), which expressly eliminated judicial jurisdiction over all pending and future habeas corpus cases brought by aliens in Guantanamo, while preserving the limited review of the CSRT tribunals in the D.C. Circuit Court of Appeals. The MCA 2006 did not require that all detainees undergo a CSRT in order to continue to be detained.[22]

Guantanamo detainees now challenged the constitutionality of the jurisdiction stripping provision of MCA 2006. In a 5-4 opinion authored by Justice Kennedy, the Court ruled in *Boumediene v Bush* that the petitioners had a constitutional right to habeas corpus because the MCA 2006 jurisdiction stripping provision violated the Suspension Clause of the Constitution.[23] (Justice Kennedy retired from the Court on July 1, 2018.) That provision provided that the writ of habeas corpus may not be "suspended" except in certain circumstances when public safety was at stake, perhaps during a rebellion or an invasion. These conditions did not exist in *Bouemdiene*. Thus the Court looked at whether Congress had provided for an "adequate substitute" remedy for the writ, thereby precluding a finding that there had been an unconstitutional suspension.[24]

Before getting to the issue of an adequate substitute, the Court took up the question of whether aliens designated by the Executive as enemy belligerents and detained outside the United States enjoy the privilege of habeas corpus. The Court, after an extensive examination of the history of the writ and precedent, concluded that yes, they do. The determination of the extraterritorial reach of the writ and the suspension turned on three considerations: (a) the citizenship and status of the detainee and the adequacy of the process through which that status determination was made; (b) the nature of the sites where apprehension and then detention took place; and (c) the practical obstacles inherent in resolving the prisoner's entitlement to the writ. Regarding the matter of "status," the Court noted that these detainees were denied their status as enemy belligerents. Next the Court addressed the issue of the adequacy of the substitution, and noted that the process afforded the

21 *Hamdan v Rumsfeld* (cited in note 2). As noted in a previous chapter, the Court in this same case struck down the military commissions established by President Bush saying the military commissions had to follow procedural rules more in conformity with the Uniform Code of Military Justice.

22 Jennifer K. Elsea and Michael John Garcia, *Enemy combatant detainees: Habeas corpus challenges in federal court*, 22 (Congressional Research Service, February 3, 2010, R33180).

23 Cited in note 2.

24 *Swain v Pressley*, 430 US 372 (1977); *United States v Hayman*, 342 US 205 (1952).

detainees thus far did not involve a full adversarial process. As for (b), the Court noted that in every practical sense Guantanamo was not "abroad," because it was in the "constant jurisdiction of the United States." As for (c), the Court noted the government presented no credible arguments that the military mission at Guantanamo would be compromised if the courts had jurisdiction to hear petitions for the writ of habeas corpus.

Regarding the question of the adequacy of the substitute, the Court concluded that the procedures made available by the CSRT, MCA 2006 and DTA were not an adequate substitute for a habeas hearing in a federal court. In essence, the problem was the CSTR procedures themselves could too easily end up reaching an erroneous judgment, and given the limited review in the D.C. Circuit Court of Appeals, there was not much of an assurance that an erroneous status determination in the CSRT would be corrected.

It should be noted that the CSRT itself was not struck down by the Supreme Court. As flawed as the procedure was, it could still be used by the military to determine the status of a detainee; but a detainee's right to a constitutionally adequate procedural hearing would thus rest on the habeas hearing in a court.

The *Boumediene* decision has also served to keep the writ available to challenge not just the fact or duration of detainment, but also the conditions of confinement, such as forced feeding by means of nasogastric tubes.[25] (The court ultimately rejected this claim on the merits. See Chapter 8.) The availability of the writ for these claims is especially important in light of the fact that federal law bars all other suits, e.g., for damages, based on conditions of confinement.[26]

Putting *Boumediene* together with the decision in *Hamdi*, the following two categories of detainee have access to habeas corpus: U.S. citizens held anywhere and aliens held in Guantanamo or in the United States. Whether non-citizens held *anywhere* have access to the writ of habeas corpus – say, at the Bagram Airfield in Afghanistan – has not been ruled on by the Supreme Court. The D.C. Circuit Court of Appeals has ruled that they do not.[27]

An important issue that will not be pursued here is whether individuals lose the right not to be deprived of one's freedom of speech rights, equal protection rights, and due process of law rights as protected by the First, Fifth, and Fourteenth Amendments, when the writ has been properly suspended according to the requirements of Article I, Section 9, Clause 2. Would it be permissible for the Executive, during a lawful suspension of the writ, to detain all opponents to the President? All Jews? Issues such as these have been addressed in the scholarly literature.[28]

25 *Aamer v Obama*, 742 F3d 1023 (DC Cir 2014).

26 28 USC §2241(e)(2). See *Al-Zahrani v Rodriguez*, 669 F3d 315 (DC Cir 2012); Dycus, Berney, Banks, Reven Hansen, Vladeck, *National security law*, 6th ed., at 873 (cited in note 1).

27 *Al Maqaleh v Gates*, 605 F3d 84 (DC Cir 2010).

28 Martin H. Redish and Colleen McNamara, *Habeas corpus, due process and the suspension clause: A study in the foundation of American constitutionalism*, 96 Va L Rev 1361 (2010).

III. Habeas corpus procedures

While the Supreme Court took steps to assure the availability of the writ, the protection offered by the writ could be undermined. After the petition is filed, a habeas hearing is triggered to determine if the detainee is an unprivileged enemy belligerent. But the hearing might be neither a serious inquiry into the Executive's legal authority, nor a serious inquiry into the facts the Executive used when it declared the detainee an unprivileged enemy belligerent.

An ordinary criminal trial is designed to avoid the criminal conviction of the truly innocent. While the criminal trial's procedures may be the gold standard, the Supreme Court in *Boumediene* said that "Habeas proceedings need not resemble a criminal trial, even when detention is by executive order." This, by itself, is not a radically new observation, in that it has long been recognized that criminal defendants are entitled to more extensive procedural protections in their actual trial than when they "collaterally challenge" using the writ of habeas corpus.[29] But those challenges usually occur post-conviction, after all the protections of a criminal trial have been applied. The challenges mounted by Guantanamo detainees are pre-conviction (albeit post-detention) and in this circumstance the Supreme Court said "Where a person is detained by executive order, rather than, say, after being tried and convicted in a court, the need for collateral review is most pressing," and the "writ must be effective. The habeas court must have sufficient authority to conduct a *meaningful review* [italics added] of both the cause or detention and the Executive's power to detain."[30]

What then are the procedural components that make possible a "meaningful review?" A starting point is 28 USC §§2243 and 2246. As described by Justice O'Connor, these provisions provide that the person detained may deny under oath the facts set forth in the government's return. But evidence in a habeas hearing may be taken by deposition, affidavit, or interrogatories.[31] 28 USC §§2243 and 2246 provide only an incomplete and skeletal outline, as noted by Justice O'Connor, of a hearing. Thus the Supreme Court in two opinions put a bit of flesh on the bones. Unfortunately, what the Court said was ambiguous in important respects, and did not address a large number of issues that would have to be addressed in order to work out the details of a habeas hearing. These details were left to the lower courts to decide. As will be seen, because of these details, commentators have suggested that habeas hearings today do not provide a "meaningful review."

29 Stephen I. Vladeck, *The D.C. Circuit after Boumediene*, 41 Seton Hall L Rev 1451, 1467 (2011).

30 *Boumediene v Bush*, at 782 (cited in note 2).

31 *Hamdi v Rumsfeld*, 542 US 507 (2004). The Court upheld the authority of the government to detain enemy combatants but ruled that United States citizen detainees had a due process right to challenge status before an impartial authority.

The Supreme Court's procedural requirements for habeas hearings are summarized below.

From *Boumediene*:

- Detainee must have an opportunity to rebut the factual basis for the government's assertion that he is an enemy combatant.
- The court must have the authority to look at the relevant law, including the claim that the President does not have authority to detain them.
- The court must have some authority to assess the sufficiency of the government's evidence.
- The court must have authority to admit and consider relevant exculpatory evidence even if it was not introduced in a prior proceeding, e.g., in the CSRT.
- The court must have the authority to issue an appropriate order for relief including an order directing the detainee's release.

From *Hamdi*:

- A citizen-detainee must receive notice of the factual basis of his classification as an enemy combatant.
- The detainee must have a fair opportunity to rebut the government's claimed facts before a neutral decisionmaker.
- The right to be heard must be granted at a meaningful time and in a meaningful manner.
- "[T]he exigencies of the circumstances *may* demand that, aside from these core elements, enemy combatant proceedings may be tailored to alleviate their uncommon potential to burden the Executive at a time of ongoing military conflict." [Italics added.]
- "Hearsay, for example, *may* need to be accepted as the most reliable available evidence from the Government in such a proceeding." [Italics added.]
- "[T]he Constitution would not be offended by a *presumption in favor of the Government's evidence*, so long as that presumption *remained a rebuttable* one and fair opportunity for rebuttal were provided. Thus, once the Government puts forth *credible evidence* that the habeas petitioner meets the enemy-combatant criteria, the onus could shift to the petitioner to rebut that evidence with more persuasive evidence that he falls outside the criteria." [Italics added.]
- The burden of proof on the government must be more than merely coming forward with "some evidence."

These guidelines, because of their ambiguity and omissions, forced the lower courts to address many crucial issues regarding the required procedures for a habeas hearing without guidance from the Supreme Court.

In developing the doctrines in this area the judiciary has had to consider how a given rule would, on the one hand, risk the erroneous deprivation of liberty of a non-terrorist, and, on the other hand, create a risk to national security by leading to the release of an actual terrorist. When it comes to ordinary criminal law the famous dictum of Blackstone holds sway: "It is better that ten guilty persons escape than one innocent suffer." This is certainly not the precept that has been followed by the judiciary when it comes to formulating habeas procedures for dealing with a petition for the writ by someone accused by the Executive of being an unlawful enemy belligerent. For example, Judge Traxler of the Fourth Circuit would require that detainees be afforded "the normal due process protections available to all" unless the government can demonstrate that "this is impractical, outweighed by national security interests, or otherwise unduly burdensome."[32] Other judges would shift even further from the Blackstone precept. Judge Wilkinson, also on the Fourth Circuit bench, said insisting on Judge Traxler's approach would frustrate the democratic branches of the government in their effort to promote public safety.[33] The bluntest statement came from Judge Silberman on the D.C. Circuit Court of Appeals, who wrote "candor obliges me to admit that one cannot help but be conscious of the infinitely greater downside risk to our country, and its people, of an order releasing a detainee who is likely to return to terrorism."[34]

Here follows a brief summary of what appears to be the prevailing position regarding each bullet listed above:

Right to an attorney: Petitioners have been afforded a right to an attorney, but not at government expense. The Sixth Amendment right to an attorney paid for by the government is not applicable since these habeas hearings are not criminal cases.[35]

Burden of proof: The prevailing view is that the government has the burden of proof to establish its claim that the detainee is an unprivileged enemy combatant, and that the government will prevail if the proof satisfies a "preponderance of the evidence" test.[36] But at least in the District of Columbia, that test may not be securely in place.[37] The D.C. Circuit in one decision said its approval of the preponderance test was not an endeavor to identify the "minimum required by the Constitution."[38] Most courts have rejected the position that the government can prevail by only producing "some evidence." The "beyond a reasonable doubt" test used in ordinary criminal proceedings has also been rejected.[39]

32 *Al-Marri v Pucciarelli*, 534 F3d 213 (4th Cir. 2008) (en banc), (Traxel, J. concurring).

33 Id (Wilkinson J., concurring in part and dissenting in part).

34 *Esmail v Obama*, 639 F3d 1075 (DC Cir 2011) (per curiam) (Silberman J., concurring, 1077).

35 *Al Odah v United States*, 346 FSupp 2d 1 (D DC 2004).

36 *Al Odah v United States*, 611 F3d 8 (DC Cir 2010).

37 Benjamin Wittes, et al., *The emerging law of detention 2.0*, 16 (Harvard Law School/Brookings April 2012), archived at https://www.brookings.edu/research/the-emerging-law-of-detention-2-0-the-guantanamo-habeas-cases-as-lawmaking/; Vladeck, *The D.C. Circuit after Boumediene*, at 1469–1471 (cited in noted 29). See, also, *Al-Adahi v Obama*, 613 F3d 1102 (DC Cir 2010).

38 *Al-Bihani v Obama*, 590 F3d 866 (DC Cir 2010).

39 Id.

Admissibility of hearsay: Federal courts in the District of Columbia have ruled that hearsay should generally be admitted.[40] To manage dozens of post-*Boumediene* petitions, District Court Judge Hogan issued a case management order that established the following approach to the admission of hearsay evidence: hearsay could be admitted "if the movant establishes that the hearsay evidence is reliable and that the provision of non-hearsay evidence would unduly burden the movant or interfere with the government's efforts to protect national security."[41]

Presumption of regularity/accuracy and authenticity: A presumption of regularity means the habeas court presumes that the government official who prepared a document with hearsay statements accurately identified the source and accurately summarized the statements. The presumption does not involve accepting the truth of the nongovernment source's statement. The D.C. Circuit Court of Appeals has said that government documents enjoy a presumption of regularity.[42] If the detainee rebuts the evidence in the document, that in turn leads to an inquiry as to the credibility of the *detainee*.[43] Any detainee that provides incredible exculpatory statements will find that their statements will be used as evidence to prove that they are an unprivileged enemy belligerent.[44] The presumption of accuracy may effectively switch the burden of proof in habeas hearings from the government to the detainee.[45]

As for authenticity, the question is whether the evidence is what the proponent claims it to be. The approach of a majority of judges is that authenticity must be established prior to admission of the evidence into evidence.[46]

Discovery, classified information, exculpatory evidence: When the government relies on a declaration prepared by a governmental official alleging that the detainee is an unprivileged enemy belligerent, the detainee may seek discovery of the underlying evidence and documents on which the declaration is presumably based. The Fourth Circuit in the *al-Marri* case said the discovery effort of al-Marri could only be denied if the government demonstrated that the hearsay declaration it relied on should be accepted as "the most reliable available evidence" it could produce without undue burden or serious jeopardy to national security.[47] Judge Hogan's case management order in

40 Id.; Vladeck, *The D.C. Circuit after Boumediene*, 1468 (cited in note 30).

41 Case Management Order, *In Re Guantanamo Detainee Litigation* *5 Misc. No. 08-0442 (TFH), Civil Actions Nos. 02-cv-0828 etc. (DC DC Nov 6, 2008), archived at http://www.scotusblog.com/wp-content/uploads/2008/11/hogan-case-mng-order-11-6-08.pdf.

42 *Latif v Obama*, 666 F3d 746 (DC Cir 2011).

43 Id.

44 Wittes, et al., *The emerging law of detention 2.0*, at 20 (cited in note 37).

45 Id at 12.

46 Id at 54.

47 *Al-Marri v Pucciarelli*, at 253 (cited in note 32).

the District of Columbia set forth a narrow rule regarding discovery rights of the detainee – a right to documents or objects that are referenced in the documents the government files in response to a habeas corpus petition; the statements of and circumstances of the statements of the detainee also referenced in the same government document; and "for good cause" additional limited discovery.[48]

Regarding classified information that the detainee may seek, the government must provide the detainee with an "adequate substitute." As for the detainee's counsel, he or she is to be provided with the classified information if the counsel has a security clearance, but even given that, might not gain access if the government objects. After such an objection, the judge is *in camera* to decide if the information is to be disclosed, and if not, whether the government may be permitted to rely on the information. Thus, the possibility exists that undisclosed information will be used to detain the detainee. Judge Hogan's rules also require the government to disclose all "reasonably available" evidence in its possession that is exculpatory.

Detainee (inculpatory) admissions: Several issues arise regarding the use of the statements made by the detainee prior to a habeas hearing. The courts have said the statement should not be discredited merely because it was given without the benefit of a Miranda warning.[49] The use of these statements also raises the same issue that arose regarding the presumption of accuracy – have they been accurately translated and transcribed by the government?[50] These prior statements may be used by the government to discredit statements made in the hearing by the detainee. Bringing the credibility of the detainee's exculpatory statements into doubt may further cement the case against the detainee.

Interpretative approaches: Other rulings have further tilted the habeas hearing in favor of the government. These rulings include how the habeas judge should approach the interpretation of a specific piece of evidence in conjunction with the total body of evidence brought forward in the hearing. The Circuit Court of Appeals for the District of Columbia has embraced a "mosaic" or "conditional probability" approach to the evidence. This means that even if a particular fact does not prove the ultimate proposition that needs to be proved, it may not be tossed aside and the next fact evaluated as if the first fact did not exist. Under a conditional probability approach one fact may make more probable another fact. For example, if there was proof that a detainee had communications ties with al-Qaeda, that by itself does not prove the person was a member of al-Qaeda. Likewise, staying in a guest house of al-Qaeda, by itself may not be sufficient. But taken together, these

48 Case Management Order (cited in note 41).

49 Wittes, et al., *The emerging law of detention 2.0*, at 91 (cited in note 37).

50 Id at 75–78.

disparate pieces may establish the probability that the detainee was a member of al-Qaeda.[51] The evidence should be viewed collectively, not piece-by-piece. Even unreliable disparate piece aspects should be taken into account. (Recall here from Chapter 8 the ambiguities regarding the definition of unprivileged enemy belligerent.)

Scope of review on appeal: The ruling of the district court judge may be appealed to a circuit court of appeals. In the District of Columbia, that standard of review favors upholding the district court's findings of fact – the district court will only be overturned if there were "clear error(s).E[52]

In sum, the dynamic in these cases appears to be one in which the government mounts a circumstantial "credible" case, and then the detainee is required to come forward with an alternative credible explanation. If the detainee's alternative explanation is not found credible, it is then assumed that the government has met its burden of proof.[53]

The government's "case" may consist of a "declaration" written by a governmental official that purports to lay out accurate information about the comings-and-goings of the detainee, and that may incorporate statements made by the detainee prior to the hearing, and interrogation reports (hearsay statements of other individuals not available for direct questioning at the hearing). The government is likely also to use information about the behavior of other unnamed individuals said to be terrorists to suggest that the petitioner followed the same behavior patterns, e.g., traveling a particular route used by other terrorists, or information from people associated with the detainee who are said themselves to have ties to al-Qaeda. It is even possible that the judge might consider classified evidence not made available to the detainee or to the detainee's attorney.

The detainee must then choose between standing mute, or offering an alternative explanation that the court might conclude is not credible. If that happens, it is concluded that the government's case has been proved by a preponderance of the evidence.

There is also a marked asymmetry when it comes to interpreting the government's case and the alternative narrative of the detainee. While the government's case is looked at in its totality (mosaic theory), the claims of the detainee are looked at individually; each element of the detainee's set of claims is examined separately for credibility.

51 Id at 116–122; Vladeck, *The D.C. Circuit after Boumediene*, at 1468, 1471–1473 (cited in note 29).

52 *Awad v Obama*, 608 F3d 1 (DC Cir 2010).

53 *Al Odah v United States*, 648 F Supp. 2d 1 (D DC 2009), aff'd 611 F3d 8 (DC Cir 2010).

SELECT BIBLIOGRAPHY

Law

Carr, James G., and Patricia L. Bellia. *The Law of Electronic Surveillance*, August 2015 ed. Thomson Reuters, 2015.

Cole, David, and James X. Dempsey. *Terrorism and the Constitution: Sacrificing Civil Liberties in the Name of National Security*. New Press, 2006.

Donohue, Laura K. *The Future of Foreign Intelligence: Privacy and Surveillance in a Digital Age*. Oxford University Press, 2016.

Dycus, Stephen, and others. *National Security Law*, Aspen Casebook Series, 6th ed. Wolters Kluwer, 2016.

Fisher, Louis. *Military Tribunals & Presidential Power: American Revolution to the War on Terrorism*. University Press of Kansas, 2005.

———. *The Constitution and 9/11: Recurring Threats to America's Freedoms*. University Press of Kansas, 2008.

Kris, David, and J. Douglas Wilson. *National Security Investigations and Prosecutions*, 2nd ed. Thomas West, 2012.

Said, Wadie E. *Crimes of Terror: The Legal and Political Implications of Federal Terrorism Prosecutions*. Oxford University Press, 2015.

Setty, Sudha. *National Security Secrecy: Comparative Effects on Democracy and the Rule of Law*, ASCL Studies in Comparative Law. Cambridge University Press, 2017.

Miscellaneous

Greenberg, Karen J. *Rogue Justice*. Crown Publishers, 2016.

Greenwald, Glenn. *No Place to Hide: Edward Snowden, the NSA, and the U.S. Surveillance State*. Metropolitan Books, 2014.

Kraft, Michael B., and Edward Marks. *U.S. Government Counterterrorism: A Guide to Who Does What*. CRC Press, 2011.

Savage, Charlie. *Power Wars: Inside Obama's Post-9/11 Presidency*. Little, Brown & Company, 2015.

Schneier, Bruce. *Data and Goliath: The Hidden Battles to Collect Your Data and Control Your World*. W.W. Norton & Company, 2015.

INDEX

For Product Safety Concerns and Information please contact our EU
representative GPSR@taylorandfrancis.com
Taylor & Francis Verlag GmbH, Kaufingerstraße 24, 80331 München, Germany

www.ingramcontent.com/pod-product-compliance
Lightning Source LLC
LaVergne TN
LVHW011125300926
849160LV00008B/519

* 9 7 8 1 1 3 8 3 6 9 6 9 6 *